Microsoft®
ACCESS® 2

Roadmap

DANIEL A. TAUBER and BRENDA KIENAN

SYBEX®

San Francisco • Paris • Düsseldorf • Soest

ACQUISITIONS EDITOR: *Joanne Cuthbertson*
DEVELOPMENTAL EDITOR: *David Peal*
EDITOR: *Armin Brott*
PROJECT EDITOR: *Valerie Potter*
TECHNICAL EDITOR: *Kurt Hampe*
ASSISTANT EDITORS: *Michelle Khazai and Kris Vanberg-Wolff*
BOOK DESIGNER, AND SCREEN GRAPHICS ARTIST: *Helen Bruno*
PRODUCTION ARTISTS: *Helen Bruno, Rhonda M. Holmes and Ingrid Owen*
TECHNICAL ILLUSTRATOR: *Cuong Le*
ROADMAP GAMEBOARD ILLUSTRATOR: *Kistler Design*
PAGE LAYOUT AND TYPESETTER: *Thomas Goudie*
PROOFREADER/PRODUCTION ASSISTANT: *Sarah Lemas*
INDEXER: *Matthew Spence*
COVER DESIGNER: *Ingalls + Associates*
COVER ILLUSTRATOR: *Robert Kopecky*

Library of Congress Card Number: 94-66145
ISBN: 0-7821-1548-9

Manufactured in the United States of America
10 9 8 7 6 5 4 3 2 1

TABLE DATASHEET TOOLBAR

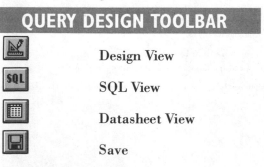

	Copy
	Paste
	Find
	Sort Ascending
	Sort Descending
	Edit Filter/Sort
	Apply Filter/Sort
	Show All Records (Remove Filter/Sort)
	New Query
	New Form
	New Report
	Database Window
	AutoForm
	AutoReport
	Undo Current Field/Record
	Undo
	Cue Cards
	Help

QUERY DESIGN TOOLBAR

	Design View
	SQL View
	Datasheet View
	Save

	Run
	Properties
	Add Table
	Totals
	Table Name
	Select Query
	Crosstab Query
	Make-Table Query
	Update Query
	Append Query
	Delete Query
	New Query
	New Form
	New Report
	Database Window
	Builder Window
	Undo
	Cue Cards
	Help

QUERY DATASHEET TOOLBAR

	Design View
	SQL View
	Datasheet View
	Print

continued…

For every kind of computer user,
there is a SYBEX book.

All computer users learn in their own way. Some need straightforward and methodical explanations. Others are just too busy for this approach. But no matter what camp you fall into, SYBEX has a book that can help you get the most out of your computer and computer software while learning at your own pace.

Beginners generally want to start at the beginning. The **ABC's** series, with its step-by-step lessons in plain language, helps you build basic skills quickly. Or you might try our **Quick & Easy** series, the friendly, full-color guide.

The **Mastering** and **Understanding** series will tell you everything you need to know about a subject. They're perfect for intermediate and advanced computer users, yet they don't make the mistake of leaving beginners behind.

If you're a busy person and are already comfortable with computers, you can choose from two SYBEX series—**Up & Running** and **Running Start**. The **Up & Running** series gets you started in just 20 lessons. Or you can get two books in one, a step-by-step tutorial and an alphabetical reference, with our **Running Start** series.

Everyone who uses computer software can also use a computer software reference. SYBEX offers the gamut—from portable **Instant References** to comprehensive **Encyclopedias**, **Desktop References**, and **Bibles**.

SYBEX even offers special titles on subjects that don't neatly fit a category—like **Tips & Tricks**, the **Shareware Treasure Chests**, and a wide range of books for Macintosh computers and software.

SYBEX books are written by authors who are expert in their subjects. In fact, many make their living as professionals, consultants, or teachers in the field of computer software. And their manuscripts are thoroughly reviewed by our technical and editorial staff for accuracy and ease-of-use.

So when you want answers about computers or any popular software package, just help yourself to SYBEX.

For a complete catalog of our publications, please write:

SYBEX Inc.
2021 Challenger Drive
Alameda, CA 94501
Tel: (510) 523-8233/(800) 227-2346 Telex: 336311
Fax: (510) 523-2373

SYBEX is committed to using natural resources wisely to preserve and improve our environment. As a leader in the computer book publishing industry, we are aware that over 40% of America's solid waste is paper. This is why we have been printing the text of books like this one on recycled paper since 1982.

This year our use of recycled paper will result in the saving of more than 15,300 trees. We will lower air pollution effluents by 54,000 pounds, save 6,300,000 gallons of water, and reduce landfill by 2,700 cubic yards.

In choosing a SYBEX book you are not only making a choice for the best in skills and information, you are also choosing to enhance the quality of life for all of us.

This Book Is Only the Beginning.

● *Machines should work;
people should think.*

Acknowledgments

OUR thanks go to the many people who contributed their efforts to the creation of this book.

At Sybex, thanks to Dr. R.S. Langer, who provided encouragement and helpful suggestions—especially for the material on links and joins; to David Peal, who made many suggestions; and to Barbara Gordon, Chris Meredith, and Celeste Grinage, who indulged us as much as they could. Thanks to Armin Brott, Val Potter, and Kurt Hampe for cleaning things up, checking them twice, and making them right. Thanks also to Helen Bruno and Thomas Goudie for making the book look so snappy; to Sarah Lemas, Michelle Khazai, Kris Vanberg-Wolff, and Matthew Spence for contributions in their areas of expertise; to Cuong Le for technical illustrations; and to Kistler Design for translating our gameboard illustration with such wit.

Our appreciation goes again to Lonnie Moseley and the folks at CRT Inc., a consulting company and Microsoft Training Center in Philadelphia; and to Sharon Crawford, Ms Murphy herself.

We'd also like to express gratitude to our friends and family for their past and ongoing support:

○ Margaret Tauber, Ron and Frances Tauber, Jessica Grant, and the rest of the Tauber family.

○ Rion Dugan, Thaisa Frank, Fred Frumberg, Bruce Gelfand, Carol Heller, Bob Huber, Xuan Mai Le, Mrs. W. Moseley and her family, Cordell Sloan, Robert Williams, Jerry Doty, Shari Levine, Carolyn Miller, Sally Borie Wilson, the Undercoffer/McArdle family, and (in remembrance) Maureen Seitz and Felix Favre.

Roadmap QuickKey

Roadmap QuickKey

▶* Putting Data In

▣⁄ Changing Data

▣⊞ Looking at Data Selectively

▨ Mailing Labels and Form Letters

▨ Making Reports

▤ Printing and Displaying Data

Roadmap QuickKey

Roadmap QuickKey

Setting Up Access

Making Tables Work

Definitions of Technical Terms

Roadmap QuickKey

Definitions of Technical Terms

Cool Things You Can Do with Access

Contents

PART 2

○ Access A to Z

· ·

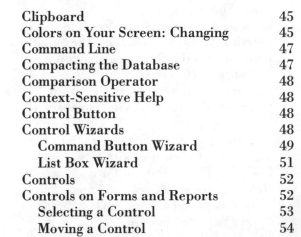

G

H

I

J

KL

M

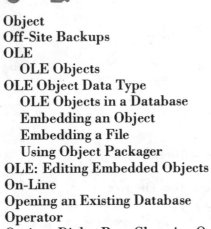

V

W

XYZ

Introduction

THIS book is meant to guide you through the ins and outs of Microsoft Access, giving you the answers you need—before you even know you need them.

It's no accident they called it Access. The folks at Microsoft wanted you to get the idea that Access was easy to use, that it would give you access to your information and to the power of databases. They wanted you to think you wouldn't have to pay a programmer to set up your database, and that you yourself wouldn't have to learn programming to run the thing.

All this is true, but nothing is as easy as it looks. Any database must be set up with care. In *Microsoft Access 2 Roadmap*, we're going to assume that you're a regular Jack or Jane, with some kind of data that you, your boss, or your clients want organized. We're also going to assume that you don't know much about databases, relational theory, or Access itself. You shouldn't have to know these things—after all, you don't have to be an engineer or even a mechanic to drive a car, right?

HOW TO USE THIS BOOK

This book is written in plain English, and will provide answers in a snap. This book is broken into two parts, each of which is further broken into bite-sized, easy-to-follow sections.

You can breeze through Part 1's orientation and overview of databases, then flip around from topic to topic in the alphabetically organized Part 2. If you use the skipping-around method, the alphabetical organization, Roadmap QuickKey Table of Contents, and Index will help you find exactly what you're looking for.

You'll find lots of cross-references in this book. This is because we don't like to repeat ourselves and because you wouldn't want to hear it again, anyway.

WHAT'S IN THIS BOOK

Here's what you'll find in the two parts:

PART 1: THE BIG PICTURE

We start with the basics. We'll tell you a thing or two about databases, then show you around Access, and finish off with the grand finalé: designing your database on paper in preparation for translating it into Access. At the end of Part 1 you'll find a big, two-page roadmap that will guide you through the steps you'll need to take to create your electronic database. If you already know the stuff in Part 1, you can skip ahead to the other part of the book.

PART 2: ACCESS A TO Z

Here's where you'll find out how to create a brand new database with all its parts working together—a powerful tool for dealing with your data. We'll tell you how to add, change, retrieve, and delete data so you can start digging around in your database.

We'll also tell you how to use your database as a tool for manipulating data—asking questions of it and getting quick answers. To do this, though, you'll need to know how to phrase the questions so Access can understand them, and how to link your lists of data to each other to net you the most information with the least effort. That's all in Part 2.

So is information about how you can look at data (on-screen in *forms*, or on paper in *reports*), and how to make the creation of forms and reports magically easy. Access's many *Wizards* will ask you a few questions, hum and whir, then—poof!—present you with what you asked for in one of its most popular, professional-looking formats.

Of course, what the Wizards create may not be *exactly* what you want, so we'll tell you how you can make what the Wizards come up with even better, and how to do really special things with forms and reports—things some people claim just can't be done.

We'll also tell you the almost supernatural things you can do yourself—how to use Object Linking and Embedding (OLE) to place documents from other programs, pictures, and even sound and video into the records in your Access database; and how to import and export data between Access and other popular programs. We'll even show you how to customize Access to make it fit your own, unique vision.

Throughout the book, we assume you have Access installed on your machine. But just in case you don't, we've included a section to tell you how to do the installation yourself, with as little hassle as possible.

You won't have to know any specialized jargon to understand this book. But if you find some word a little puzzling, you'll be able to look it up and get your linguistic bearings.

All of this is in Part 2, arranged alphabetically for your easy reference.

TOOLBAR CHARTS

The toolbars in Access change depending on what you're trying to do. This is not meant to confuse people but it sometimes does. On the inside front and back covers of this book, you'll find listed all the most commonly used Access toolbars.

CRIB SHEET

At the front of this book you'll find a handy "crib sheet" that will walk you through the basic steps of the procedures you do most often in Access: Creating a Database File, Creating a Table and Fields, Creating a Query, Adding a Field to a Query, Creating a Form, and Creating a Report. Tear this crib sheet out of the book and keep it near your desk for instant reference while you work.

WHAT'S THAT STUFF IN THE BOXES?

Throughout this book, we've highlighted certain text by putting it in boxes:

These are notes, pointing out some gem of information you should probably pay attention to or some little side matter on the topic at hand.

Tip

These are tips—alerting you to some extra cool tidbit that's not to be missed if you want to make the most of Access.

These are warnings. If you ignore some of these warnings, something's likely to go wrong, but it won't kill you (or your system). Others alert you to real danger, though, so pay attention if you see this icon.

You Can Skip This Stuff

When things get really involved, or when we're giving you the historical background, it's set aside in these gray boxes, called sidebars. This stuff is often technical, or specialized, or interesting only to crazies like us who want to know why things are the way they are.

JUST FOLLOW THE BOUNCING BALL...

Rather than sticking with one database that might not be relevant to your project or business, we've tried to describe a variety of possibilities in our examples.

When it comes to the nuts-and-bolts "how-to" sections, we've presented the explanations in simple, step-by-step lists, not geared to any particular example, so you can follow along—whatever your database project might be.

Anything you have to type as you do things is shown like this in this book. And for certain keys on the keyboard, we've used what you actually see on the keys—Enter is represented by the symbol ⏎, Control is abbreviated Ctrl, Delete is generally represented by Del, and Escape as Esc.

In this book you're sometimes going to find directions like "select File ➤ Save." This means you should point the mouse pointer at File on the menu bar and single-click, then point at Save and click again.

CAN WE TALK?

We learned a lot about Access by trial and error in our own work, and we've written this book to get what we've learned off our chests and to keep you out of trouble. If you think we can make anything more clear, more complete, or more entertaining, or if we just plain blew it, please write:

Dan Tauber & Brenda Kienan
c/o SYBEX Inc.
2021 Challenger Drive
Alameda, CA 94501

We'll try to incorporate your suggestions in the next edition of this book.

the
Big Picture

· ·

WHAT IS A DATABASE?

It's really pretty simple. You could keep your clothes in a heap in the corner and sort through the whole thing every time you wanted to find a pair of blue socks, or you could buy a dresser, make one drawer the sock drawer, and look there when you want your blue socks. Knowing that this was the *sock* drawer, you'd just search for the color *blue*.

A *database* is a system that lets you organize and store pieces of information in an electronic file so that they're easier to find and use. It's more complicated to arrange than your dresser, but it operates on fundamental principles that are as simple as organizing drawers.

WHAT A DATABASE IS FOR

Nearly everyone has information that should be stored in a database—perhaps that's why they're among the most widely used of computer applications. In this section, we're going to tell you about the basic parts of a database.

Joe keeps the names and phone numbers of his friends and associates on scraps of paper in his wallet. One scrap to a person, and each has a name, phone number, and maybe an address on it.

Each of these scraps is what's called (in database lingo) a *record*. *Data* is what is scribbled on the scraps. If Joe organized

all that data in alphabetical order into an address book with a-b-c tabs along the side, he'd have a *database*. A database is just a bunch of information broken down into discrete pieces and organized in a way that's easy to use. An encyclopedia is a database. So are recipes on index cards in a box. A magazine is *not* a database, because, while it is full of information, the material is not broken down and organized around a reference point (it's not arranged alphabetically, or by number, or by any other system that makes it easy to look things up).

If you have only a few friends and associates, and you don't mind rifling through scraps of paper stuck in your wallet, you don't need a database. But the more bits of data you're trying to keep track of, the easier it will be if you move a notch up in technology—you can keep more data organized in an index card file than in your address book, and you can keep *much* more data organized in an electronic database program like Access than you ever could on paper. Access 2 will let you work with up to 1 *gigabyte* of data in your database. That's roughly equivalent to *10 million* index cards!

Just think about how long it would take to find the address and phone number for John Emerson Smith III from among 10 million index cards if you had to go through them all by hand.

See **Byte Sizes; Data**

WHAT A DATABASE PROGRAM LIKE ACCESS CAN DO

A database needn't be limited to dealing with phone numbers and addresses. You can use Access to store, organize, and analyze other kinds of data you use every day.

With a database program like Access you can:

- ✪ Create an on-screen daily organizer— just like the leather-bound one you carry.

- ✪ Print out mailing labels for your business or your after-work sports team.

- ✪ Make corrections to your mailing list as people come and go.

- ✪ Keep track of customers, transactions, and products in separate tables, and then draw selected pieces of data from each table to create invoices and reports of everything from paper clip purchases to profits/losses.

You could set up an organized *list*—a database that includes the name, mailing address, and phone number of each of your customers. When you want to send letters to them, Access' features make it a snap to combine the names and addresses stored in Access with a letter written in your favorite Windows word processor to create individually addressed communications that look nothing like form letters. Monthly invoices are no problem either: no more retyping the same names and addresses you did last month, no more calculations, no filling out the forms. Access does all this work for you.

A Brief History of Databases

· · · · · · · · · · · ·

Access is not the first database program. One of the first computers built in the United States in the 1880s was nothing more than a mechanical database "engine" for the U.S. Department of Census. It performed statistical calculations on the data census takers had collected.

By the 1960s, big companies were using multimillion dollar mainframe computers to run their databases. Those mainframes had to be run by specially trained personnel in air-conditioned rooms—a situation that discouraged the use of the computer for anything but the most important calculations.

PC versions of database programs—such as all the incarnations of dBASE—have been around since the late 1970s. But to make these early programs really useful, you had to know a lot of obscure commands, or at least get an expensive programmer to customize the database program for your purposes.

In the 1990s, database programs that used Windows technology appeared. Instead of typing in long, confusing commands to get the database to do things, you could point and click with the mouse on icons, buttons, or commands listed in multiple-choice menus. Access, the first of these Windows-based database programs, represented a giant leap toward making powerful database technology available to developers and non-programmers alike.

Now many of the individual tasks involved in setting up your database are further automated with Access' "Wizards," tools that are included in the program to make creating and using your database a snap. Access' Windows-based graphical interface also makes this a really simple-to-use but powerful database program.

A DATABASE IS JUST RECORDS...

Remember Joe, with his wallet full of loose "records"? Joe can write information down on the papers in his wallet in any order; it doesn't matter. When he wants to call up Olivia Clark, he looks at every scrap of paper to find the one with Olivia's number on it.

If Joe used an address book, he could instead turn to "C" for Clark, and there he'd find some boxes on the page, including one where he'd written Olivia's name on one line, her address on another, and her phone number on a third. In database lingo, each of these lines of data is called a *field*. Every record in a database includes the same set of fields. When Joe gets a new address book, all of the boxes, which are *records* on the page, have identical fields—and that, along with the alphabetical tabs on the edge, makes it

easy for Joe to look up his friends' addresses and phone numbers. Figure 1.1 shows you Joe's address book.

Access does things a little differently from database programs like dBASE for DOS. Access stores records in organized lists called <u>tables</u>. One or more tables in Access make up a whole database. (Well, there are a few other things that make up an Access database—more on this as we go along...)

...That Make Up Tables

A *table* is just a collection of records with the same structure: all of the records in the table contain the same kind of information. Access allows you to set up tables and *link* them to other tables. Think of tables as the building blocks of your database.

It's like this: Olivia maintains a database for her small business. In her database, she has one table that functions as her customer address book. It's pretty basic, a lot like Joe's "address book." Then she's got another table that functions as her invoice book, in which each record contains the particulars of an order. The Customer Address table, which tells her *who* placed the order, is linked to the Invoice table, which tells her *what* was ordered. (In Olivia's order-entry system, every invoice is linked to a customer, but not every customer is linked to an invoice.)

Figure 1.1

In Joe's address book, there are
<u>fields</u> for First and Last Name,
Address, City, State, ZIP Code, and
Phone Number.

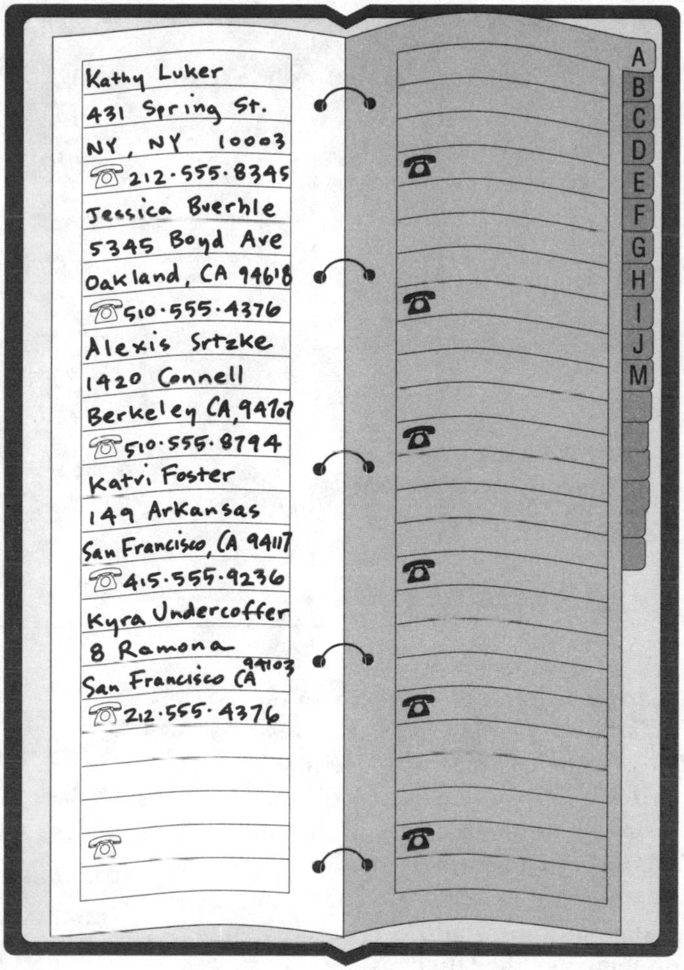

Remember that all the records in a table contain the same fields. (In other words, each record in the Invoice database contains lines for Date of Order, Product Ordered, Quantity Ordered, Price, and so on.) While you enter data into a record, you build your Access database with tables. Figure 1.2 shows a set of related tables that are linked to form one big database.

Microsoft Access is a *relational* database. This means that the data in several tables is *linked* through one or more fields they have in common. For example, the

Figure 1.2
....

Each table in this database is
linked to other tables.

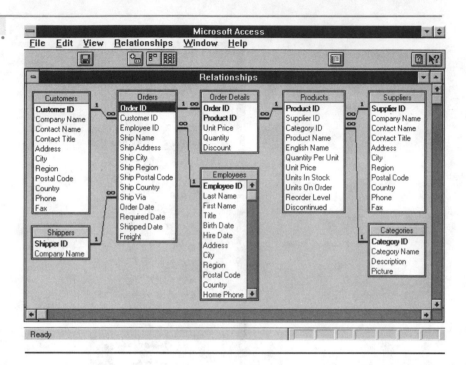

names, addresses, and phone numbers in
Olivia's client list are the same as those
that appear in her invoice list. When
Olivia writes invoices with her Invoice table, Access will automatically pull the customer's name and address from her
Customers table.

A flat-file database could get complicated for someone like Olivia as soon as
one of her customers placed two orders, because she'd have to repeat (by typing it in)
the same data over and over—meaning
that each record would have to be larger
(to include all the customer info) and there
would be a lot of room for mistakes (for example, the spelling of a customer's name
might not be repeated consistently).

66 **It's this business of linked tables
that separates database programs
like Access from the other type of
database—a _flat-file_ database—
which allows you only a single table
in which to store all your information. When you think about and plan
your database (as described in upcoming sections), _tables_ and their
links should be your most important
consideration.**

If you were keeping a database for a nonprofit arts organization, you might keep data in several tables:

- A Mailing List table to hold everyone's name, mailing address, phone number, and account number.

- A Contributions table to hold a list of contributions. In this table, you do not store names or other mailing list information. Instead, you store a piece of data (a unique identifier, such as the account number) in each record that *links this record* to the person's record in the Mailing List table.

- A Membership table to hold a list of members of the organization and the date their memberships expire. Again, you would store a piece of data that links each record to the record for the same person in the Mailing List table.

Each person would have a record in the Mailing List table. They may or may not, however, have a record in the Contributions or Membership tables. (Imagine a large database with tables and fields set up like those set up for the business shown in Figure 1.2.)

...That Make Up Objects

Access is not only a *relational* database, it is also an *object-oriented* database. Everything in Access—fields, records, tables, and more that we'll get into later—is called an *object*.

"Object-Oriented" Explained

There's a lot of talk about "object-oriented" these days. The difference between a more conventional system and an object-oriented one is that in a conventional system you apply an outside function to data, while in an object-oriented system you tell the data to do something to itself.

Objects are actually rather old technology, developed in the late '60s, that is just now making a big commercial appearance. If you really want to explore object-oriented technology, check out Smalltalk—a completely object-oriented language originally designed by Xerox PARC in the 1970s.

...That Are Stored in Files

All the various objects that make up your database—the data in records, tables, and more that we'll talk about later—are stored in a single database file.

While you are using Access, you can save, rename, and even delete these objects. In many other database programs, the *database file* contains the database's records and fields. In Access, *tables* contain the records and fields. The tables are then stored along with other things in a single file—your database file.

Storing all the database's objects in a single file makes things both simpler and more complicated at the same time. The good part is that you don't have to remember which file contains each of the objects you've created—they all move around together. In dBASE for DOS and other flat-file database programs, you had one file for the original records that formed the database, another file (with a different name) for the mailing labels you created from the database, and still more files with more different names for any versions of the database that you had indexed or sorted.

In Access, all of the objects are kept together, which seems a lot better. But problems can arise when you create an object in one database and want to use it in another. Since the object is stored within the first database file, it's hard to track the thing down and copy it into your new database. You may find it better in some cases to split your database into two or more files to help with this situation.

See   **Attaching; Joins and Relationships**

ACCESS ADVANTAGES

Separating your data into several tables has a number of advantages—one is that it allows you to use Access' *security* features to restrict access to certain pieces or types of data. (You can, for example, keep private information confidential—such as *how much* your contributors gave, or who gave and who didn't.)

Using multiple tables also allows you to avoid storing empty, meaningless fields in your tables. Using a flat-file database, you would have to have a field in each and every record for contributions and another field for expiration dates, whether that information was relevant to every record or not. Every detail would have to appear as a field in every record—many of these fields would go empty. While this may not appear at first glance to be important, eliminating empty fields can reduce the size of your database and make your data much faster to access.

Access also includes a number of Wizards—almost supernatural tools that let you create the most commonly used Access objects in the blink of an eye, simply by answering a few questions as they appear in dialog boxes.

But the real advantage in Access is its *interface* (the face it presents to you, the user, to interact with). Let's take a look at what you need to run Access, and what Access looks like when it's running.

See   **Wizards**

WHAT YOU NEED

To run Access, you need to have three programs installed on your machine: DOS, Windows, and Access. Almost all PCs come with DOS already installed. DOS takes care of the most fundamental aspects of your PC and, in the same way you don't have to think about breathing, you shouldn't have to think about DOS as long as you've got Windows. Some machines will also arrive on your desk with Windows pre-installed. Windows gives you intuitive control over the somewhat less-fundamental aspects of your machine—things you have to do consciously, but not with a lot of thought, like moving your arms and hands. If you take this a little further, Access is then like a tool in your hands that you use consciously to perform some kind of work.

To run Windows (and Access) properly, you should have at least 6 MB of RAM (preferably 8 MB or more), at least 10 MB of free hard-disk space, a color graphics card and monitor supported by Windows, and a machine with at least a 386SX CPU.

If you don't know how to get around in Windows, refer to Sybex's Murphy's Laws of Windows. It will tell you everything you need to know about Windows basics.

See **Installing Access; Random Access Memory**

LOOKING AT ACCESS: A GUIDED TOUR

In this section, we'll use a sample database (called Northwind Traders) that comes with Access to give you a brief guided tour of the Access interface and those objects you'll use most often:

- Tables
- Queries
- Forms
- Reports

You don't have to turn on your computer and follow along here, but you can if you want to.

STARTING ACCESS AND OPENING THE SAMPLE DATABASE

To start Access, double-click on the Access icon (shown here).

Microsoft Access

When you start Access, the Welcome screen may appear. Double-click on its control box (the box with the – in it, in the upper-left corner of the screen) to move along.

Select Open Database from the File menu to display the Open Database dialog box shown in Figure 1.3. Then select NWIND.MDB from the SAMPAPPS directory and click on the OK button to open the Database window for the Northwind Traders database.

See **Database: Opening an Existing; Directories; Starting Access**

Figure 1.3

The Open Database dialog box

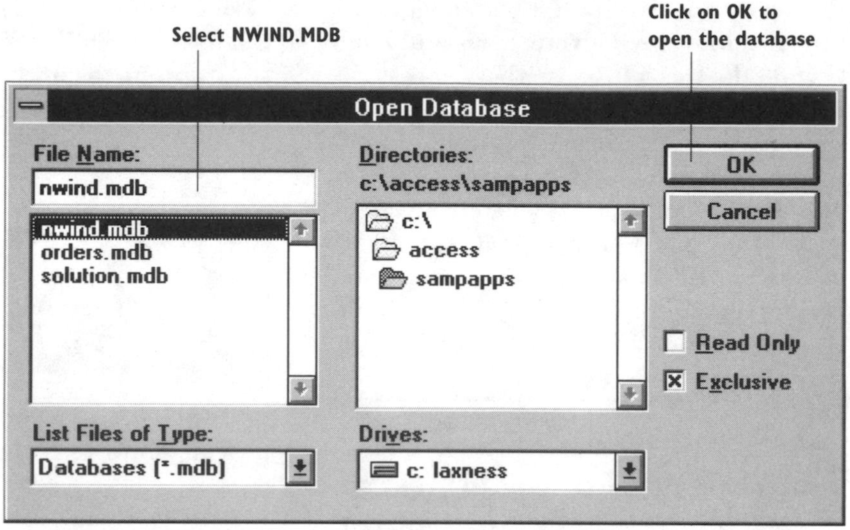

Select NWIND.MDB

Click on OK to
open the database

LOOKING INTO THE DATABASE WINDOW

The Database window is where Access lists all the objects that make up the current database. The Database window is also sometimes called the *Database container window*, because it holds all the objects of the database. Access uses the name of the database file without the file's extension—which is .MDB—to name the container window. For example, the title of the container window for Northwind's database is "Database: NWIND," because the database is stored in the file NWIND.MDB.

> *See*   **Database File: Naming;**
> **Database Window; Directories**

Listing Different Objects

The buttons along the left side of the Database window control which type of object is shown. When you click on one of these buttons to select it, it looks raised. Right now, the top button along the left side—the Table button—should be raised, like it is in Figure 1.4, so a list appears of all the objects of that type (tables) in the NWIND database file. (You can display other types of Access objects by pushing down other buttons. If you do that now, when you're finished, make sure the Table button is raised and a list of tables appears in the window.)

Figure 1.4

The Database window showing all
the NWIND database tables

LOOKING AT TABLES IN DATASHEET VIEW

Tables, which are the most fundamental objects in Access (and the source of data for queries, forms, and reports), can be displayed as *datasheets*. Select the Employees table by clicking on its name, then click the Open button. The table will appear, displayed in a datasheet, a format that looks very much like a spreadsheet, with the data laid out in column-and-row style. Here, in Datasheet View, columns are labeled with field names, and each row of data represents one record (Figure 1.5).

See **Datasheet View**

CHANGING EXISTING DATA IN DATASHEET VIEW

Sometimes, you're going to want to change the data in your tables—when your customers move, for instance, or when a product or an employee's phone number changes. You can modify the data in a table from Datasheet View.

Access uses *current record indicators*—which appear as icons, or little pictures—to show you what's happening with the current record. For example, in Figure 1.5 the small right-pointing arrow at the leftmost end of the first row (the first record) means that record is the current one.

You can edit or type data as you like in the *current field* of the current record—the current field has the blinking cursor in it. To change the current field, you can

Figure 1.5

The NWIND Employees table in Datasheet View

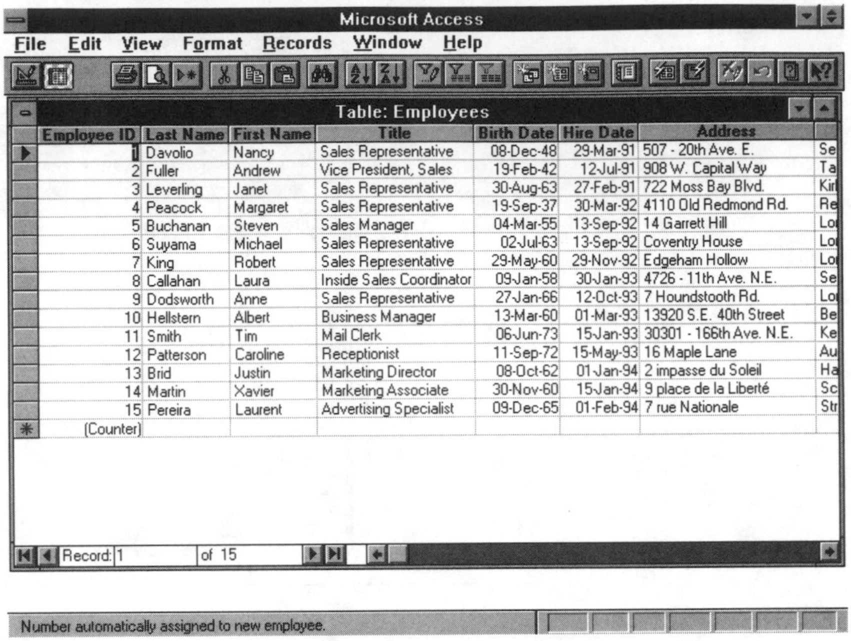

Employee ID	Last Name	First Name	Title	Birth Date	Hire Date	Address	
1	Davolio	Nancy	Sales Representative	08-Dec-48	29-Mar-91	507 - 20th Ave. E.	Se
2	Fuller	Andrew	Vice President, Sales	19-Feb-42	12-Jul-91	908 W. Capital Way	Ta
3	Leverling	Janet	Sales Representative	30-Aug-63	27-Feb-91	722 Moss Bay Blvd.	Kir
4	Peacock	Margaret	Sales Representative	19-Sep-37	30-Mar-92	4110 Old Redmond Rd.	Re
5	Buchanan	Steven	Sales Manager	04-Mar-55	13-Sep-92	14 Garrett Hill	Lo
6	Suyama	Michael	Sales Representative	02-Jul-63	13-Sep-92	Coventry House	Lo
7	King	Robert	Sales Representative	29-May-60	29-Nov-92	Edgeham Hollow	Lo
8	Callahan	Laura	Inside Sales Coordinator	09-Jan-58	30-Jan-93	4726 - 11th Ave. N.E.	Se
9	Dodsworth	Anne	Sales Representative	27-Jan-66	12-Oct-93	7 Houndstooth Rd.	Lo
10	Hellstern	Albert	Business Manager	13-Mar-60	01-Mar-93	13920 S.E. 40th Street	Be
11	Smith	Tim	Mail Clerk	06-Jun-73	15-Jan-93	30301 - 166th Ave. N.E.	Ke
12	Patterson	Caroline	Receptionist	11-Sep-72	15-May-93	16 Maple Lane	Au
13	Brid	Justin	Marketing Director	08-Oct-62	01-Jan-94	2 impasse du Soleil	Ha
14	Martin	Xavier	Marketing Associate	30-Nov-60	15-Jan-94	9 place de la Liberté	Sc
15	Pereira	Laurent	Advertising Specialist	09-Dec-65	01-Feb-94	7 rue Nationale	Str
(Counter)							

press the Tab key. (If you're on the last field of the current record and you press the Tab key, the cursor goes to the first field of the next record.) To get from field to field you can use the arrow keys. The two "VCR-type" controls along the bottom of the window let you get from record to record. (VCR-type controls *look like* the controls on your home VCR.)

If you're following along on your computer, double-click on the control box to close the datasheet.

See **Current Record Indicators; Datasheet View; Datasheet View: Navigating; Editing Data in Datasheet View**

WHAT IS A QUERY?

Among the Access objects you will most commonly use is the *query*. A query is a set of rules that can bring together data from many tables and simultaneously filter it according to criteria you set. A query, then, is really just a *question*, or a set of questions bundled together. For example, a query might ask, "In the Employees table, what are the first names and last names of all the people who were hired after 1/1/93?" In that case, any employee hired on or before 1/1/93 would *not* be listed in the results of the query. The results of the query (called a *dynaset*) are treated as another table in Access and can be used in the same way as a table (Figure 1.6).

Figure 1.6

Because Access places the answers to your query in a new set of records (a dynaset), you can actually base one query on another.

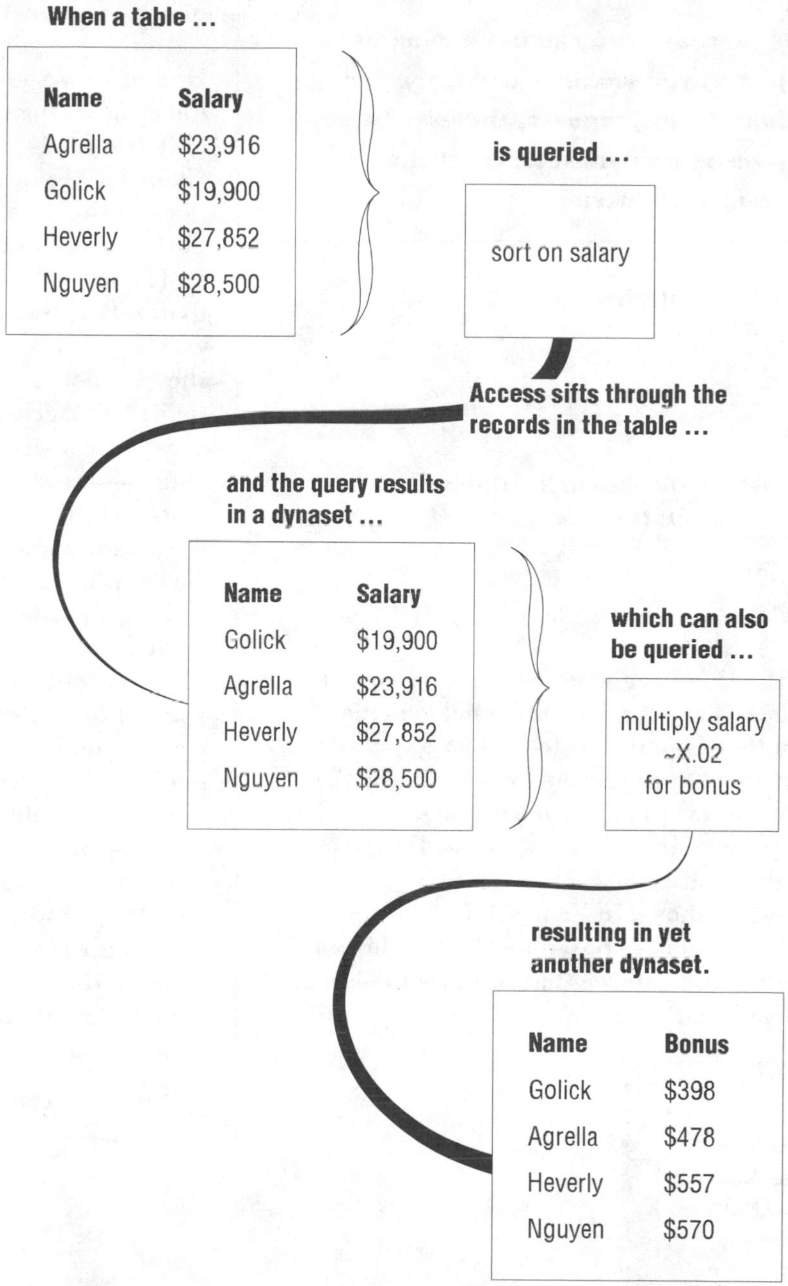

When a table ...

Name	Salary
Agrella	$23,916
Golick	$19,900
Heverly	$27,852
Nguyen	$28,500

is queried ...

sort on salary

Access sifts through the records in the table ...

and the query results in a dynaset ...

Name	Salary
Golick	$19,900
Agrella	$23,916
Heverly	$27,852
Nguyen	$28,500

which can also be queried ...

multiply salary ~X.02 for bonus

resulting in yet another dynaset.

Name	Bonus
Golick	$398
Agrella	$478
Heverly	$557
Nguyen	$570

Because you can use a dynaset just as you would a table, you can base forms, reports, and even other queries on dynasets, which are the results of queries.

See   Queries

Looking at Existing Queries

To list the queries in a database, click on the Query button

in the Database window. Then select the Employee List query and click on Open. Another layout that looks like a spreadsheet will appear, this time including the name of every employee in the table and an employee ID. Now click on the Design icon in the toolbar to see the query in Design View, as shown in Figure 1.7.

This query is based on the Employees table—you can see that because the Employees table

is displayed in a smaller window within the query's Design View window.

In the grid along the bottom part of the Design View window you can see that the query is asking for the data contained in only two fields from the table—Employee Name and Employee ID. That means that none of the data in any of the other fields in the table (addresses, phone numbers, and so on) will show up in the results (the dynaset) of this query.

The word Ascending (which appears in the Sort column under the Employee Name field) tells Access to sort this dynaset in ascending order based on the Employee Name—so in the dynaset that eventually results from the query you'll see a list of people's names and employee ID numbers, sorted *alphabetically*.

If you wanted to change the Sort order— if for example, you were sorting a list of the dates people were hired and you wanted to know who was hired most recently, you could click in the Sort cell, click on the word Ascending, then click the down- arrow and select Descending from the drop-down menu. You could also, if you wanted, choose Not Sorted, in which case the list would not be sorted.

If you're following along now, double-click on the control box to close up the Query Design View window. The Database window will reappear.

See   Filters and Sorts; Queries:
Sorting Data in a Field

Figure 1.7
....

The Employee List query shown in Design View. Because we added the criterion asking for Employee Name "Like Davolio*," all the records that include an Employee Name that starts with "Davolio" will appear in the results of the query.

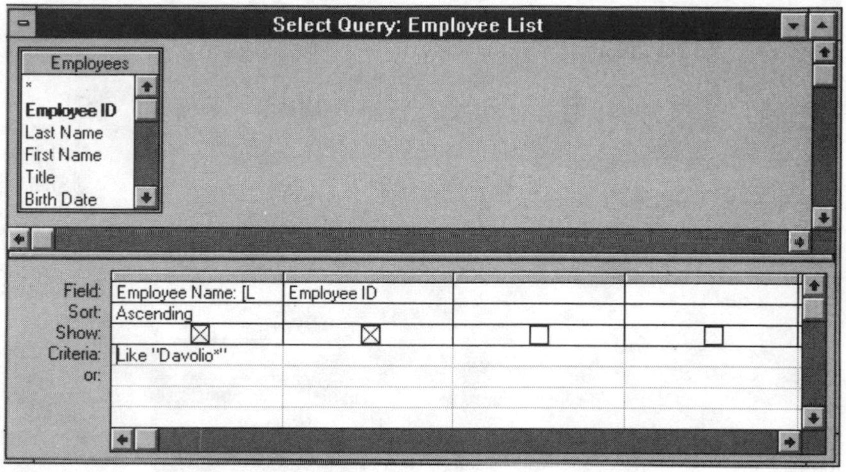

TABLES ARE CONNECTED WITH IDS

How does Access know how to link the data from one table to the data in another? Well, in every record in every table, one field is set aside for this purpose. In our sample NWIND tables, those fields have been called ID fields. In the diagram of NWIND tables shown in Figure 1.8, for example, the Customers table includes a Customer ID field (at the top of the field list). The Orders table includes an Order ID field (again at the top of the field list); but it also includes a Customer ID field. It is through that *shared* (common) data—the Customer ID in this case—that the Orders table is *linked* to the Customers table. The link, then, is the shared field.

See **Joins and Relationships**

LOOKING AT YOUR DATA IN FORMS

Sometimes you just want to look around your data, or maybe change things a bit. For that, Datasheet View is fine. But when it comes to entering new data or analyzing data, all that "cursoring" around can get tiresome.

Access allows you to look at records (whether they're part of a table or a dynaset) on screen in a format that looks like a form to be filled out. *Forms* arrange data in a nice, neat window.

Forms can be based on *dynasets*—the results of *queries* (questions you ask of your data)—just as they can be based on a table.

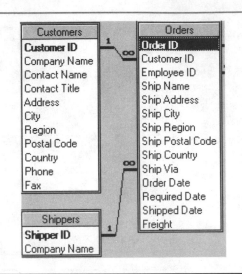

Figure 1.8

Tables are linked through special fields that are held in common by those tables you want to be linked. Here, the Customer ID appears in both the Customers table and the Orders table, forming the link between them.

To look at one of the forms that come with the Northwind Traders database, click on the Form button

(along the left side of the NWIND Database window). A list of the forms included in this particular database will appear (Figure 1.9).

To open the Employees form, highlight "Employees" by clicking on it, then click on the Open button. Figure 1.10 shows one record from the Employees table, viewed as a form.

With a form open, you can quickly switch to Datasheet View by clicking on the Datasheet button in the toolbar:

In Datasheet View, you will see the whole table, laid out once more in column-and-row format. From Datasheet View, you can switch back to the form by clicking again on the toolbar's Form button (the one to the left of the Datasheet button). You can switch back and forth by alternately clicking the Datasheet button and the Form button.

Click on the Form's control box to close it, and the Database window will reappear.

See **Forms and Form Wizards; Datasheet View**

REPORTS: LOOKING GOOD ON PAPER

Of course you don't always handle your data as a list, even as a customized one like a form. Often you want to tell other people something about your data, so you make some kind of

Figure 1.9

The NWIND Database window
showing all the forms.

Forms usually show one record at
a time. Here's one record from the
Employees table, in the form
of a form.

Figure 1.10

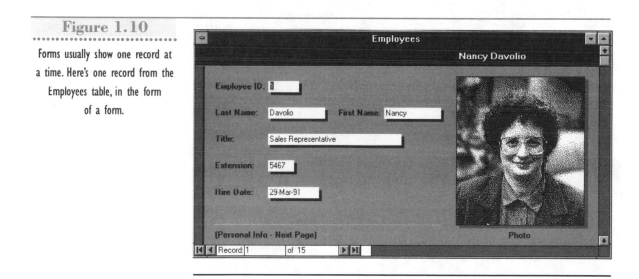

meaningful printed report that may include the entire contents of a table or may be just a summary of information. Access can print out very professional-looking reports based on your data (see Figure 1.11). Reports in Access are handled similarly to forms, except that they are designed to be printed rather than displayed on the screen.

Figure 1.11

Sample of a printed report

Employee Sales by Country
06-Apr-94

Country:	Salesperson:	Order ID:	Sale Amount:
UK			
	Buchanan, Steven		
		10463	$713
		10474	$1,249
		10477	$558
		10529	$946
		10549	$3,554
		10569	$890
		10575	$2,147
	Total for Buchanan, Steven:		$10,058
	Dodsworth, Anne		
		10475	$1,505
		10501	$149
		10506	$416
		10538	$140
		10557	$1,153
		10566	$1,761
		10577	$569
		10586	$24
	Total for Dodsworth, Anne:		$5,716
	King, Robert		
		10458	$3,891
		10483	$669
		10490	$3,163
		10496	$190
		10497	$1,381
		10507	$749
		10512	$525
		10513	$1,942
		10520	$200
		10523	$2,444
		10527	$1,503
		10531	$110
		10532	$796
		10550	$683
		10573	$2,082
		10585	$143
		10597	$718
		10601	$2,285
	Total for King, Robert:		$23,475

1

The Report Wizards can help you create reports in the wink of an eye, and the Mailing Label Report Wizard is a special feature that makes laying out mailing labels no trouble at all.

See **Mail Merge to Microsoft Word; Modifying Forms/Reports: Adding a Logo; Printing; Reports and Report Wizards**

HOW ACCESS OBJECTS INTERACT

You're probably wondering how all these Access objects interact. Well, let's say you have a Mailing List table with everyone's name and address in it. You make a query that pulls out all the people in California by making the criterion for State CA. You can then base a form (on screen) or a report (on paper) on the dynaset. If you hadn't queried for CA, you'd be basing your form or report on the entire original table, and *everybody* would be included in the final form or report.

ACCESS SAVES AS YOU GO

Access anticipates the dynamic nature of your database, and updates the data in your table as soon as you change it. The copy of the table that's on disk is *always* up to date. You'll find this a big advantage if you're on a network and many people are using the same tables or databases at the same time. You should still keep a backup copy, however, so your most recent data will be safe.

See **Backup; Save/Save As**

LEAVING ACCESS

To exit Access, pull down the File menu and select Exit. Access will prompt you to save any objects you've created or modified before it closes up shop—in this case, we wouldn't want to save anything, so click on No.

Now that you've become acquainted with the program, let's take a closer look at what you have to do to set up a database.

See **Exiting Access**

DESIGNING A DATABASE

There are three basic steps to setting up the simplest Access database:

✪ Plan the database's structure on paper.

✪ Create and name a database file to hold the objects (the tables, queries, forms, and so on) that will make up your database.

✪ Set up tables to hold your data.

First, we're going to talk about *plans*, because your finished database won't hold together without a good one.

Planning Your Database's Structure

You don't need to know a lot of relational database theory to set up an Access database.

Access makes it easy to create and modify tables—but you do have to plan beforehand. This calls on your organizational skills more than on your technical skills. You don't have to be a programmer, you just have to be willing to look at the data you use every day in a fresh way.

If you already have a set of paper forms into which you enter data, you can use them as a model. Turn your computer off, and grab some paper and a pencil.

Assessing Your Needs

First, you must map out on paper the information you use in your business and what you do with it. As you do this, think about what data you use and how it flows through the processes of your business. Plot that on paper with pencil, asking yourself as you do:

- What kinds of data do you need to store?

- What general categories might the data fall into?

- What data-entry forms do you use, and how do you need them to be formatted?

- How do you validate or verify data?

- What reports do you want to generate from the data?

- What calculations, formulas, and statistics do you want in your reports?

- What criteria do you use for selecting data to include in your reports?

- What type (alphabetical/numeric) and order (ascending/descending) of sorting will you want to perform on your data?

- What will you do to maintain your systems?

You don't have to work through this list in a linear way—maybe you'll find it more comfortable to think first about the individual pieces of data, the fields that will contain that data, the tables, or the reports you want to print. Start anywhere you like, but do try to cover each of the points in the list; that will help you think through your systems.

If you already have a paper-based system, assemble its pieces in front of you. Look at your paper forms. Perhaps you have a list of customers, a folder full of invoices for each one, and a ledger listing payments. Or maybe you have subscription cards, personnel records, or project tracking schedules that describe your business. Get them all together. Scrutinize them for their content (on which you can base your data-entry and other forms) and to jog your thinking about what data you might want to include in your new automated system.

66 You don't have to follow your old system verbatim. This, of course, is your opportunity to revamp and enhance it. Think, as you go, of a <u>wish list</u> of items that might make your system smoother or more complete. Jot that down as you go. Think also about the maintenance procedures you've used in the past and those you'd like to use in the future). Figure into your planning some processes for <u>purging</u> (erasing) old data that's become useless or <u>archiving</u> (saving in some formal storage system) data that you don't need now, but that might be important again later. Jot that down, too.

Planning Your Tables

Now go through your material and organize it into the general categories you think you'll want. (This is in preparation for setting up tables.) Let's say you're going to have to report on the costs of editing different book projects. If you were keeping track of freelance editors working on those different book projects, you'd have three kinds of data to track:

Editors The freelance editors' social security numbers, names, addresses, phone numbers, special skills, and rates of pay.

Book Projects Each book's identification number, title, publication date, and description, along with the amount budgeted for editing the book, and the editor assigned to edit it.

Invoices The freelance editors' invoices for book projects, which probably include the editor and cost per project for each editor on each project.

Grab three pieces of fresh paper now and assign one sheet to each of the categories, assuming that each one will become a table.

The point here is that you want to make an educated guess about what you're going to do with your data, and organize your thinking before you start randomly setting up tables. On the paper that represents each table you think you'll need, write down the fields—the basic pieces of data—you think will go into the records in that table.

You should avoid repeating data as you do this. In our editors/book projects example, notice that the name of the editor is a piece of data that can be shared between all three tables. We don't want to store that data in all the tables—we just want to put it into *one* of them (you could call this a *master* table). In the other two tables, we'll store a unique identifier (perhaps the editor's social security number, if the Editors table is the master table), or *primary key*, as a pointer to the other tables, so Access can retrieve data that's actually stored in the master table. (Only in the Editors table do we store detailed information about the editor.)

Tip

As you look into the potential structure of tables for your database, if you start to see data appear in more than one table, think about creating a link between tables or even a new table to hold the common data.

From a Paper-Based Database to an Electronic Database

Looking again at our editors/book projects example, when you get to the electronic database, you'll set up three tables, based on the categories of data you've plotted:

Editors   The master table with detailed information about each editor: first and last name, address, phone number, *social security number*, rate of pay, and special skills.

Book Projects   A subordinate table with each book's *identification number*, title, publication date, and description, along with the amount budgeted for editing the book, and a *link* (the *social security number*) that points to the editor assigned to edit the book.

Invoices   Another subordinate table, this one containing the freelance editors' invoices for book projects, each *linked* (via the *social security number*) to the Editors table, where names, addresses, and so on are filed, and *another link* (this time via the book's

identification number) to the Book Projects table, where information about the books' budgets is kept.

Later, when you want to figure out how much it has cost to edit a certain book, you're going to have to set up a query that pulls pieces of information from each of three tables:

- The editor's name and rate from the Editors table
- The book project's number, title, and budget for editing from the Book Projects table
- The editor's invoices for that project from the Invoices table

Planning the Fields in Your Records

Next, you'll enter into your paper-based tables those fields you think will be contained in each record in that table.

Breaking Down Your Data Now for Maximum Flexibility Later

If you've been listing your customers by their full names on index cards or printed forms since you started your business, it's time to learn to break that data down further. You'll be robbing Access of its power if you don't do this. If you store the City, State, and ZIP Code in your mailing list in a single field called "Address," for example, you'll have a hard time sorting your database by ZIP Code. No ZIP Code sort, no cheap bulk rate on mail. It's a lot easier to create separate fields now for each piece of data than to have to split it up later. This is also important so that, when you want a list of say, *Smiths*, you can ask Access to get it for you. You don't want to have to think up all the possible first names for the Smiths—you can let Access do the work.

Figuring Out the Type of Each Piece of Data

As you know, each individual item of data you want to store in a record is stored in a field. Now you need to know that each field can store a certain *type* of data, based on the field's assigned *data type*—most data is of the Text type, but some is of the Number type, or some other type. There are specific instances for assigning types to different pieces of data.

66 Each data type has its own specific properties, and some of what determines which data type to use is the properties of that data type.

Glossing Over the Data Types Just to Get You Going

Access allows for specific types of data. When you design your tables, use Table 1.1 to figure out what *types* of data you want to include.

See **Data Types; Data Types in Access**

A Note on Properties

Objects in Access have <u>properties</u>. This isn't as weird as it might sound. Properties are just characteristics, so in the same way that a fire hydrant is an object that has properties—its "color" is red, it's "material" is metal—objects in Access have properties. For example, data of the Number type might have properties specified under "Format," like whether negative numbers will be shown in red (or another color), or in brackets, or some other way. An Access form has properties specified under "Sort," which describe in what order data is sorted, and under "Filter," which describe which data is sorted.

Establishing the Primary Key

The *primary key*, a piece of data that uniquely identifies each record, has three purposes:

- To provide each record with a unique identifier
- To determine in what order the records will be displayed in Datasheet View
- To support the relationships established between tables

Table 1.1

The Access Data Types

Data Type	What It's Used For
Text	Letters, characters, or any numbers with which you want to do no calculations (a ZIP code)
Memo	A note or text to detail or remind you of something
Number	Numbers (formatted the way you want) with which you want to do calculations
Date/Time	The date and/or the time
Currency	Numbers formatted like money
Counter	A unique, incremented number Access assigns to each record as it is created
Yes/No	A true/false, yes/no, or other two-choice answer to a simple question
OLE Object	An embedded object—for example, a spreadsheet or document from another program, a graphic, or even a small piece of digitized movie footage

Often you'll find that a primary key is suggested among the data in your paper-based system: a social security number, an account number, something of that sort.

You can let Access assign its own primary key. For its own internal purposes, Access automatically assigns a Counter field (containing a unique number) to every record, and you can just let Access make that the primary key if you don't have a more specific one in mind.

See   **Joins and Relationships**

MAPPING RELATIONSHIPS

Having plotted the structures of each table in your database, and generally filled in the fields you expect to use, now it's time to map out the relationships between the tables.

You can do this simply by drawing lines. Start by assigning one table—the one that seems more central to your other tables—as the master table. Locate a piece of data that appears in that table and in *another* table. Draw a line from the piece of data in the master table to the same piece of data where it appears in the second table.

This will illustrate for you the relationships between your tables, and will help you when it's time to form links between tables in your Access database.

A Note on Normalization

Normalization is identifying and removing redundant data and repetitive fields from your tables. This is something you do when working out the fields in your tables and mapping relationships between tables.

Say you have an Orders table containing orders from different purchasers for a lot of different products. If more than one purchaser is ordering Widget 2041, for example, the field containing Widget 2041 is going to show up a lot in the table. That's redundancy. Redundancy is bad because it uses up storage space. To get rid of redundancy, just create a new table to hold the product list. Then you can link the Orders table to the Products table, using your database more efficiently.

Now let's say you have the purchasers' names and addresses in the Orders table and then you have them again in the Invoices table—that's repetition. Repetition, like redundancy, is a waste of valuable storage space. To solve a repetition problem, again, you'd create a new table—this time, for our example, you'd create a table called Customers, and establish links to the Orders and Invoices tables so they could both pull the names and addresses from the same place.

For more on linking tables and joins in general, see Joins and Relationships.

CREATING THE DATABASE IN ACCESS

Now that you have your paper-based database converted into an overall plan for your electronic database, you're ready to set things up in Access. The basic steps are pretty simple; they follow the same logical order as the steps you took to plot the pieces of your database on paper.

1. Create a database file to hold all the objects in your database. (This is like creating one big folder into which to place all the stuff that makes up your system.)

2. Create the tables, and then—by setting up the fields—the records.

3. Define relationships and establish links (joins) between the tables.

4. Enter data (using either the datasheet or a convenient data-entry form).

The big roadmap illustration you'll see at the end of Part 1 shows the route to follow in Access (and this book) as you set up your new database. In Part 2, you'll also find illustrations from the big roadmap picture marking those entries in that most closely describe steps along the route.

See Database File: Creating

WHAT TO DO WITH YOUR ACCESS DATABASE

After you create a database file and tables to hold your data and fill your tables with data, you'll want to create other Access objects to let you retrieve, view, edit, sort, question, and print your data.

> *See*   **Datasheet View; Forms and Form Wizards; Printing; Queries; Reports and Report Wizards**

Tip

As you're setting up your electronic database and creating new objects to make the most of it, remember to review your paper-based plan often—you'll probably think of new, more creative ways to handle things as you go along, but it's your basic plan that will give your database it's firm foundation.

PART 2

Access
A-Z

ACCESS

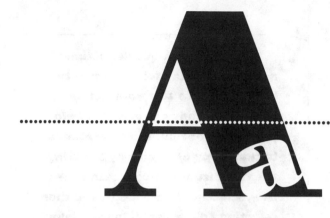

ACCESS

Access is a powerful relational database management program that will let you create systems for storing, organizing, and using data (basic pieces of information)—even if you have no programming skills.

See **Part I**

ACCESS BASIC

The programming language that comes with Access is called Access BASIC.

ACTION

Commands inside macros are called *actions*. Action queries are something else altogether.

See **Action Queries; Macro**

> 66 **We don't cover programming in this book. That's because the beauty of Access is its ease of use, and you're not supposed to have to know how to program it. But if you're the type who likes to stay up late nights tinkering, and you're itching to get under the program's skin, you can check out Access' programming features on your own. With Access you can create objects called Modules that contain Access BASIC programs. All that is explained in the Building Applications book provided by Microsoft with the program.**

ACTION QUERIES

Action Queries let you systematically change data in your tables. You can create an Action Query to delete all records from a table that meet some criteria—say people who have not responded to some mailing you sent out.

Some queries pull data out of existing tables or dynasets (based on some set of criteria) and produce a new dynaset of data. Those are *select* queries.

Sometimes you're going to want to *modify* the data systematically—for example, you might want to change the area codes of all the phone numbers in Santa Monica when the phone company assigns that city a new area code. That's what an *action* query does—it actually modifies the data stored in the tables upon which the query is based.

Access gives you four types of action queries from which to choose:

✪ Make Table

✪ Update

✪ Append

✪ Delete

> *See* **Append Action Query; Delete Action Query; Make Table Action Query; Queries; Query Wizard; Update Action Query**

Because action queries actually modify the data stored in your tables, be sure to test your action query on a <u>copy</u> of your data before you use it for real. You can create a backup copy of a table by selecting the table from the Database window, selecting Edit ➤ Copy, and then selecting Edit ➤ Paste. In the dialog box that appears, enter a new table name for the backup copy of your table. Now you can test your action query.

ACTION QUERY WIZARD

See **Query Wizards**

ACTIVE CELL

The *active cell* is the cell that's currently being used in a datasheet, also known as the *current* cell. The active cell is the highlighted cell.

ADD-IN MANAGER

The Add-In Manager allows you to add, remove, and customize add-ins. When you access the Add-In Manager (select File ➤ Add-Ins ➤ Add-In Manager), a dialog box will appear, displaying all the libraries of add-ins currently installed.

To remove an already installed add-in, highlight its name in the Available Libraries list and click the Uninstall button. The check box next to the newly uninstalled library will disappear, telling you that it has been un-installed. (The library will actually still be available until you quit and restart Access. Libraries are all loaded when Access starts.) To close the dialog box, click on Close.

To add a new add-in, open the Add-In Manager as described above. The same dia-log box will appear. You needn't highlight anything, just click the Add New button. The Add New Library dialog box will ap-pear, listing files with an .MDA extension. Highlight the name of the add-in you wish to add and click on OK. Close the dialog box by clicking on Close, then restart Ac-cess. (The add-in will be installed only af-ter you've quit and then restarted Access.)

Some add-ins include customizable fea-tures. The specific process involved in cus-tomizing an add-in varies depending on the add-in. The documentation for a particu-lar add-in should tell you about options for customizing.

See   **Add-Ins**

ADD-INS

Add-ins are libraries of Access BASIC code you can use even if you're not a program-mer. Add-ins were used by the developers of Access to create Wizards; in Access 1.1, add-ins were "hidden," meaning they were difficult for you to use.

You can see evidence of the existence of add-ins when you use the Wizards, each of which is actually written as its own library of Access BASIC code. New add-ins may become available as add-on products. You can install add-ins yourself, as they be-come available. Add-ins are accessible from the File ➤ Add-Ins menu.

See   **Add-In Manager; Attachment Manager; Database Documentor; Import Database (Add-In)**

AGGREGATE FUNCTIONS

See   **Queries; Totals Query**

ALIGNMENT

See   **Controls: Properties; Text: Toolbar Shortcuts for Changing**

ALPHABETIZING

See   **Filters and Sorts; Queries:
Sorting Data on a Field; Quick Sort**

APPEND ACTION QUERY

An Append action query is a query that
will, when it is run, append (copy) records
to the table. An Append action query *adds*
data to an *existing* table; it doesn't create a
new table.

This is going to come in handy when you
want to copy an entire dynaset to an existing table. For example, you might want to
take all the records for people who are simply not going to resubscribe to your magazine (despite your repeated urging), and,
rather than simply tossing out their names
and addresses, append them to your general mailing list, so you can inform them of
upcoming events.

To create an Append action query, first
design a Select query that produces the dynaset you want to append to another table.
Once this is done, convert your Select
query into an Append action query by
doing the following:

1. Select Query ➤ Append.

2. Access displays the Query Properties
   dialog box shown in Figure A.1. If you
   want to append the data to a table in
   another database file, select the Another Database option, then enter the
   path and the filename in the File Name
   box. The Table Name pull-down list
   will appear. From that list, pick the table from which you want to append.
   The Append To row will appear in the
   QBE grid.

3. Now enter the name of this field in the
   table to which you're planning to append data.

4. Once you have the Append To row all
   set up, click on the Execute button on
   the toolbar to run the query.

Figure A.1

The Query Properties dialog box

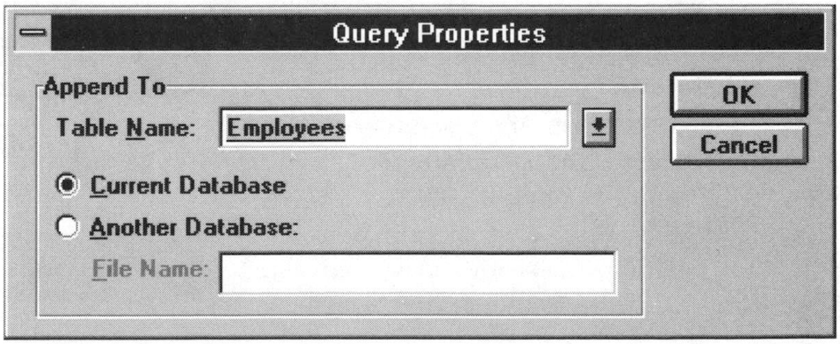

5. Access displays a dialog box telling you how many records are about to be appended. You can either click OK to have Access append the records, or click Cancel to stop.

Microsoft Access

141 row(s) will be appended.

OK   Cancel   Help

66 If you forget that you have executed an Append action query and do it again, the same records will be appended a second time to the database. Then you'll need to know how to delete the query.

See Database Window; Datasheet View: Deleting Records; Queries; Query Wizards

APPLICATION

An *application* is a computer program designed to specialize in some area (database management, spreadsheet analysis, word processing, desktop publishing, etc.). Microsoft Access is an application.

ARCHIVE QUERY WIZARD

See Queries; Query Wizard

ASCENDING ORDER

Ascending order goes from the lowest number or value to the highest (from A to Z, for example, or from 1 to 100). Case is not taken into account here; an A is the same as an a. If numbers and letters are mixed, Access puts numbers before letters.

See Filters and Sorts; Queries: Sorting Data on a Field; Quick Sort

ASCII TEXT FILES

See Importing; Importing from a Text File

ATTACHING

Attaching gives you a way to work in Access on data that's actually in another format—without changing the format of the data permanently. Attaching is handy when you need to share data with other people who aren't using Access. If, for example, you're doing database work with or for someone who uses Paradox, you can use the exact same Paradox file they do, fiddle around with it in Access, and return it to them, fiddled with but not transformed into an Access file. In Paradox, they will see the changes you have made to the data, but the file will still be a Paradox file. Attaching is also very useful when you want to use the same Access table in more than one database. You keep one copy of the table in a single database and then attach to it in your other databases.

You can tell which tables listed in the Database window are attached because this icon

appears next to their name.

Once you have added an attached table to your database file, you can use that table much like any other. The only restriction is that you cannot modify the structure of the table.

See **Attachment Manager; Importing**

ATTACHING TO AN ACCESS TABLE

When you need to use the same Access table in more than one database, store the table in a single database and then attach to it in the others.

You can attach an Access database to a table in another Access database by following these steps:

1. You must have the Database window open for the database to which you want to attach a table. Then Select File ➤ Attach Table. The Attach dialog box will appear (Figure A.2).

2. In the Attach dialog box, select Microsoft Access as the data source.

3. In the Select Microsoft Access Database dialog box that appears next, select the name of the file that contains the table you want to attach to your database. Then click on the OK button.

Figure A.2
....

The Attach dialog box

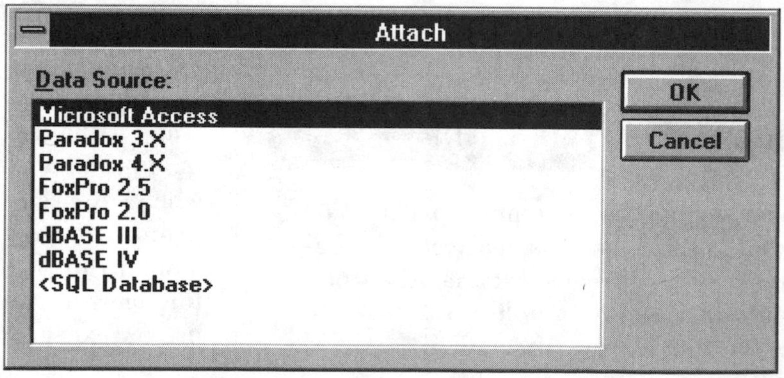

4. Access will display the Attach Tables dialog box, showing a list of all the tables that are stored in the database file you chose in step 3. Select the name of the table to which you want to attach your database. Then click the Attach button.

5. Access will display a dialog box telling you that it was able to attach the table. Click on OK.

6. Repeat the process, beginning with step 4, until you have attached all the tables you want from the database file.

7. When you are done, click on the Close button.

The newly attached tables will show up in the list of tables in the Database window. You can tell they're attached, because the icon next to them will have an arrow on it.

See **Attaching; Importing**

ATTACHING TO A PARADOX TABLE

If you need to share data with people who are using Paradox, you can attach to the Paradox table. It's pretty much the same as attaching to an Access table.

To attach to a Paradox table:

1. You must have a Database window open for the Access database to which you want to attach the Paradox table. Select File ➤ Attach Table. The Attach dialog box will appear.

2. In the Attach dialog box, select Paradox 3.*x* or 4.*x* (whichever you're using) and click on OK. The Select File dialog box will appear.

3. In the Select File dialog box, select the name of the file that contains the Paradox table. Once you have selected the file, click the Attach button.

4. Access will display a dialog box saying that it has attached to the Paradox table. Close the box.

5. You'll be returned to the Select File dialog box. If you want to attach more tables, start at step 3 and do it all again.

6. When you are finished, click on Close.

Once you have attached to a Paradox table you can use and modify it just like any other Access table. (You cannot, however, change the table's structure.) The data itself will be stored in the Paradox table file, so other people using Paradox can use the data and can see any changes you make.

See **Attaching; Importing**

ATTACHMENT MANAGER

Keep in mind that *attached* tables are tables that are in other database files but that are attached to the table you're working in so data can be shared between database files as well as between tables. Access "knows" where to find the attached table because it's been set up to know where that table is located (in what file). The Attachment Manager add-in allows you to review and modify the locations of attached tables. In other words, it lets you:

❍ Tell Access to find the table in a file other than the file where it was originally stored

❍ Tell Access to find the table in the same old file, but that the file's now in a new directory

To use the Attachment Manager, you must first open the database file (File ➤ Open), then:

1. Select File ➤ Add-Ins ➤ Attachment Manager from the menu bar.

2. A dialog box will appear, showing a list of all the attached tables in the current database (Figure A.3). The Attachment Manager must first check to see if the file is in the old location; then, if it's

not, you'll be able to reassign the location. Next to each filename is an empty check box. Click on the check box for the filename with which you want to work.

3. Click on the OK button.

❍ If the Attachment Manager finds the tables you've selected in their original database files and directories, a message will appear telling you the attachments have been "refreshed." Click on the OK button to get rid of the message. You'll be returned to the Attachment Manager dialog box, listing the attached files and their locations.

❍ If the Attachment Manager is unable to find any of the attached tables, a Select New Location dialog box will appear. In this box, click on the name of the file you want to locate. Then click on OK. The Attachment Manager will find the file for you, and will indicate that it

---

Figure A.3
••••••••••••••••••••••••••••••••
The Attachment Manager dialog box

Attachment Manager		
Select the attachments to be updated:		
◆▦ Suppliers	C:\ACCESS\SAMPAPPS\NWIND.MDB	☐
◆▦ Shippers	C:\ACCESS\SAMPAPPS\NWIND.MDB	☐
◆▦ Products	C:\ACCESS\SAMPAPPS\NWIND.MDB	☐
◆▦ Orders	C:\ACCESS\SAMPAPPS\NWIND.MDB	☐
◆▦ Order Details	C:\ACCESS\SAMPAPPS\NWIND.MDB	☐
◆▦ Employees	C:\ACCESS\SAMPAPPS\NWIND.MDB	☐
◆▦ Customers	C:\ACCESS\SAMPAPPS\NWIND.MDB	☐
◆▦ Categories	C:\ACCESS\SAMPAPPS\NWIND.MDB	☐

[OK]   [Cancel]

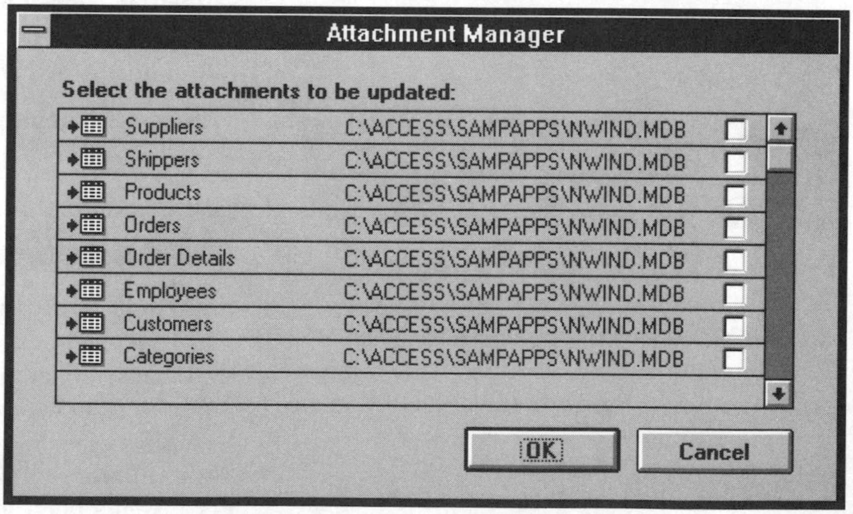

has done so by displaying the message saying attachments have been refreshed. Click on the OK button to get rid of the message. You'll again be returned to the Attachment Manager dialog box, listing the attached files and (this time) their new locations.

4. To close the Attachment Manager dialog box, click on Close.

See   **Add-Ins; Attaching**

AUTOFORM WIZARD

Using the AutoForm Wizard, you'll get a snappy, no-questions-asked look at your data in the form of a form. (Normally, you have to answer the Wizard's questions before you see the form, but in this case, the Wizard just whips up a generic form.)
   To use the AutoForm Wizard:

1. Open the database file, select a table or query, and click on Open to open it.

2. Click on the AutoForm Wizard button

   on the toolbar.

3. A form will appear, showing one record in your table. (You can also do this by selecting AutoForm in the Form Wizard dialog box instead of clicking the AutoForm button.) You can do all the usual form-type things with this form.

See   **Forms and Form Wizards**

AUTOREPORT WIZARD

Don't have time to answer the Wizard's few questions before printing a quick report? The AutoReport Wizard will quickly compile a report summarizing the data on the datasheet you're viewing. You can have a printed report like this in no time flat.
   To use the AutoReport Wizard:

1. Open the database file, select a table or query, and click on Open to open it.

2. Click on the AutoReport Wizard button

   on the toolbar.

3. A report will appear on-screen, showing one record in your table. (You can also do this by selecting AutoReport in the ReportWizard dialog box instead of clicking the AutoReport button.)

You can print the report by selecting File ➤ Print from the menu bar or by clicking on the Print button.

See   **Printing; Reports and Report Wizards**

A
B
C
D
E
F
G
H
I
J
KL
M
N
O
P
Q
R
S
T
U
V
W
XYZ

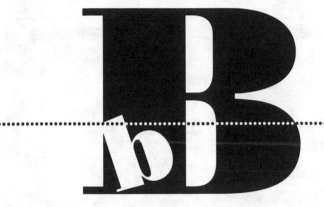

BACKUP

A *backup* is a copy of your data or program files (on floppy disk or tape), which you should store carefully as insurance against loss or damage.

> *See* **Save/Save As**

BANDS

In Access, both forms and reports are divided into distinct areas called *bands*. Essentially, a band is a horizontal strip of the form or report (see Figures B.1 and B.2). The band may be of any width, depending on what it contains. You place different types of information in each band. For example, you place *controls* that hold titles and other information that you want to appear on the top of every page of a report in the Header band. In Group/Totals reports, each group you told the Wizard to create has its own Detail band, where the Wizard places column heads to describe what's in the column.

> *See* **Controls; Forms and Form Wizards; Reports and Report Wizards**

BAR GRAPHS

> *See* **Forms and Form Wizards; Graph Wizard**

"BETWEEN" CRITERIA

> *See* **Criteria; Queries; Query Wizards**

Figure B.1

Reports have bands to
separate areas.

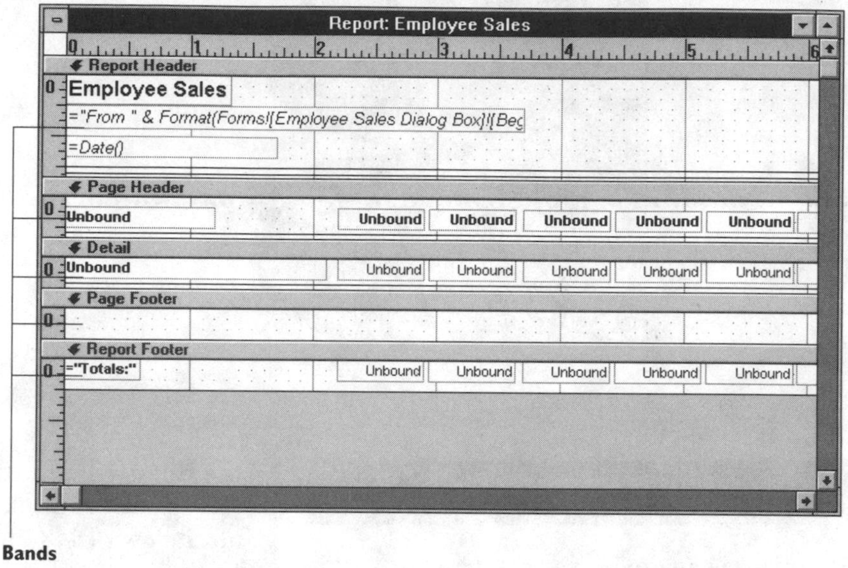

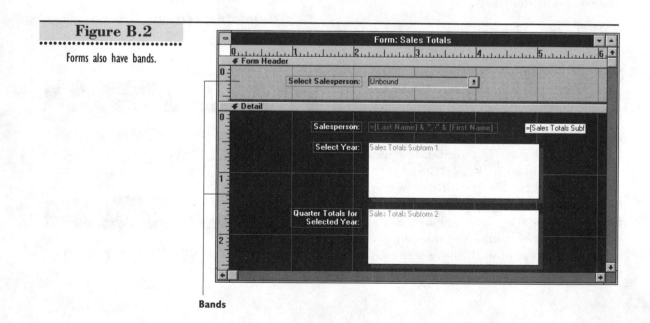

Bands

Figure B.2

Forms also have bands.

Bands

BIT

Bit is the cool way to say Binary digIT. Eight bits make a byte.

See **Byte Sizes**

BITMAP

An electronic file that represents an image with a collection of bits is known as a *bitmap* file and has the extension .BMP.

See **Modifying Forms/Reports: Adding a Logo; OLE; OLE Object Data Type**

BOLD TEXT

See **Text: Toolbar Shortcuts for Changing**

BOOKMARKS

See **Help**

BOOT

To start your computer is to *boot*. (To *re*-start your computer is to *reboot*.)

BOUND CONTROL

A control on a form or report that displays data from a table or dynaset is a *bound control*.

See **Controls**

BRACKETS: USING

When you type a field name in Access, if the field name includes spaces or colons, you must surround it with square brackets. To enter the field name Ship Date, you'd type [Ship Date]. This helps Access to know where the field name begins and ends.

See **Field Name**

BUTTON BAR

In Access, they call it a toolbar; some other programs call it a *button bar*. The toolbar is the strip of icons at the top of your screen, each of which represents a tool you can use in Access.

See **Toolbar; Toolbox**

BUTTONS (CONTROLS)

See **Control Wizards**

A
B
C
D
E
F
G
H
I
J
KL
M
N
O
P
Q
R
S
T
U
V
W
XYZ

BYTE SIZES

Byte is the basic unit of measurement in computer storage. Approximately 1,000 bytes are a kilobyte (K), 1 million bytes are a megabyte (MB), and 1 billion bytes are a gigabyte (GB). To put it another way, 1 *GB* is 1024 *MB*, which is 1024×1024 *K*, which is $1024 \times 1024 \times 1024$ bytes—a very big number. A double-spaced typewritten page is about 1024 bytes of information.

To get further into this, a byte is 8 *bits* (at least on a PC), and each bit has one of two values: *one* or *zero* (sometimes called *true* or *false*, or *on* or *off*). Another way of thinking about a byte is that a byte represents a single character—a letter, number, piece of punctuation, or a *blank space*.

C

CALCULATED FIELDS

See **Expressions: Using; Queries: Creating; Queries: Fields Combined With**

CENTERING TEXT

See **Text: Toolbar Shortcuts for Changing**

CLIPBOARD

The Clipboard is a kind of memory trick: you copy or cut something, and then you can paste it in somewhere else. Where was it in between?...It was on the Clipboard.

> **The Clipboard is a feature of Windows that works in every Windows application, including Access.**

You can copy or cut and then paste in Access—between a form and a datasheet, for example, or between one place on the datasheet and another, *whatever*. You can also copy or cut and paste between different Windows applications—for example from a Microsoft Word document to a table in your Access database.

See **Copy, Cut, and Paste**

COLORS ON YOUR SCREEN: CHANGING

Access comes with a pretty generic color scheme. It's fine for everyday business use, but if you want to wake yourself up while you're doing data entry, or if you're color blind and all the windows run together, you might want to change a thing or two. You can change the colors on your Access screen using the Windows Control Panel. (To do this, you need to be *out* of Access, and *in* Windows.)

In the Program Manager's Main window, double-click on Control Panel, then on Color. The Color dialog box will appear (as shown here) with all the pieces of your windows and desktop laid out.

can choose. Select a new color, then close the Color Palette window. You'll see the results of your choice shown in the sample in the Color dialog box. When you're happy with the color scheme, click on OK. All of your windows will appear in the new color scheme until you decide to change it again.

If you aren't up to designing your own color scheme, Windows provides a choice of well-coordinated, attractive combinations (with colorful names like Black Leather Jacket or Hot Dog Stand) from which you can choose. In the Color dialog box, double-click on the Color Scheme button and select something that appeals to you from the drop-down list. If you don't like it, you can always go back to the default color scheme by clicking on Windows Default in the Color Scheme drop-down list.

See **Customizing Access**

66 **Any color settings you choose will appear in all your Windows applications, and in the windows of Windows itself.**

COLUMN WIDTH

See **Datasheet: Modifying Columns and Rows**

You can change any aspect of the color settings you want. Click on the part of the desktop you want to change, then on the Color Palette button. The Color dialog box will expand, as shown in Figure C.1, to include a palette of colors from which you

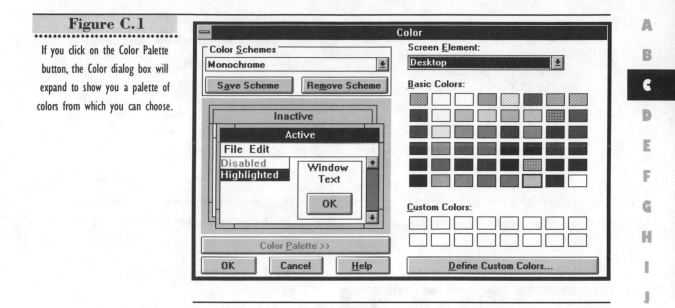

Figure C.1

If you click on the Color Palette button, the Color dialog box will expand to show you a palette of colors from which you can choose.

COMMAND LINE

The *command line* is the list of instructions you type in at the C:\> prompt (the DOS prompt) to make something happen.

COMPACTING THE DATABASE

So you delete a record from a table in Access, and the record seems to be gone—it *looks* like it's gone. Well, it is deleted, but the database file is still holding a place for it, just in case. You don't want all your hard disk space crowded with database files full of old, unwanted records. To reclaim space that held records you've deleted, you'll need to *compact* your database file.

To compact a database file:

1. *No database files should be open.* Select File ➤ Compact Database.

2. The Database to Compact From dialog box will appear. In the dialog box, select the database file in which you've deleted records—the one you now want to compact.

3. Click on OK.

4. The Database to Compact Into dialog box will appear. In the File Name text box, type in the name you want for the file after it's been compacted. (This can be the same name it had before—and in fact, you can just click on that filename if you want and it will simply appear in the File Name text box.)

5. Click on OK.

6. If the name of the file you're compacting from is the same as the name of the file you're compacting to, a dialog box will appear asking you to confirm that it's okay to go ahead. Click on Yes if it's okay, or No if you want to bail.

As Access compacts the selected database file, a progress meter—a moving horizontal blue bar that looks kind of like a thermometer—will appear in the status bar to show how things are going.

See   **Datasheet View: Deleting Records; Forms: Deleting Records**

COMPARISON OPERATOR

A *comparison operator* is a relational operator that compares two values—for example, less-than (<).

See   **Expressions: Components**

CONTEXT-SENSITIVE HELP

A Help system—like the one in Access—that notices what you are doing, and addresses its instructions to you in that context, is known as *context-sensitive*. This means you don't have to read through a lot of irrelevant gobbledygook to get help with the particular thing you're trying to do.

See   **Help; Cue Cards**

CONTROL BUTTON

The *control button* is the little button in the upper-left corner of every window in Windows. When you click once on the Control button, a drop-down menu appears, giving you the option to close, move, or resize the window.

> **66** **The control button is not to be confused with button controls.**

See   **Windows Basics; Controls**

CONTROL WIZARDS

Among the new Wizards in Access 2 are the Control Wizards, with which you can place some of the more complicated types of controls on forms and reports. With a form or report open in Design View, you'll see a toolbox, which will include the Control Wizards tool:

This is a toggle button; to select or deselect it, click on it. When the button is selected it looks pressed down.

66 **If the toolbox does not appear on screen in Design View, select View ➤ Toolbox from the menu bar.**

Now, you can place any kind of control you want; if it's one that a Wizard exists for, the Wizard (a series of dialog boxes) will appear when you click to place the control. These following are only a few of the many Wizards available throughout Access:

- ○ List box
- ○ Combo (drop-down) box
- ○ Options group
- ○ Command button
- ○ Graphs

To use the Wizard, just answer the questions as they appear. A Wizard might ask you what action you want a button to perform when you click on it, or where (in what table) to find items you want to include in a list box, for example. (Each of the Control Wizards works a little differently and asks different questions, but they're all easy to use.) When you've answered the questions in a Control Wizards dialog box, click on the Next button to move to the next questions (in the next dialog box). If you want to go back at any point (to the previous dialog box), you can click on the Back button.

When you've answered all the questions in all the dialog boxes, you'll know because you won't have any other options except Back or Finish. Click on Finish and—voilà!—the control will appear on the form or report, in the location you first clicked (before the Wizard appeared to help you).

Most of the Control Wizards are for items that are more useful on forms than reports, so we're going to stick to forms in the rest of this section. You can apply everything we say about forms here to reports.

See **Modifying Forms and Reports**

Command Button Wizard

The Command Button Wizard allows you to quickly place command buttons—buttons that do something when you click on them—on your forms. For example, you might want to place a button on your form that lets you click on it to go back to the previous record.

To use the Control Wizard to place a Command Button on a form, you should have the form open in Design View and the toolbox should be visible. If the toolbox is not displayed, select View ➤ Toolbox from the menu bar. You should also have the Control Wizards enabled.

The Command Button Wizard works a little differently depending on what kind of button you're placing. Let's look at a commonly used example. To place a button

A
B
C
D
E
F
G
H
I
J
KL
M
N
O
P
Q
R
S
T
U
V
W
XYZ

that will take you back to the previous record if you click on it, do the following:

1. Click on the Command Button tool

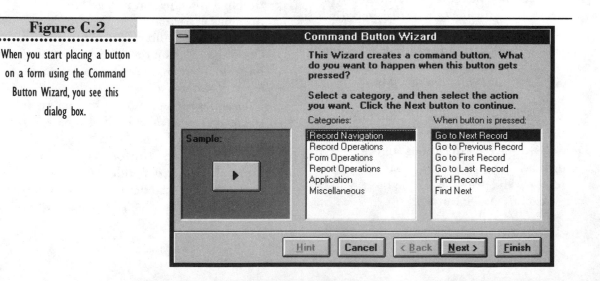

in the Toolbox.

2. Click on the form where you want the command button located. The first of the Command Button Wizard dialog boxes will appear as is shown in Figure C.2.

3. In this first dialog box, you'll tell Access what action you want performed when the button you're placing is clicked. General categories of actions (i.e. Record Navigation, Form Operations, Applications, etc.) are listed as Categories on the left side of the dialog box. The action we want the button to perform is grouped under the Record Navigation actions, so select Record Navigation.

4. A list of actions on the right side will be continually updated to reflect the selected Categories as you change them. Select Go to Last Record from the list and click the Next button. Another dialog box will appear.

5. In this dialog box, you'll tell Access what you want the button to look like. You can specify text or pick a picture that will be displayed on the button. To specify text, click on the check box next to Text:, and type the text into the text box. To select a picture, click on the check box next to Picture:, then select any of the pictures listed by clicking on its name. As you click on picture names in the Picture: list box, Access will display a sample of the picture in the Sample box. Click on Next to continue.

Figure C.2

When you start placing a button on a form using the Command Button Wizard, you see this dialog box.

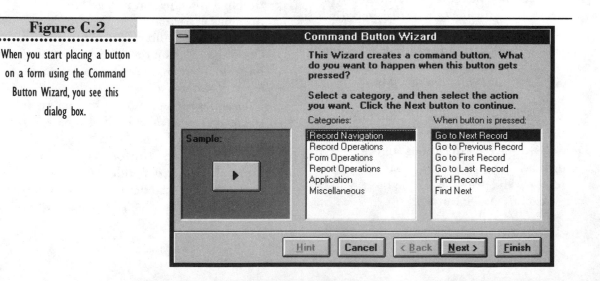

6. The last of the Command Button Wizard dialog boxes will appear. Here, you can type a control name for the button into the text box. When you're finished, click on the Finish button. Access will display your form in Design View, including your new button.

Now, every time you display the form in Form View, it will include a button you can click on to move to the next record.

List Box Wizard

The List Box Wizard allows you to place a list on a form. This can come in handy when data from only a certain set of possibilities should be entered into a field. The data entry person can just pick from the list when entering data. The list of possibilities can come from a field in one of your tables or queries, or can be a set of values you've specified.

To use the List Box Wizard to place a list box on a form, you should have the form open in Design View and the toolbox should be visible. If the toolbox is not displayed, select View ➤ Toolbox from the menu bar. You should also have the Control Wizards enabled.

The List Box Wizard works a little differently depending on whether you're specifying the values to display or asking it to pull the values from a table or query. To place

a list box that always displays the same set of choices on a form, do the following:

1. Click on the List Box tool

in the Toolbox.

2. Click on the form in the location you want the List Box to appear. The List Box Wizard dialog box will appear.

3. In the dialog box, two choices appear, asking if you want the List Box as it appears on your form to display values that originate in a table or query, or if you wish to provide a list of values. In our example, we want to type in a list of values, so select that option by clicking on its option box. Click the Next button.

4. The next List Box Wizard dialog box will appear. Here, you'll tell the Wizard first the number of columns you want in the list and then what to display in each row of the list. The default in the Number of columns: box is 2; we want just one column, so type 1. Then click in the Col 1 cell in the little grid you see, next to the right arrow. The Col 2 cell will vanish, leaving just one column in the grid.

5. In this cell, you'll start entering the values that will appear later in the list on the form. Say you want a list of shoe sizes to appear; you would type the sizes here, pressing Tab after each one to move to the next cell. Figure C.3 shows the dialog box all filled in. When you're done, click on Next to move to the next dialog box.

6. Here, you'll tell Access in what field to place what the user picks from the list box. Click on the option box for Store that value in this field:. Then click on the down arrow next to the drop-down box, and from the list of fields in the table, select the one you want. When you're done, click on the Next button.

7. In the next dialog box that appears, you can enter a name for the control you just created—for example, Shoe Size—by typing the name into the text box. Once you have named the control, click on the Finish button. You will be returned to the Design View of your form, which will now include the list box.

CONTROLS

A *control* is any of the gizmos you place on a form or report in Design View. A *field* is a control, and so is the *label* for that field. A line or border that will appear on the form or report is also a control.

> *See*   **Controls on Forms and Reports; Controls: Properties; Design View; Forms and Form Wizards; Modifying Forms and Reports; Reports and Report Wizards**

CONTROLS ON FORMS AND REPORTS

Everything that appears on a form or report is called a *control* in Design View. Every line, every field, every button, every

Figure C.3

We have filled in the List Box Wizard's dialog box so it will display a list of shoe sizes.

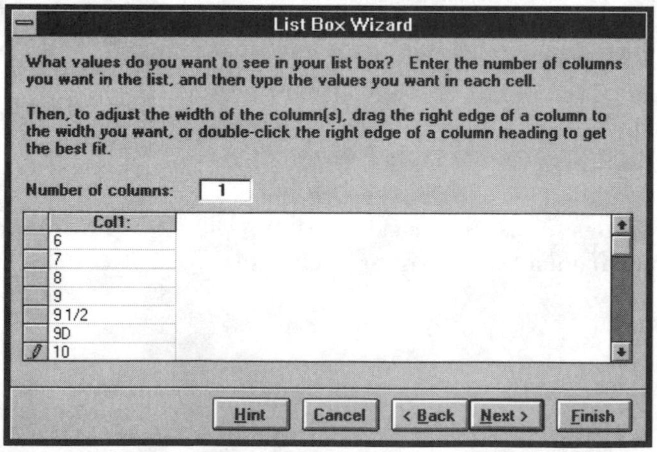

66 **Most controls that are on forms are also on reports, but some—those that require a graphical interface, such as drop-down boxes, command buttons, list boxes, and toggle buttons—are not useful on a report. We'll talk in this book about the controls you'll find most useful. You can do a lot using just the simple controls we'll talk about here. If you want more information on controls, check Access' on-line Help and User's Guide.**

Sub form, every label—everything. Every control has a set of properties associated with it that determines how the control

looks. Simply put, you modify the look of anything on your form or report by selecting the control and then modifying the control's properties in the Property box.

Selecting a Control

Before you can do much of anything to one of the controls being displayed in Design View, you have to select it. You select a control on a form or report by pointing at it with the mouse pointer and clicking. Once you've selected a control, little handles will appear around it, as shown in Figure C.4. You use these handles just as you would use the handles on a suitcase—to move the thing around—but in this case you have to grab the handle with the mouse pointer.

Click on the control at the handle with the mouse and hold down the mouse button as you drag the handle along to manipulate

Figure C.4

When a control is selected, little handles will appear around its edges so you can move it around with the mouse and resize it.

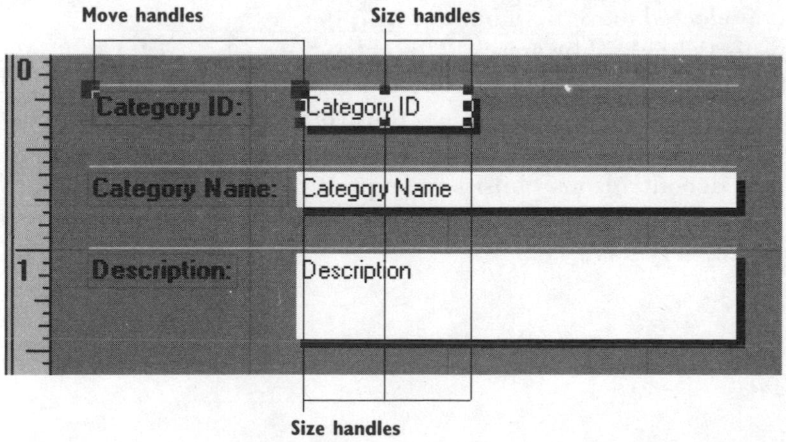

Move handles   Size handles

Category ID: Category ID

Category Name: Category Name

Description: Description

Size handles

the control—you can resize it using the Size handles, or move it to a new place on the form or report using the Move handles.

You can select more than one control at a time—hold down the Shift key and click on each control in turn. (Don't let up on the Shift key as you do this.)

If the Property box is not already on screen, you can display it in one of three ways:

✪ Select View ➤ Properties from the bar.

✪ Click on the Properties button on the toolbar.

✪ You can click with the right mouse button on any control displayed and then select Properties from the shortcut menu that appears.

The Property box will display the properties of the control that's selected. If you have selected more than one control, the Property box will be empty. This is because the properties of one control that's selected might be different than those of another control selected at the same time. Since all controls are considered equal, none of them get their properties listed in the Property box.

Moving a Control

You can move controls all around on your form or report. Moving controls around takes some pretty exact mouse work. But don't worry… the worst thing that will happen is you will end up with a control in the wrong place. You can always select Edit ➤ Undo from the menu bar to undo your last move or resizing of a control.

To move a control from one place to another:

1. With the form in Design View, unselect the control you want to move. You can tell what each control displays because they show the field that they get their information from inside of them while you view the form or report in Design View.

2. Click and hold down the mouse button over the control you want to move.

3. Now you can drag the control to a new location.

Now when you display the form the control will appear in the new location. You can move a control on a report in the same way.

It's one thing to move two controls around together—say a label for a field and the field itself—without changing the location of one compared to the location of the other. But sometimes you're going to want to move one without the other—maybe you want to drop the label to a position *above* the field instead of next to it.

66 **Many controls are attached to labels, which are also controls, so when you move the control the label moves with it.**

If you want to move a control *and* change its position relative to any other controls that it is attached to, you'll have to use the Move handles on one of the controls to drag it around.

To do this, select the control by clicking on it. Once the control is selected, the Move handle will appear in the upper-left corner of the control. You can grab the Move handle by moving the mouse over it. When you've done this, the mouse pointer will change to a pointing hand. While the pointer looks like a hand, click on the Move handle and drag the control to its new location.

Resizing a Control

There are a few things the Wizards can't seem to get just right, and one of those is the width of fields. It seems that no matter what type of data you want to display, the Wizard creates a control that is either too narrow or too wide to display what you want. You can manually change the width of a control by following these steps:

1. Select the control that you want to resize.

2. Move the pointer around to one of the Size handles. The pointer will turn into a two-headed arrow.

3. While the pointer is a two-headed arrow, you can click on the control and drag it to its new size. A faintly drawn box will appear around the control, indicating its new size, as you drag the mouse around. When you're happy with the size of the new control (as represented by the box), release the mouse button. The control will appear in its new size.

Tip

When you resize a control to make it wider or narrower, it's really easy to botch the control's height. A control that is just the right width to display the data is useless if it is also so short that it cuts off the bottom half of the letters or numbers. You can have Access set the height of a control to accommodate whatever font and size is associated with the control by selecting Format ➤ Size ➤ To Fit while the control is selected. You can also fix the height of multiple controls at once by selecting them all, and then selecting Format ➤ Size ➤ To Fit.

A
B
C
D
E
F
G
H
I
J
KL
M
N
O
P
Q
R
S
T
U
V
W
XYZ

Adding a New Control to the Form or Report

If you want to display information that appears in a field in the table or dynaset your form or report is based on, but that does not appear in your form or report, you can add a new control for that field. Do this by opening the form or report to which you want to add the field, and viewing the form or report in Design View. Then, to add the new control (which will essentially add a field to your form or report):

1. If the Field List box is not being displayed, select View ➤ Field List to make it show up.

2. Select the field you want to add to the form or report from the Field List box.

3. Now drag that field down to the form or report. Release the mouse button when the field is located where you want it to appear on the form or report. The new control will then appear on the form or report.

If you now switch to Form View (if you are modifying a form) or Print Preview (if you are modifying a report), you will see the control you just added, appearing on your form or report as a new field.

CONTROLS: PROPERTIES

Remember that things (such as tables) in Access are called *objects* and objects have *properties*. Fields within tables, and controls on your form or report are objects too and therefore also have properties.

Some of the more complex types of controls have more properties than others. A control that displays a field has a long list of properties—font type, size, weight, and more. In contrast, a control that just displays a rule (line) has only a few properties, like the thickness and color of the line.

In Access 2, properties are categorized to make it easier for you to find them. The categories for properties are:

All Properties   Includes *all* of the properties for the object or control

Data Properties   Includes properties related to the data

Layout Properties   Includes properties related to the way the object or control looks

Event Properties   Includes properties related to defining the behavior of the object (trust us—just stay out of this one)

Other Properties   Includes all those miscellaneous properties that don't fit in elsewhere

You set a control's properties from the Property box, where different options will be listed depending on what type of control you have selected. If the Property box is not being displayed on the screen, you can make it appear by clicking on the Properties button on the toolbar. The Properties button looks like this:

(66) **A little weirdness common to many Windows programs is that drop-down lists aren't in alphabetical order. The Properties list, for example, seems to have been organized by whim. You'll have to look up and down the list (using the scroll bars if necessary) to find the property you want.**

Changing a control's property can be done like this:

1. Select the control for which you want to change properties.

2. If the Property box is not open, open it by clicking on the Properties icon (shown above) on the toolbar.

3. At the top of the Property box, you'll see a box with a down-arrow at its rightmost end. To find the category of properties you want, click on the down-arrow and a drop-down list will appear. Select the category of property you want to change by highlighting it in the drop-down list.

✪ If no properties of that category exist for the control you're working with, the Property box will be blank.

✪ If there are properties of that category associated with the control, a list of those properties will appear in the Property box.

4. Scroll around in the Property box until you see the property you want to change.

5. Enter the new value for the property.

6. Repeat steps 3 to 5 until you have changed all the properties you want to change.

Now that you have changed the properties of one control you can move on to the next one.

✪ You can save lots of time by leaving the Property box on the screen while you work on other things. As you select different controls to modify, the Property box will automatically change to show you the properties of that control.

✪ If the Property box starts getting in your way, you can either move it to another part of the screen by clicking on its title bar and dragging it, or make it go away by double-clicking on its control box.

Some of the More Useful Properties to Change

We could double the size of this book by listing every property of every control that you can change, but we're going to spare you. Instead, we're going to cover some of the more useful controls, and their more commonly used and changed properties. These are controls you can change right now to modify the way your forms and reports look or behave.

A
B
C
D
E
F
G
H
I
J
KL
M
N
O
P
Q
R
S
T
U
V
W
XYZ

Just as we're not covering pro-gramming in this book, we're not going to talk about properties associated with Access macros or Access BASIC objects. You can do some very groovy things by associating macros with controls, though. For example, you can create a pushbutton that says Find, which will bring up the Find dialog box every time you push it. If you want to get into this sort of thing, check out either the Access manuals or **Understanding Microsoft Access 2** (Sybex, 1994).

Remember—not all controls have all the properties we list here. Some have more, some have fewer. Access will tell you (when you select a control) what properties that control has.

Properties in the Property box are grouped into categories as follows:

The **Data Properties** group contains properties that relate to the data displayed in a control.

Control Source: The source of the data that is displayed in the control can be a field name in the table or dynaset the form is based on, or an expression that will calculate a value.

Format: The formatting information that appears here determines what the data in the control will look like when it is displayed.

Decimal Places: The information shown here controls the number of decimal places number data will have.

Default Value: You can enter a default value for a field into this property. If this default value is not the same as the default value property you set when you designed the table, this one will win out.

Validation Rule: Gives you another chance to enter a validation rule. Note that validation rules in a table are always enforced, but validation rules in forms are in effect only when you're using the form. Remember too, that validation rules are not useful on reports since you do not use a report to enter data.

Validation Text: Here, you can enter a message to be displayed when the validation rule is violated.

The **Layout Properties** determine how controls appear when they are displayed on-screen.

Size Mode: Determines how Access makes graphics fit into the control that displays them. You can clip graphics, scale graphics to fit inside of the control, or zoom graphics to fit within the control.

Scroll Bars: If the field is too long for the control, you can have Access display scroll bars next to the field, so you can scroll around to view what's not showing up in the display. Because scroll bars are a screen element and not something that can be printed, scroll bars are useful on forms, not reports.

Can Grow: If the Can Grow property is set to Yes, Access will increase the height of the field so that all of the data of the field is visible at once. Because the field can grow both on screen and in print, this property is a good way to handle variable length fields on both forms and reports.

Can Shrink: This is less useful than the Can Grow property, but it's still fun. Setting Can Shrink to Yes allows Access to reduce the number of lines a field can display until only the data in the field fits. It's a sort of shrink-to-fit property. (Usually, you'll find that creating a field as wide as you want it and only high enough to display a single line, then setting the Can Grow property to Yes without messing with Can Shrink is the best way to go.)

Special Effects: This property lets you assign the control a raised, sunken or normal look. By far the easiest way to set these values, though, is to use the *Palette*.

Font Name: Changes the font in which the field is displayed. You can display a field in any font you have installed on your system.

Font Size: Changes the size of the font in which the control is displayed.

Font Italic: Lets you display the data in italics.

Font Underline: Allows you to display the data underlined.

Text Align: Lets you choose how text is aligned within the control—left, right, centered, or general. If you pick general, the alignment depends on the type of data you are displaying in the field.

The **Other Properties** group contains properties that do not fit in under any of the other categories.

Name: Every control on a form or report needs a unique name so Access can keep them all straight. A control's name may be the same as the name of the field from which it gets data, or it may be some meaningless name like *Text27* that was given to it by Access.

Status Bar Text: Contains the text that Access displays in the status bar at the bottom of the window while the control is active.

CONTROLS: SELECTING A FONT AND POINT SIZE

Let's say you don't like the *font* (style of type) and *point size* (size of the type) as they show up on your form or report. This is one of the many things the Wizard decided for you, but you can change what the Wizard has done.

To modify the font and point size a control is displayed in, change the control's Font Name and Font Size properties, as described here:

1. Select the form or report that includes the text for which you want to modify the font, and view it in Design View.

2. Select the control that represents the text you want to change.

3. If you do not have the Property box on the screen, select View ➤ Properties.

4. Click on the down-arrow at the right-most end of the box at the top of the window, and select Layout Properties from the drop-down list that appears. This limits the properties that appear in the Property box to those about the layout of the selected object. A list of properties that fall under the Layout Properties category will appear in the Property box.

5. In the list of properties, find Font Name. (The list is long, and Font Name appears near the bottom of the list, so keep moving down 'til you find it.)

6. Click on the Font Name property box. A little box with a down-arrow in it will appear.

7. Click on the down-arrow, and a drop-down list of all the fonts that are installed on your computer will appear.

8. Pick the font you want from the list.

9. Once you have picked the font you want to use, you can enter a point size (if you want to change it) in the Font Size box.

66 **Some fonts are bigger than others. For example, 12-point Courier is slightly larger than 12-point Courier New. You may need to change the size of the control to accommodate larger font sizes.**

Now you can click on either the Form View (if it's a form) or Print Preview (if it's a report) button on the toolbar to see the results of your work.

See **Controls: Properties; Text: Toolbar Shortcuts for Changing**

COPY, CUT, AND PASTE

To copy a single cell in a datasheet, or to move data between two cells, do the following:

1. Select the cell that holds the data you want to copy or move.

2. Select Edit ➤ Copy from the menu bar to copy the data to the Windows Clipboard. (If you want to move the data, select Edit ➤ Cut instead.)

3. Now select the cell into which you want to copy the data.

4. Select Edit ➤ Paste. This will copy the contents of the Clipboard into the cell you just selected.

You can also copy an entire record—a very handy feature that saves typing, and allows more time for more important chores, or maybe a trip to Hawaii. To copy an entire record, just follow these steps:

1. Select the record you want to copy. You can select a record by picking Edit ➤ Select Record from the menu or by clicking in the area just to the left of the first field in the record.

2. Select Edit ➤ Copy to copy the record to the Clipboard.

3. Select Edit ➤ Paste Append to create the new record. Access adds the new record at the bottom of the datasheet.

If you have cut a record, or copied one to the Clipboard, and you then select another record and choose Edit ➤ Paste, you will overwrite the record that the pointer is on...without warning!

See **Data Entry Shortcuts; Clipboard**

COUNTER DATA TYPE

The Counter data type holds a number that increases sequentially with each new record. The first record, for example, would be 1, the second record, 2, and so on. (Using the Counter data type, Access *counts* the records as they are entered, and gives each its own unique number.)

Access uses the Counter data type when it creates a primary key field, because the primary key field must be unique. A counter field is comparable to a number field with a Field Size of Long Integer. This can be very useful when you're relating tables, because you must join tables on compatible fields.

See **DataType; Data Types in Access; Joins and Relationships**

Counter Data Type Properties

Access pretty much handles the counter business. You cannot modify the number stored in a counter field. Once you say that a certain field is going to be a counter field, Access fills it in. There are three properties associated with counter fields:

- Format
- Caption
- Indexed

You can specify **Format** properties, and you might find it useful to do so. All the formats that are good for numbers are also acceptable for counters, so refer to the section on Number Fields Properties to get the scoop on this.

You can set up a **Caption** to be displayed on the status bar when you view it in a form or report. This might be helpful if you want to tell the person doing data entry that he or she can't and shouldn't mess with the counter field.

You can also change the **Indexed** property, but since the only thinkable reason to use a counter field is for the primary key, you should just keep the Indexed property set to "Yes (No Duplicates)."

See **Data Type; Data Types in Access; Number Data Type; Primary Key; Text Data Type**

A
B
C
D
E
F
G
H
I
J
KL
M
N
O
P
Q
R
S
T
U
V
W
XYZ

CREATING A TABLE

See   **Part 1; Tables: Creating in Design View; Table Wizard**

CRITERIA

The specific instructions you give, telling Access what data and records to include and not to include when it runs a query or retrieves data to place in a form, are known as *criteria*.

Specifying Criteria in Queries

"Specify criteria" is just a formal phrase for "make a set of rules to follow." The criteria you specify tell Access which records to include in the dynaset that results from your query. Those records that do not match the criteria you specify will not be included.

To set up criteria, you type it into the Criteria box of the QBE grid, under the name of the field to which it's going to apply. For example, in Figure C.5, if you wanted to specify a criteria for the Company Name field, you'd follow that column

Figure C.5

Follow down the field name column of your choice, and across the Criteria row, 'til the column and row meet. That's where you'll set up criteria for that particular field.

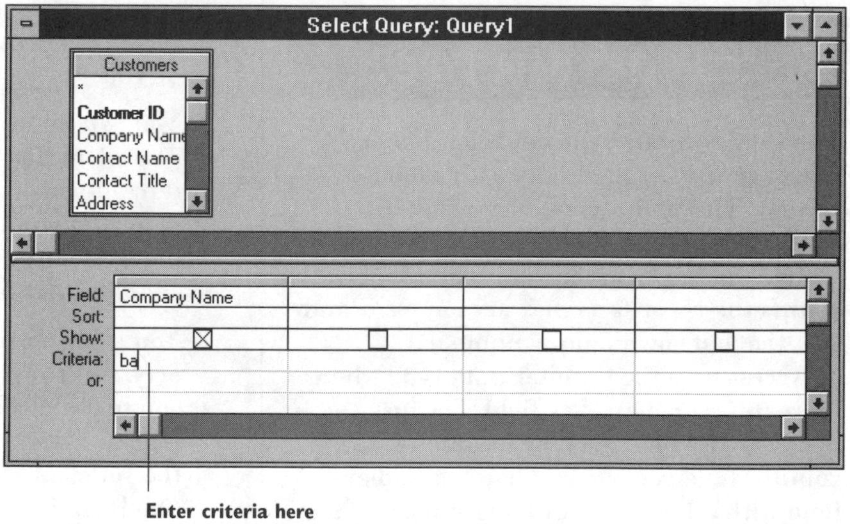

Enter criteria here

down, and you'd move across the Criteria row, and in the cell where the column and row meet, you'd specify criteria.

Here are some sample criteria for text fields:

Criteria	Matches
CA	All fields that match the string "CA"
Ca*	All fields that start with the letters "Ca"
a*7	All fields that start with an "a" and end with a "7"
*quack	All fields that end with "quack"

Tip

You can use wildcard characters here, just as in the Find dialog box. Look in "Datasheet View: Finding and Replacing Text" for more details.

You can also specify criteria for Number fields. Here are some sample criteria for Number fields:

Criteria	Matches
Between 10 and 20	All fields that are between 10 and 20
< 40	All fields that are less than 40
> 10	All fields that are greater than 10
< > 5	All fields that do not equal 5

And here are some criteria you might use for Date fields:

Criteria	Matches
Date( )	Fields with today's date
Between Date( ) - 7 and Date( )	All fields with a date within the last seven days
#1/1/96#	Fields with the date: January 1st, 1996

Tip

When you enter a date into criteria (or anywhere else in Access, for that matter), you must place # signs at the beginning and end of the date. The only exception to this is when you are entering the date into a table—in that case, Access very considerately places the # signs for you.

A B **C** D E F G H I J KL M N O P Q R S T U V W XYZ

You can also use other fields from the source tables and queries as part of the criteria. For example, if you had a table of salaries and bonuses and you wanted to see the names of everyone whose bonus totaled more than 20% of his or her salary, you could use the following criteria in the bonus field:

```
>[Salary]*0.2
```

·············· **Tip** ····················

Access can get confused when you are entering field names that include spaces. To make things clearer, place square brackets around field names. That helps Access know where one field name ends and the next field name begins.

Criteria is made up of a *comparison operator* followed by an *expression* to compare to the field value. (A comparison operator finds something that is different from something else. An expression is a mathematical "sentence"—like "1+1"— that has a result—like "=2.")

You can use the following comparison operators when you specify criteria:

Operator	Meaning
<	Less than
< =	Less than *or* equal to
>	Greater than
> =	Greater than *or* equal to
=	Equal to
< >	*Not* equal to

See **Expressions; Expression Builder; Filters and Sorts; Queries**

Multiple Criteria in Queries

The world might be a fine place if all questions were simple. But because things usually don't work out that way, you need a way in your database program to ask more complicated questions. To allow for complex queries, Access lets you combine multiple criteria, using "and" and "or" to connect more simple queries.

You can, for example, take two queries:

❂ "Which customers bought less than 100 units last year?"

❂ "Which customers get a discount greater than 10%?"

and connect them with the word "and" to form a more sophisticated query:

❂ "Which customers bought less than 100 units last year *and* got a discount greater than 10%?"

Of course the dynaset that resulted from this query would tell you whether any low-volume customers were getting hefty discounts, and then you could decide what to do about it!

In Access, you specify "and" criteria by typing the criteria in the Criteria row in the QBE grid. You specify "or" criteria by typing the first possible criteria in the Or row of the QBE grid, and the second possible criteria in the next, empty row of the QBE grid.

In the example of an Employees table, let's say you want to see the First and Last Name fields of all the employees who meet the criteria: "Had a bonus of over 20% of salary *or* lived in California *and* were reimbursed for education." For Access to run that query, you would specify the criteria:

```
([Bonus]>[Salary]*0.2) or ([State]
= "CA" and [Education] > 0)
```

In Figure C.6, you'll see the QBE grid that describes that question. Notice how the criteria for State and Education is in the same row—that's because they are connected by "and." The criteria for Bonus is in a separate row, because it is connected by "or" with the rest of the criteria.

Variables in Criteria

Access allows you to specify different values in a criteria each time you run the query that uses the criteria. The program will even prompt you to supply the values when you run the query. Access does this using a special type of query called a *parameter query*.

See   **Queries; Queries: Prompts to Enter Data**

Figure C.6

The criteria shown in this QBE grid includes both "and" and "or."

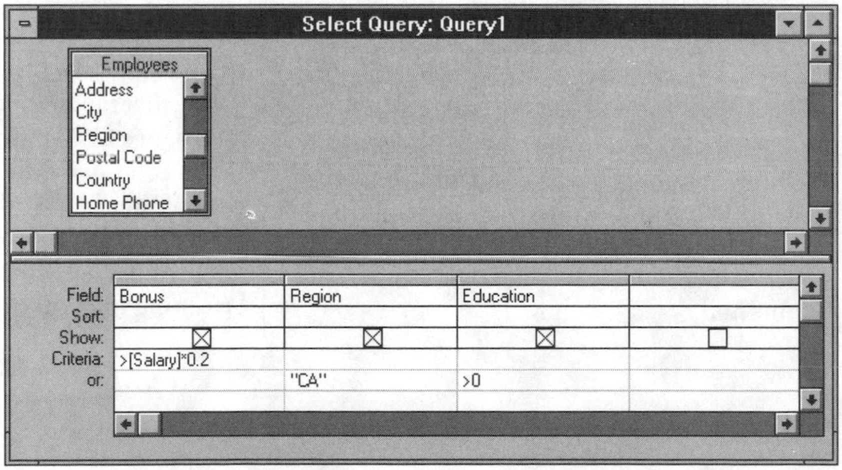

CROSSTAB QUERIES: CREATING

A crosstab query displays your data in a column-and-row grid format like the Datasheet View, but where the data is *cross tabulated*, meaning that all the data is shifted around: column heads are taken from one field, row heads from another field, and then the values pulled from a single field fill in the cells. This can produce a kind of summary of your data, which will make it easier for you to get a comprehensive look at things.

For example, if you have a table of prices for a number of stocks, you can display the following fields in a crosstab query:

✪ Company Name

✪ Date

✪ Closing price

Creating a Crosstab Query without the Wizard

To create a crosstab query:

1. Create a new query based on the table or query you want to summarize. You can do this using either the click-and-drag method or the pull-down menu method.

2. Select Query ➤ Crosstab to turn the query into a crosstab query. This adds two new rows to the QBE grid: Total and Crosstab.

3. Add the two fields you want to use as column and row heads, either by clicking and dragging them into the first two field cells on the QBE grid, or by using the pull-down menu method. In the Total box for each of these fields, select Group By.

4. Now add the field you want to display as data, again using either the click-and-drag or the pull-down menu method to move the field from the Field List to the next blank field cell on the QBE grid.

5. In the Total box for this field, select an aggregate function (*See* Functions: Aggregate) to perform on the data.

6. In the Crosstab box, select data for the field you are using as data.

Now, having designed your crosstab query, you can view it just like you would any other select query, by clicking on the Datasheet icon in the toolbar.

Figure C.7 shows the Design View of a crosstab query that uses company names as column heads, dates as row heads, and the closing prices of sample stocks as the data. Figure C.8 then shows the results of running this query.

Figure C.7

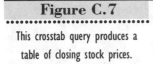

This crosstab query produces a table of closing stock prices.

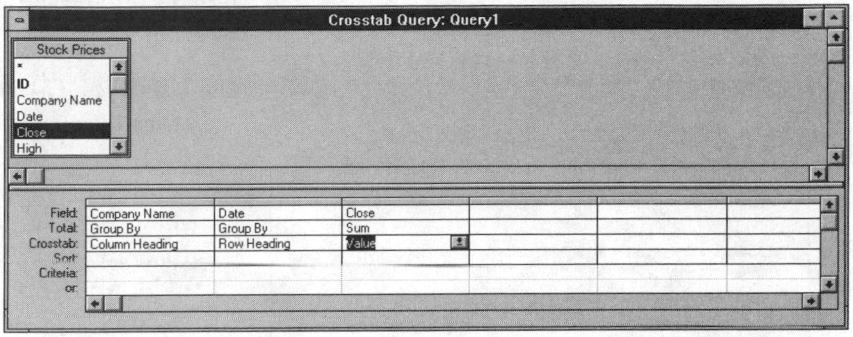

Crosstab Query: Query1

Stock Prices
*
ID
Company Name
Date
Close
High

Field:	Company Name	Date	Close			
Total:	Group By	Group By	Sum			
Crosstab:	Column Heading	Row Heading	Value			
Sort:						
Criteria:						
or:						

Figure C.8

The results of running the query shown in Figure C.7

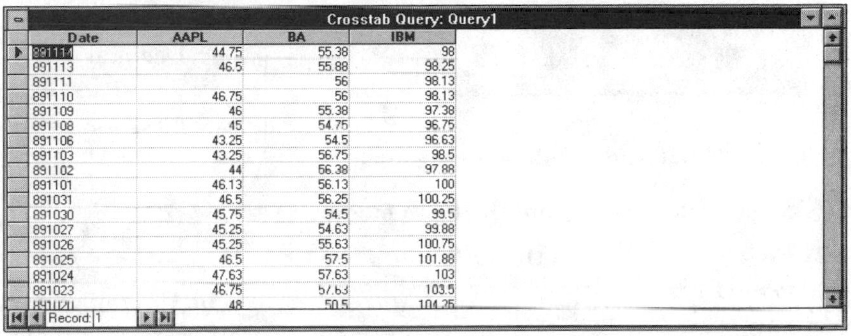

Crosstab Query: Query1

Date	AAPL	BA	IBM
891114	44.75	55.38	98
091113	46.5	55.88	98.25
891111		56	98.13
891110	46.75	56	98.13
891109	46	55.38	97.38
891108	45	54.75	96.75
891106	43.25	54.5	96.63
891103	43.25	56.75	98.5
891102	44	56.38	97.88
891101	46.13	56.13	100
891031	46.5	56.25	100.25
891030	45.75	54.5	99.5
891027	45.25	54.63	99.88
891026	45.25	55.63	100.75
891025	46.5	57.5	101.88
891024	47.63	57.63	103
891023	46.75	57.63	103.5
891020	48	50.5	104.25

Record: 1

Creating a Crosstab Query with the Wizard

See **Queries; Query Wizards**

CUE CARDS

An on-screen Help system in Access—Cue Cards—tells you what to do step-by-step, and then waits for you to do it before proceeding to the next stage of whatever you're doing. Cue Cards are especially handy for beginners.

Cue Cards look like small dialog boxes that stay on the screen while you do the things they describe, like create a table or a new form.

A
B
C
D
E
F
G
H
I
J
KL
M
N
O
P
Q
R
S
T
U
V
W
XYZ

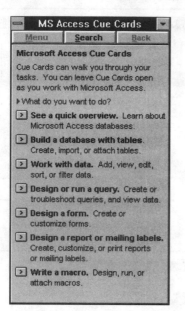

To use Cue Cards, follow these steps:

1. Select Cue Cards from the Help menu.

2. Pick a Cue Card on the task you want to perform.

3. Follow the directions in the Cue Card. When you are finished with the directions, click on the arrow button to move to the next card.

See　**Help; Context-Sensitive Help**

CURRENCY DATA TYPE

The Currency data type is used to store numbers *formatted to represent money.* Access can store numbers between −922,337,203,685,477.5808 and 922,337,203,685,477.5807. You can perform all the mathematical calculations you like on the data stored in currency fields. Keep in mind these points, though:

○ Using the Currency data type, you can store only four digits to the right of the decimal point. If you need more accuracy than that, or a larger range, you should not use the Currency data type. Instead, you should use a Number field, and you should set the Format, Decimal Places, and Validation properties to make the field look like money.

○ You can store foreign currency amounts in Currency fields (even if Windows is set to U.S. format on your machine), again by setting the Format, Decimal Places, and Validation properties in accordance with the foreign system you want to use.

Currency Properties

The Currency data type has the following properties associated with it:

○ Format

○ Decimal Places

○ Input Mask

○ Caption

○ Default Value

○ Validation Rule

○ Validation Text

○ Required

○ Indexed

Format is usually the local currency, so you should leave this property set to Currency unless you want the data formatted for some other currency. We cover the format properties of numbers—and currency—in the section on Number Fields Properties, so look there for more details.

Leave **Decimal Places** set to Auto, and Access will use the proper number of decimal places for currency—here in America, that's usually two. If you have some reason to split money into fractions of pennies, you can specify up to four digits after the zero.

Input Mask controls what fields look like before you enter any data. Since this is a Currency field, you should enter something like 0.00.

Caption is the label that will appear next to the field on forms and reports. You might want the caption to be "Enter US Dollars," or "Minimum payment is $20.00."

Default Value is a value Access will place into the field every time it creates a new record. If most of your customers pay $42.00, you could have this field default to $42.00— then, if some people pay more, you could change the number in this field just for them. Really, all this does is save the data-entry person some time in typing in a lot of data that's the same.

Validation Rule holds a rule against which Access is going to check any data that anyone tries to enter in the field. An example of this in a Contributions

table might be that the number must be a positive number. (You wouldn't want anyone making a *negative* contribution, would you?) To ensure that only positive amounts are entered, as you would want in a Contributions table, enter >0 as the Validation Rule.

Validation Text is the place where you would specify a message to be displayed by Access if the Validation Rule were violated. Let's say someone did make the mistake of entering a negative amount in a Contributions field. A message that says, "You must enter a positive number!" would alert the person to the mistake.

Required makes it so the data entry person absolutely *must* enter data in this field for every new record in the table.

Indexed (in a currency field) determines whether Access creates an index based on this field. Valid values in this field are: No, Yes (Duplicates OK), and Yes (No Duplicates).

When you use a **Number data type** to store currency, watch out—Access rounds numbers in a number field differently from how it rounds numbers in a currency field. Your results may be off by as much as a few cents, which will make a big difference in serious accounting.

See   Data Type; Text Data Type;
Number Data Type

CURRENT CELL

The current cell is the one currently in use. This is, presumably, the highlighted cell (also known as the *active* cell). You can make a cell in a datasheet active using one of three techniques:

✪   Click on the cell.

✪   Use the arrow keys to move around while you have an entire cell selected.

✪   Use the Tab key and Shift-Tab to move the current record forward or backward. When you are at the cell at the end of a record these keys will move the current record to the next record.

See   Datasheet; Datasheet View:
Navigating

CURRENT RECORD INDICATORS

Access uses *current record indicators*—a fancy term for little pictures—to show you what's happening with the current record in a datasheet. The current record's status shows as one of these icons:

Indicator	Meaning
	Indicates the current record
	You've changed the record and changes are not yet saved
	The current record is locked and you can't make changes

See   Datasheet View

CUSTOMIZING ACCESS

Some car owners just can't be happy unless they're hanging over the engine with ratchets and a screwdriver, tinkering. Maybe you're that kind of computer user, and you're just dying to see what you can soup up in Access. Well, there isn't much—Microsoft thinks Access is just fine the way it is, thank you—but there are a few things you can change that might save you time and make Access more usable for you.

See   Colors on Your Screen:
Changing; Options Dialog Box:
Changing Options

CUT AND PASTE

See   Copy, Cut, and Paste

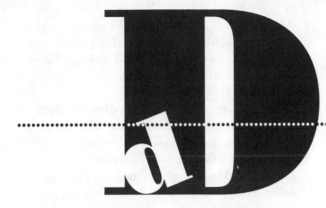

DATA

Data is the stuff that makes up information, broken down into its most basic pieces. For example, a list of first names (not the first names of actual people, just *first names*) is data. When first names are combined with last names so they describe actual people (or when you can imagine faces that go with the first names), those two pieces of data—the first name and the last name or the first name and the face, become *information*.

See Part I

DATABASE

A *database* is a collection of data, organized around a specific reference point. Your address book is a database on paper. The same information, in an electronic format, would be a mailing list database.

See Part I

DATABASE: CREATING

Creating an Access database involves:

1. Creating a database file to hold all the objects in your database.

2. Creating the tables, and then—by setting up the fields—the structure of the records in the tables.

3. Establishing links between the tables.

4. Entering the data.

66 **With the pieces of your database in place, you'll be able to create queries, sort and retrieve data, and run reports as necessary.**

See   **Database File: Creating; Entering Data; Joins and Relationships; Tables: Creating in Design View; Tables: Creating Fields In; Table Wizard**

DATABASE FILE

In Access and many other relational databases, a single database file contains tables of data as well as *all* the other objects (records in tables, queries, forms, reports, and more) that relate to the database. Access database files have the extension .MDB.

DATABASE FILE: CREATING

After you've planned your database on paper—but before you do anything else to set it up—you have to create a database file to hold all the objects that make up your database.

If you don't have Access running, start it up by double-clicking on the Microsoft Access icon in the Windows Program Manager. Then close the Welcome screen by double-clicking its control box (in the upper-left corner of the screen). (*See* Starting Access)

To create a database file from scratch:

1. Open the File menu.

2. Select New Database.

3. The New Database dialog box will appear. You'll be asked to name your new database (see Figure D.1). Type in a name (*See* Database File: Naming).

Other programs allow you to work on unnamed files until you are ready to save them, but Access makes you name your database file right away. Access requires a filename so it can immediately save the changes you make to your tables in the database file.

66 **We're not talking here about naming your tables—this is about naming your database file.**

Figure D.1

The New Database dialog box

```
┌────────────────────────────────────────────────────────────┐
│ ▭            New Database                                     │
│                                                              │
│ File Name:              Directories:          ┌──────────┐  │
│ ┌──────────┐            c:\access             │    OK    │  │
│ │ clients  │                                  └──────────┘  │
│ └──────────┘            📂 c:\                 ┌──────────┐  │
│ ┌──────────┐ ▲          📂 access             │  Cancel  │  │
│ │          │            📁 sampapps           └──────────┘  │
│ │          │            📁 setup              ┌──────────┐  │
│ │          │                                  │ Network… │  │
│ │          │                                  └──────────┘  │
│ │          │ ▼                         ▼        ☒ Exclusive  │
│ └──────────┘                                                 │
│ List Files of Type:     Drives:                              │
│ ┌──────────────┐ ▼     ┌──────────────┐ ▼                   │
│ │Databases[*.mdb]│      │ 💾 c: laxness │                    │
│ └──────────────┘       └──────────────┘                     │
└────────────────────────────────────────────────────────────┘
```

If you don't pick a name for your database, Access will do it for you—with a generic, meaningless name. Here's how the generic, meaningless name system works: Access calls your unnamed database DB*n*.MDB, replacing the *n* with a number (like 1 for the first time this happens, 2 for the second time…). Don't let this happen; it's very bad, because when you look later at your list of database names, you won't know which is which.

See   **Database File: Naming**

DATABASE DOCUMENTOR

The Database Documentor is an add-in that allows you to view and print detailed information about the objects in your database. To use the Database Documentor, open the database you want to document

and follow these steps:

1. Select File ➤ Add-ins ➤ Database Documentor from the menu bar. The Database Documentor dialog box will appear.

2. In the Object Type drop-down list, pick the type of object in your database about which you want to print information. Your choices are:

✪ Database

✪ Tables

✪ Queries

✪ Forms

✪ Reports

✪ Macros

✪ Modules

✪ All Object Types

Selecting Database allows you to generate information about the actually database that holds all of your other Access objects. Picking All Object Types from the list allows you to generate information about any combination of objects in your database. The rest are pretty obvious.

3. As you change the selection in the Object Type drop-down list, the list labeled "Print Definitions of Objects" will change. This list displays all of the objects of the type you selected in step 2. Click to the right of each of the objects about which you want to generate information. An × will appear next to the name of each object you select; once you have selected all the objects about which you want to print information, click on the OK button.

Tip

You can pick *all* the objects very quickly by clicking on the Select All button.

4. Access will work for a few seconds and then display an on-screen report in Print Preview, showing information about the objects you selected. You can print the report by selecting File ➤ Print.

See   **Add-Ins: Printing**

DATABASE FILE: NAMING

You can use up to eight characters in your database name. Access will add a period after that, and a three letter extension—MDB—that will help Access recognize that your file is an Access database.

Give your database a name that will help you remember what's in it. MY.MDB is no good; instead, something more like RENTALS.MDB or CLIENTS.MDB will tell you what's in the file.

The database filename rules are pretty lenient, but there are some things you can't do. You can't use a space in your database filename, and you can only use standard letters and numbers, some punctuation marks, and the following special characters:

$$- \ \& \ ! \ \# \ \hat{} \ @ \ \{ \ \} \ [\ ] \ (\ ) \ \sim \ \% \ \$$$

Giving Your Database Files Their Own Home

Not only should you give your database files names that make them easy to identify, you should also put them in a directory *other* than the Access home directory. That makes it easier to find and back up your files. You can create a new directory to hold your database files. Do this either from the Windows File Manager or the DOS command line.

To store your database file in a directory other than the Access directory:

1. From the File menu, select New Database. The Database File dialog box appears.

2. Select the drive (usually A:, B:, or C:) and the name of the directory you created to store your database.

3. Type the filename in the File Name box, then click on OK.

If everything worked out when you followed the steps outlined in "Database File: Creating," an empty window will have appeared on your screen, as shown in Figure D.2. It's empty because you haven't typed in data yet. You only created a database *file*—a place to put your information—like a box with no index cards in it.

Now you are ready to create a *table*. (Remember, tables are nothing more than a further breakdown of how you store your information. A table is just a list of data.)

If you need a refresher on what makes up a database, reread Part I.

DATABASE: OPENING AN EXISTING

See   **Database Window; Opening an Existing Database**

Figure D.2

When you create a new database, the Database window is displayed, but it doesn't include any objects.

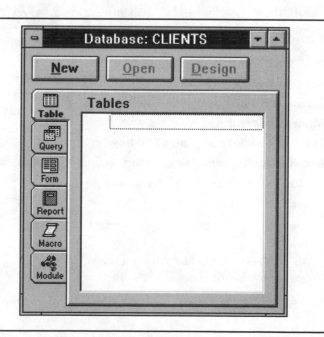

DATABASE WINDOW

The Database window is a kind of entry way into your database file—in it, Access lists the objects contained in the database file that's currently open. ...Well, actually only objects of one type are listed at a time; you can make a list of objects of one type or another appear by clicking on the buttons along the left side of the Database window (see Figure D.2).

Along the top of the window is another set of buttons; these allow you to take certain actions. For example, you can open an object by highlighting the object's name and clicking the **Open** button. You can start the process of creating a new object by selecting the button for that type of object along the left side of the Database window and then clicking the **New** button. You can open an object in Design View—where you can modify it—by highlighting the object's name and clicking the **Design** button.

> You can delete objects from your database file by highlighting their name in the Database window and pressing the Delete key on your keyboard. Access will display a dialog box asking you to confirm the deletion; click OK to go ahead.

You can preview reports by clicking on the Report button along the left side of the window, highlighting the report's name from the list that appears, and then clicking on the **Preview** button. (The Preview button appears in place of the Open button when you are listing reports.)

When you are listing Macros or Modules, the Open button will be replaced by a **Run** button, but we're not getting into that in this book.

> *See*   **Datasheet View; Forms and Form Wizards; Queries; Reports and Report Wizards; Table Wizard; Tables: Creating in Design View**

DATA: ENTERING

> *See*   **Entering Data**

DATA: ENTERING INTO AN EXISTING RECORD

In Datasheet View, to replace data in an existing record, you can just move to the cell that contains the old information and type new information in over the old. (This is really just a variation on adding a new record.)

You can also enter data into a blank cell in an existing record by moving to the blank cell and typing in the new stuff.

> *See*   **Copy, Cut, and Paste; Datasheet View: Adding a Record; Data Entry Shortcuts**

Saving Changes and Sharing Files

Once that little pen icon along the left side of your datasheet goes away it means Access has updated the table in the database file on disk and you can no longer undo any changes you've made.

Access does this because some people use their database on a <u>network</u>, a lot of computers wired together so they can share information and resources. In a network situation, it is possible for one person to be working on a database at her machine in one room while another person is working on the <u>same</u> database on his machine in a separate room. You don't want people repeating or undoing each other's work—not only would that be wasteful, it would also make everyone concerned completely crazy.

To keep the database file consistent for multiple users, Access can be set up to perform <u>record locking</u>. In this nifty system, as soon as person A starts to edit a record, all other Access users on the network are locked out of that record. Two people can't work on the same record at the same time. Only after Access commits the changes to disk can another Access user that has the same database open and edit the record.

DATA ENTRY SHORTCUTS

You can use these keys in Form View and in datasheets to make data entry faster and easier.

Press **Ctrl-;** to insert the date.

Press **Ctrl-:** to insert the time.

Press **Ctrl-Alt-Spacebar** to insert the default value for a field.

Press **Ctrl-'** *or* **Ctrl-"** to insert the value from the same field in the previous record.

Press **Ctrl-Enter** to insert a new line in a field, a label, or the Zoom box.

Press **Ctrl-+** to add a new record.

Press **Ctrl-−** to delete the current record.

Press **Shift-Enter** to save changes to the current record.

Press **Spacebar** to toggle a form's check box or option box on and off.

See **Copy, Cut, and Paste**

DATASHEET

The column-and-row layout in Access that contains data and resembles a spreadsheet is called a *datasheet*.

See **Datasheet View**

DATASHEET: CUSTOMIZING

See   **Customizing Access; Options Dialog Box: Changing Options**

DATASHEET: MODIFYING COLUMNS AND ROWS

In Datasheet View, you can change the width or height of a cell or a group of cells.

Changing the Width of Columns (Fields)

If *Ishkabibble* or anything else doesn't fit in a cell, you may want to increase the width of a column. To increase or decrease column width, do one of the following:

✪ Make a cell in the column you want to change the active cell. Select Format ➤ Column Width from the menu bar, and enter the new cell width in the dialog box that appears. If you change your mind and want to go back to the standard width, click in the Standard Width box and then click OK.

✪ Point the mouse at the column separator along the top of the grid. The mouse pointer will change into a two-headed arrow. Press down the left mouse button. An outline of the column will appear. You can drag the outline to make the column w i d e r or narrower.

You can always change a column's width back to the standard width. Just select Format ➤ Column Width from the menu bar, and then select the Standard Width box and click OK.

·············· **Tip** ··············

You can quickly set the width of a column to the width of the widest piece of data by double-clicking on the right column separator in the top line.

Changing the Height of Rows

Not only can you change the width of each column, you can also change the height of rows. However, all the rows in a datasheet are always the same height. You don't get to set one height for one row and another height for another row. You can change the height of rows, but if you do, you'll have to change them all.

To change the height of all of the rows in your datasheet, do one of the following:

✪ Select Format ➤ Row Height from the menu bar. Enter the new row height in the dialog box, as shown in Figure D.3.

✪ Move the mouse pointer to any row separator along the left side of the Datasheet View window. The mouse pointer will change to a two-headed arrow. An outline of the row will appear. You can click and drag the outline of the row up or down, 'til it's the height you want.

A
B
C
D
E
F
G
H
I
J
KL
M
N
O
P
Q
R
S
T
U
V
W
XYZ

Figure D.3

Enter the new row height in this dialog box.

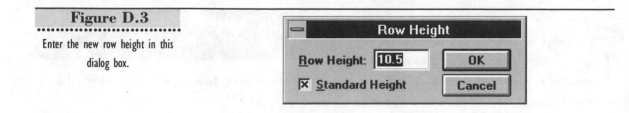

You can change the row height back to what it was—the standard height—at any time by selecting Format ➤ Row Height, then selecting the Standard Height box, and finally clicking OK.

DATASHEET: PRINTING

See **Printing; Printing Datasheets**

DATASHEET VIEW

Datasheet View—the view in which Access displays your data in a column-and-row grid that looks like a spreadsheet—makes it easy to enter data into a table or dynaset.

There are two ways to get a look at your data in Datasheet View:

✪ Open the Database window, select the table you want to see from the list that appears, and then click on the Open button.

✪ Click on the Datasheet View button when it appears on the toolbar, which will happen both when you are viewing either a table or query in Design View

and when you are viewing a form. The Datasheet View button looks like this:

On Read-Only Dynasets

You can view tables <u>or</u> dynasets in Datasheet View. A table is, of course, the structure in which you store your data. A dynaset is a collection of data that is the answer to a query.

You can usually use a dynaset as if it were a table. However, you cannot modify data that is the result of queries that are set up to produce <u>read-only</u> dynasets. Read-only means you can read them, but you can't change them. In the sections on queries, we give you more detail on those special queries that create dynasets that cannot be edited.

66 In Datasheet View, each row represents a different record and each column represents a field. If the Datasheet is very large—so large it won't fit on your screen—scroll bars will appear along the right side and/or the bottom of the window. (See Figure D.4.) You can click on the vertical scroll bars along the right side of the window to scroll up and down through the records, and you can click on the horizontal scroll bars along the bottom of the window to move to the right and left. This will allow you to see more fields. You can also click on the VCR-type buttons at the bottom-left of the screen to move to the previous or next screen.

You'll find that one cell of the now famous column-and-row grid has a blinking stick-shaped thing in it, or is highlighted. We call that blinking stick-shaped thing the *insertion point*, because that's where whatever you type will be inserted. We call the cell that contains the insertion point or is highlighted the *current cell*—and since it's the cell you are currently using, it's also called the *active cell*. (Look at Figure D.4, where the active cell in the top-left corner is highlighted.)

See **Current Cell; Database Window**

DATASHEET VIEW: ADDING A RECORD

There are two handy techniques for adding a record in Datasheet View.

One Technique

When you are in Datasheet View, scroll down to the last record that contains data, and there you will see one additional record—a blank one—marked with an asterisk along the left side:

It is into this blank row, or record, that you're going to type in the new record's data. What could be more simple?

66 You can click on cells and move between cells in this blank row just like in any other row. As long as you move horizontally, you'll be in the same record.

Type data into each cell, paying attention to the heading so you'll know what field the cell represents. When you finish typing the appropriate information into a cell, move to the next one by tapping the Tab key. Keep doing this 'til you've got all the information entered.

Figure D.4

•••••••••••••••••••••••••••

If there are a lot of records in your table, they won't all fit on the screen. In that case, scroll bars will appear on the side and/or bottom of the window. You can click on the scroll bars to scroll around the records.

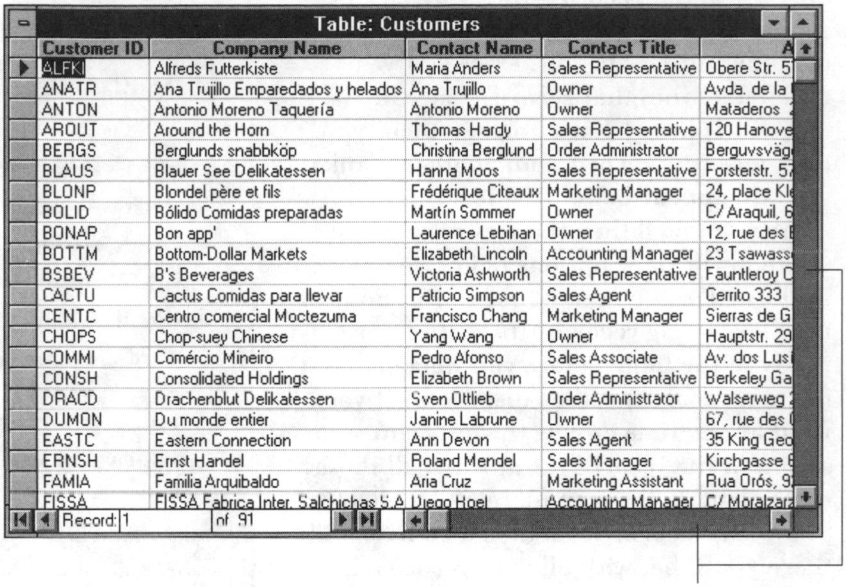

Customer ID	Company Name	Contact Name	Contact Title	A
ALFKI	Alfreds Futterkiste	Maria Anders	Sales Representative	Obere Str. 5
ANATR	Ana Trujillo Emparedados y helados	Ana Trujillo	Owner	Avda. de la
ANTON	Antonio Moreno Taquería	Antonio Moreno	Owner	Mataderos 2
AROUT	Around the Horn	Thomas Hardy	Sales Representative	120 Hanove
BERGS	Berglunds snabbköp	Christina Berglund	Order Administrator	Berguvsväg
BLAUS	Blauer See Delikatessen	Hanna Moos	Sales Representative	Forsterstr. 57
BLONP	Blondel père et fils	Frédérique Citeaux	Marketing Manager	24, place Kl
BOLID	Bólido Comidas preparadas	Martín Sommer	Owner	C/ Araquil, 6
BONAP	Bon app'	Laurence Lebihan	Owner	12, rue des
BOTTM	Bottom-Dollar Markets	Elizabeth Lincoln	Accounting Manager	23 Tsawass
BSBEV	B's Beverages	Victoria Ashworth	Sales Representative	Fauntleroy C
CACTU	Cactus Comidas para llevar	Patricio Simpson	Sales Agent	Cerrito 333
CENTC	Centro comercial Moctezuma	Francisco Chang	Marketing Manager	Sierras de G
CHOPS	Chop-suey Chinese	Yang Wang	Owner	Hauptstr. 29
COMMI	Comércio Mineiro	Pedro Afonso	Sales Associate	Av. dos Lusí
CONSH	Consolidated Holdings	Elizabeth Brown	Sales Representative	Berkeley Ga
DRACD	Drachenblut Delikatessen	Sven Ottlieb	Order Administrator	Walserweg
DUMON	Du monde entier	Janine Labrune	Owner	67, rue des
EASTC	Eastern Connection	Ann Devon	Sales Agent	35 King Geo
ERNSH	Ernst Handel	Roland Mendel	Sales Manager	Kirchgasse 6
FAMIA	Familia Arquibaldo	Aria Cruz	Marketing Assistant	Rua Orós, 9
FISSA	FISSA Fabrica Inter. Salchichas S.A	Diego Roel	Accounting Manager	C/ Moralzar

Table: Customers

Record: 1   of 91

Scroll bars

When you're finished, you can just click on an older record, or press the ↓ key to move to a blank row for a new record. The record you have just completed will be saved.

As soon as you start typing in a cell, that little current record (or new record) icon along the left side of the window will change to a pen icon. The pen icon indicates that you have modified the record. The pen icon is displayed as long as you stay with the record you've modified. During that time, you can cancel the changes you have made to the record simply by pressing the Escape (Esc) key.

All the changes you make are saved in the database file—actually written to your hard disk—either when you change to another record or when you select Records ➤ Refresh from the menu bar.

If you are on a network, and the pen icon is showing next to a record on your machine, anyone else who opens up the same database on another computer will see the little international "no" icon next to that same record, telling them that someone else is modifying the record and they can't mess with it.

Another Technique

In Datasheet View select Records ➤ Data Entry from the menu bar. Then you'll see *only the blank record*—the one you'll be typing data into—in the same old familiar column-and-row layout. Once you've typed data into that record, a new blank one will appear below. You can then type data into that record, and another blank one will appear below it, and so on.

As you do all this, the records you have created will show up, one below the other, in the order you created them. But none of the preexisting records (those that were already in the table before you started adding new records) will be displayed. If you want at any time during this procedure to see *all* of the records (or at least, all those that will fit on the screen), select Records ➤ Show All Records from the menu bar, and there you'll be, with all your records laid out in columns and rows.

·············· **Tip** ·······················

Access annoyingly gives you minuscule spaces into which you enter data. To cope with this, press Shift-F2, and a Zoom box will appear. You can then type your data into the larger space of the Zoom box. (See Zoom Box)

See also **Datasheet View: Entering Data into an Existing Record; Copy, Cut, and Paste; Data Entry Shortcuts**

Characters That Don't Appear on Your Keyboard

· · · · · · · · · · · · ·

You can enter characters besides those for which you have keys on your keyboard. To do this, use the Character Map that comes with Windows (it's in Accessories). Just copy the character you want to the clipboard and then paste it into your cell.

You can also get special characters by holding down Alt and typing in code numbers. Wherever you type in one of these special key combinations, it's corresponding symbol will appear. Some of the most commonly used symbols are shown in Table D.1.

At first, you should stick to pasting in characters from the MS Sans Serif font; that's the font Access normally uses to display the datasheet, so it'll work best.

To enter symbols from the MS Sans Serif font into a cell, hold down the Alt key while you type the number on the numeric keypad.

When you get more familiar with this stuff, check out the other fonts that come with Windows—some of them are very cool. Wingdings, the Microsoft dingbat font, for example, is a large collection of interesting glyphs and tiny pictures.

You can also use characters from any other font that your computer can display. See the sections on Printing, and on Forms and Reports.

Table D.1

Some Commonly Used Symbols from the MS Sans Serif Font

Key Combination	Symbol	Meaning
Alt-0169	©	Copyright
Alt-0174	®	Registered
Alt-0165	¥	Yen
Alt-0163	£	English Pound
Alt-0162	¢	Cent
Alt-0216	Ø	Null

66 **Access does not store font information along with each individual cell or field in your table. If you place a Wingding or other symbol in a cell, and you want it to show up in a form or report, you have to specify that font when you create the form or report. Otherwise, the Wingding or symbol won't show up.**

DATASHEET VIEW: DELETING RECORDS

When you're through with a record, you can get rid of it. To delete a record, you first have to locate it. You can scroll the Datasheet View window until you can see the record you want to get rid of, or you can use the handy Find techniques we describe in upcoming sections. (*See* Datasheet View: Finding and Replacing Text.)

Once the record you want to delete is in the window, where you can see it, you can do *one* of two things to select (highlight) the entire record:

- Click in the record selector along the left side of the record.

- If one cell in the desired record is the active cell, select Edit ➤ Select Record from the menu bar.

Tip

You can select consecutive records by holding down the Shift key while clicking on the first and last records you want to select.

With the record selected, you can delete them either by pressing the Delete key or by selecting Edit ➤ Delete from the menu bar. Access displays the message shown in Figure D.5 to confirm that you are deleting records. Click OK and Access deletes the record.

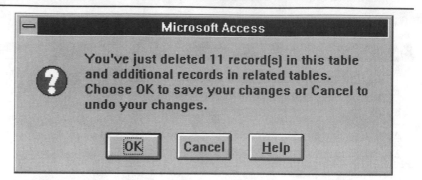

This is your last chance to change your mind before the records you've marked for deletion are gone for good.

You simply cannot undelete a record. Once you click OK, the record is gone for good. That means you'd better be sure you don't need your best customer's address any more before you click OK.

After you've marked all the records you want to get rid of, you'll have to *compact* the database.

See **Compacting the Database**

DATASHEET VIEW: EDITING DATA

See **Editing Data in Datasheet View**

DATASHEET VIEW: FINDING AND REPLACING TEXT

In Datasheet View, you can have Access search for a piece of text—either through all the data in the table or through any given field in all the records in the table. Even better, you don't have to know exactly what you are looking for. When you tell Access what to look for, you can include *wildcard* characters, which are special symbols that tell Access "anything goes" in the location of that character. *See* the section called Using Wildcards to Find Data in the Datasheet View section.

Searching for Specific Info

Sometimes you know only part of the information you want to find. Maybe you know Sally's first name, but not her last name. Maybe you know that the title of a movie starts with *The*, but that's all you remember. To find something when you have a scrap of text as a clue, you can search for a *text string*—any group of characters, strung together—anywhere in the displayed table—by selecting Edit ➤ Find or by clicking on the Find icon (it's the binoculars) in the toolbar. This will bring up the Find dialog box shown in Figure D.6.

A
B
C
D
E
F
G
H
I
J
KL
M
N
O
P
Q
R
S
T
U
V
W
XYZ

Figure D.6

The Find dialog box

Tip

Because the Find dialog box appears right in the middle of your screen, it covers part of the datasheet. If you find that the active, highlighted cell is actually *behind* the Find dialog box, don't despair. You can *move* the dialog box, by pointing at its title bar, holding down the mouse button, and dragging the little pest out of the way.

In the Find dialog box, you tell Access all about whatever it is you're looking for—or at least, as much as you know. (Psst!…This is the sort of thing the police do when you know the car that ran you over had the letter Q and the number 96 in its license plate, but you can't remember much else.)

In the Find dialog box, you can set the following controls to let Access know what it should match.

Find What   Is where you type in the text you want to find.

Where   Tells Access in which cells of your table to look for exact matches to the Find What text. You can tell Access to match the Find What text exactly with *all of the cell text* (Make Whole Field), with *only the first characters* (Start of Field) of the cell text, or with *anything anywhere within the cell text* (Any Part of Field).

Search In   Tells Access to search in either the current field only (which is shown in the title of the Find dialog box), or in all of the fields. Note that searching all of the fields for data can be time consuming—try to narrow the search if you can.

Direction   Tells Access whether you want it to search from the current record to the beginning of the table or to the end of the table.

Match Case   Forces Access to consider text to be a match only if it matches the case—uppercase or lowercase—of each character as it was typed in the Find What text.

Search Fields as Formatted Is where you can choose to search the data that is actually stored in the table, or as it is displayed on the datasheet. (Remember, they aren't always the same.) Searching fields as formatted is slower, but you're more likely to get the results you expect—especially when you are searching for dates, because Access (in its wacky inner workings) stores dates as numbers regardless of the format in which they are displayed.

Find First Sends Access searching for the first record that meets all the other requirements specified in the Find dialog box.

Find Next Searches for the next record (after the first one) that meets the requirements.

Close Closes the Find dialog box once you have found the record you are looking for.

Putting this all together, here's what you do to find specific text in Datasheet View:

1. Type whatever you want to search for in the Find What box. Remember that you can use wildcard characters (described in the upcoming section called Using Wildcards to Find Data) if you don't know every single character, or if you're unsure of the spelling of something.

2. You can determine the direction in which Access will search the table—either up or down from the current record—by selecting one of the two buttons grouped under Direction.

3. Set the other options in the Find box as you like, referring to the list above for details.

4. Click on Find First to locate the first record that meets your requirements. The first cell in the datasheet to meet your requirements will become the highlighted, active cell in the datasheet.

5. Click on Find Next if you want to continue the search in the direction (up or down) you specified.

6. When you're finished, click the Close button to close the dialog box.

············· **Tip** ·····················

If you already know which field contains the text you are searching for, search only that field. Searching all the cells in a single field is much faster than searching all the cells in all the fields. It is also faster to search for exact matches than to use Where to search for scraps of text that might appear in the front, back, or anywhere in the cell text.

Searching for a Word or a Group of Words

Sometimes you don't know exactly *what* you are searching for—maybe that's actually *why* you are looking. When you aren't sure whether the text you are searching for is a word unto itself or has something before or after it, be sure that the Where box in the Find dialog boxes reads Any Part of Field. This will make Access locate any field that contains the Find Text any place within it—even if the text string you've specified does not match the text in the field exactly.

If you're unsure of the case—uppercase or lowercase—of a string of text that you want to find, be sure that the Match Case box is *not* selected when you search.

Using Wildcards to Find Data

Although you can use the Where box to search for general patterns, it's not very flexible, and when you're looking for something nonspecific, you clearly want flexibility. By including *wildcard characters* in the Find What string, you can search your table or dynaset for very complicated patterns of data. Wildcard characters are symbols that take the place of unknown characters or numbers.

Wildcard characters available to use in Access include the following:

Symbol	Meaning
*	Match any string of characters, anything at all
?	Match any single character
#	Match any single digit
[]	Match any of the characters contained between the brackets

Symbol	Meaning
!	Match every character except the one that follows the ! (So *[!a]* matches every character except an *a*.)
-	Specifies a range of characters when used between brackets. For example, *[a-f]* matches any letter between *a* and *f*.

In searching a table of U.S. presidents, for example, *J*Q*A* finds John Quincy Adams, *M*V*B* finds Martin Van Buren, and **Adams* finds both John Adams and John Quincy Adams (his son). Table D.2 shows some other examples of wildcard combinations.

Finding Data and Replacing It

You can search for and *replace* data in a way that is very similar to the way you just searched for it. To do this, follow these steps:

1. In Datasheet View, select one cell in the field column in which you want to replace data.

2. Select Edit ➤ Replace from the menu bar. The Replace dialog box will appear, as shown in Figure D.7.

3. In the Find What box (a text box in the Replace dialog box) type in the text you want to find (and replace). You can use wildcards, if you need to.

A
B
C
D
E
F
G
H
I
J
KL
M
N
O
P
Q
R
S
T
U
V
W
XYZ

Table D.2

Some Sample Wildcard Combinations

Pattern	Matches	Also Matches	Doesn't Match
A*e	Apple	Axe	Apple II
e[a-c]	eb	dc	ee
A?B	AaB	AlB	Aaa
a#	a7	al	ab
a[ab]	ab	aa	ac
a[!a]	ab	aq	aa

Figure D.7

You can search and replace data in a table by using Edit ➤ Replace.

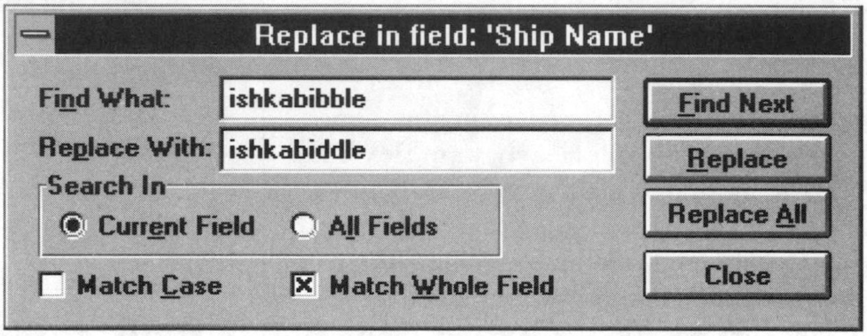

Replace in field: 'Ship Name'

Find What: ishkabibble

Replace With: ishkabiddle

Search In
- ⦿ Current Field ◯ All Fields
- ☐ Match Case ☒ Match Whole Field

Find Next
Replace
Replace All
Close

66 Access remembers whatever you last entered in the Find What or Replace What boxes. If you find something you no longer need there, just type over it to tell Access what you want to find or replace this time.

Here you have options for defining the Find What text—in fact, you have the same options you had in defining Find What when you simply wanted to *find* it.

So for more details on these options, look at the earlier sections on finding data.

4. Tell Access *what* you want to replace the found text with by typing it in the Replace With box.

Checking the check box for Match Whole Field in the Replace dialog box has the same effect as setting the Where field in the Find dialog box to Match Whole Field.

If you check the check box for Match Case, Access will have to pay attention to the case of letters (uppercase vs. lowercase) when it's looking for what you entered into the Find What box. If you do not select Match Case, Access pays no attention to case when it looks for a match.

5. Now you can click the Find Next button to have Access find the next record that matches your Find What text, without replacing the found text. Or you can click on the Replace button, and Access will replace just the first occurrence of the Find What text. (What will it be replaced with?…Well, whatever you typed into the Replace With box.)

If you want, you can continue to search through your data by clicking on the Find Next button, and to replace matching cells by clicking the Replace button.

Replacing a Similar Piece of Text in Many Records

On a large datasheet, doing this kind of two-step search and replace for a lot of stuff can take a while.

There is a way to replace *all occurrences* of the Find What data with the Replace With data. To do this, click on the Replace All button in the Replace dialog box. But be very careful when you do this, because you won't be able to undo the changes. (That will be a big problem if Access changes 10,000 records, and then you find you made some little mistake in the Replace With text.)

To use the Replace All feature:

1. Select the field on which the replace will be performed.

2. Select Edit ➤ Replace.

3. Now set things up in the Replace dialog box, just as you did before. *Be careful*, though—this time, Access won't ask you if you meant it every time it finds a match.

4. Click Replace All. If Access displays a dialog box saying it has reached the end of the records, just click Yes to continue replacing from the start of your data.

5. When a dialog box appears saying Access has reached the end of the records, this means it has searched and replaced the specified text in your entire set of data. Click on OK.

6. Now Access will give you one last warning—you will not be able to undo what Access is about to do if you proceed, so be sure you are certain it's going to be okay. If you are sure that you want to replace every smidgen of the specified data, click OK. Or, to chicken out, click Cancel.

Once you tell Access to make the changes to your data, you can't get your original data back. You can, however, do a reverse replace if you happen to make changes that you don't want to keep. For example, if you originally replaced VA with VG, try a reverse replace—VG back to VA. Be very careful, though, because you might have had a lot of VGs to begin with, and this will change them all to VAs—something you might not want.

7. Now click Close to close up the Replace dialog box. You'll be back in Datasheet View, looking at your changed data.

See **Datasheet View; Filters and Sorts**

DATASHEET VIEW: NAVIGATING

In Datasheet View, Access displays all the records that will fit at once in the Datasheet View window on the screen.

Looking at a Bunch of Records

You can increase the number of records displayed by increasing the amount of desktop space that Access can use. To maximize both the Access window and the Datasheet View window, double-click on both title bars.

Using the Keyboard and the Mouse

You can maneuver around inside the Datasheet window using either the keyboard or the mouse. Use the keys in Table D.3 to get around while you're in Datasheet View.

Using the mouse you can scroll up and down through your table in these ways:

- ❂ Clicking on the up arrow on the scroll bar (which appears when the datasheet is too big to fit in the Datasheet window) scrolls your view toward the beginning of your database one record at a time.

66 **When a cell is highlighted, the ← and → keys behave like the Tab key and Shift-Tab combination; and when the insertion point is in a cell, they move the insertion point forward or backward in the cell.**

- ❂ Pointing at the up arrow and holding down the mouse buttons scrolls smoothly toward the start of your data.

- ❂ Clicking and dragging on the vertical scroll box positions the current record at another point inside of the table.

- ❂ Clicking on the down arrow on the scroll bar scrolls your view toward the beginning of your database one record at a time.

- ❂ Pointing at the down arrow and holding down the mouse button scrolls smoothly toward the end of the table.

Jumping to Specific Records

You don't want to have to scroll through every record in the table to find the one you want (if you did, why did you buy this database program and spend your time setting up your tables?) The whole point of a database program is to get *it* to do the work for you.

Table D.3

Use These Key to Get Around in Datasheet View

Key	What It Does
↑	Moves up one record
↓	Moves down one record
Tab	Moves to the next field
Shift-Tab	Moves the current field to the left
Home	Moves to the first field in the current record
End	Moves to the last field in the current record
Ctrl-↓	Moves to the current field in the last record
Ctrl-↑	Moves to the current field in the first record
Ctrl-Home	Moves to the first field of the first record
Ctrl-End	Moves to the last field of the last record
Page Down	Advances by one screen of records
Page Up	Moves one screen of records back toward the beginning of the table
Ctrl-Page Up	Moves one screen to the right
Ctrl-Page Down	Moves one screen to the left

Using some simple Access menu commands, you can quickly move the current record in a table to some other record. You can also have Access find a particular record by searching for a piece of text you know is in that record. You don't even have to know exactly what you are looking for—instead, you can include *wildcard* characters to represent the unknown character(s).

See **Datasheet View: Finding and Replacing Text**

Going to the Ends of Your Table

You can move to the First, Last, Next, Previous, or New record by using the Records ➤ Go To command. Once you select Go To, you are presented with another menu that allows you to select the record to which you want to go.

Command	What It Does
First	Moves the insertion point to the first record in the current table

Command	What It Does
Last	Moves the insertion point to the last record in the current table
Next	Moves the insertion point from its present location to the record that's one closer to the end of the table
Previous	Moves the insertion point from its present location to the record that's one closer to the beginning of the table
New	Makes the insertion point to the blank record that always exists at the end of the table

✪ When you want to enter new records in a table, use the New command to make the blank record the current record.

✪ The Next command and the Previous command are useful only within macros, which we're not getting into in this book. You can move more conveniently from one cell to the next or the previous one by using either the mouse or the arrow keys.

See   **Datasheet View; Forms: Moving from Record to Record**

DATA TYPE

When you set up fields, you have to name them and you have to *describe the kind of data* that's going to be in them.

This is because when you want to work with data, Access is going to have to go get the data you want to use out of the tables and records and fields that contain that data. Computers take things so literally that if you sent one into a grocery store to get peaches, you'd have to tell it every detail of what "peach" was. You'd have to say that "peach" is of a food type called "fruit." Then you'd have to describe those properties of "peach" that distinguish "peach" from other foods of the food type "fruit." Those properties that describe the food type "peach" include: round(ish), peach-colored, fuzzy, and of a certain size.

When you set up a field (in a table), you have to tell Access in some detail what's going to be in that field, so Access knows what it's dealing with when it retrieves data for you. In the same way you'd describe a food of the type "fruit" as a peach, which is round, fuzzy, peach-colored, and of a certain size, you might describe data of the type "date/time" as a Date field formatted with the symbol "/" (separating the month, date, and year), and always ending in 96 (for 1996).

To use data types to their best advantage and design tables that meet your needs, you're going to have to pay attention to the specific data types that are available and the properties available for each of them. Specifying the right data type for a field when you set up your records and tables will make it easier to access and manipulate that data.

Data is just the stuff you fill your database with. The real value of your database is not the data you put into it but the information you can get out of it. Careful planning of the data types you use will greatly increase the value you can get out of your data.

See **Data Types in Access**

DATA TYPE: SPECIFYING AND MODIFYING

You can specify the data type of each field either when you create a new table or when you modify an existing table. Figure D.8 shows the Table Design View screen, which is where you specify the data type.

The basic steps for adding a new field to a database and specifying the data type are:

1. Create or open a database file and create or open a table.

2. Click on the Design button to open up Design View.

3. Enter a new field name in the Field Name column.

4. Click on the Data Type pull-down menu and pick a data type from the list that appears.

5. If it is a data type that requires a field size, you then enter this in the Properties box along the bottom of the Table Design View window.

6. Set any other Field Properties that you want to set.

Figure D.8

Specify the data type of each field in the Table Design View window.

Field Name	Data Type	Description
Shoe Size	Text	
	Text	
	Memo	
	Number	
	Date/Time	
	Currency	
	Counter	
	Yes/No	
	OLE Object	

Field Properties

Field Size	50
Format	
Input Mask	
Caption	
Default Value	
Validation Rule	
Validation Text	
Required	No
Allow Zero Length	No
Indexed	No

Table: Table1

The data type determines the kind of values that users can store in the field. Press F1 for help on data types.

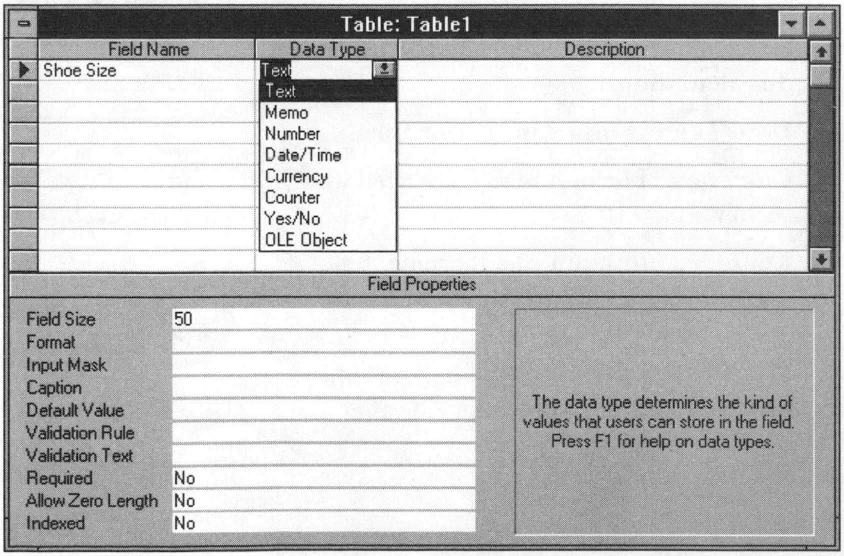

7. When you're done, close the Table Design window by selecting File ➤ Close from the menu bar.

66 **To modify an existing data type, just click on the thing you want to change and change it.**

See **Tables: Creating Fields In**

DATA TYPES IN ACCESS

Access provides these data types from which you can choose:

Text   For letters, characters, or any numbers with which you want to do no calculations (a ZIP code, for example).

Memo   For a note or text to detail or remind you of something.

Number   For numbers (formatted the way you want) with which you want to do calculations.

Date/Time   For a date and/or time.

Currency   For numbers formatted like money.

Counter   For a unique, incremented number Access assigns to each record as it is created.

Yes/No   For a true/false, yes/no, or other two-choice answer to a simple question.

OLE Object   For an embedded object—a spreadsheet or document from another program, for example, or a graphic, or even a small piece of digitized movie footage.

To find out more and get familiar with some common uses for each of them, turn to the sections for each data type.

66 **Our most complete coverage in this book is for the Text data type, because it is the one most commonly used—in fact, it's Access' default. That means Access assumes, at first, that this is the data type you're going to want. So whenever you create a new field, Access drops text into the data type. Also, most of the properties associated with any field are associated with text fields. So whatever data type interests you, read up on the text data type, too.**

See **Data Type: Specifying and Modifying**

DATE/TIME DATA TYPE

Guess what goes here? That's right—dates and times. You may want to store the date of a sale, the date an employee was hired, or the date and time a baby was born.

This, then, is the field to use. Date/Time is a data type that stores the date and/or the time, in any of a number of formats.

66 **Windows, which runs over, under, around, and through Access (See Windows), includes a number of features to localize it to the country or region where your computer is situated. When Windows was installed on your machine you (or whoever installed it) probably told it to install for the United States (assuming you're here and not somewhere else). That'll take care of a bunch of things—all the Access date formats based on the International settings will look correct to you as long as you're in the U.S. If you move somewhere else, you can run the Windows Control Panel and tell Windows to relocalize itself to your new country.**

Date/Time Data Type Properties

In a field of the Data/Time data type, you can set these properties:

- ✪ Format
- ✪ Input Mask
- ✪ Caption

- ✪ Default Value
- ✪ Validation Rule
- ✪ Validation Text
- ✪ Required
- ✪ Indexed

Format   determines what the field will look like when it is displayed. The predefined formats for dates in Access are:

General Date   If the field holds only a date, then only the date is displayed, and it will be in the form *month/date/year* (10/30/66, for example). A field that holds only the time will display the time as *hour:minutes AM/PM* (5:58 PM, for example). A field that holds both a date and time will first display the date and then the time (02/13/55 11:29 AM, for example).

Long Date   Long date means the whole date is spelled out in a formal, text-like style. The exact format depends on the International settings of your computer. The normal look is *day, month date, year* (like this: Sunday, March 27, 1995).

Medium Date   This one's going to go *dd-mmm-yy* (19-Jan-95). They call this medium, because it's medium-sized.

Short Date   Again, this depends on settings in your computer. It's another *month/date/year* thing, and the look of it is 3/27/95.

Long Time   Long Time is displayed in a style that is based on the Windows International Time settings. Assuming

A
B
C
D
E
F
G
H
I
J
KL
M
N
O
P
Q
R
S
T
U
V
W
XYZ

that you're in the United States, it will look like *hour:minutes:seconds AM/PM* (1:23:33 AM).

Medium Time This one is displayed like *hour:minutes AM/PM* (1:23 AM).

Short Time Now, Access calls military time *short time*. It's based on the 24-hour clock, so 1:00 PM is 13:00, 2:00 PM is 14:00, and so on. No need for that AM/PM stuff (that's why they call it short time). Short time looks like *hour:minutes* (13:23).

Input Mask Controls the way data is entered into the field, and how it will appear when displayed. For example, if you enter 00/00/00 into this property, the field will show the slashes before data is entered.

Caption Lets you set up a caption for the field. The caption will be displayed next to the field when the data is displayed as a form or report. The caption might, for example, tell the data entry person how to do the entry. If you don't type anything into the Caption property box, the field name will appear as the caption next to the field.

Default Value Lets you set up a default data entry for the field. For example, if you knew that most of the time your sales rep's "month" will end on the 15th, you could set that up as the Default Value.

Validation Rule Lets you set up a requirement that the data being entered meet some specified rule—for example, to limit the dates the user can enter

into the field to between January 1, 1990 and December 31, 1999, you would enter:

```
Between #1/1/1990# and #12/31/1999#
```

Validation Text Holds a message to be displayed by Access if the user tries to enter data that violates the Validation Rule. So if you've set up a Validation Rule that says the data entered must be between January 1, 1990 and December 31, 1999, you can get Access to display a message like, "Enter a date between January 1, 1990 and December 31, 1999."

Required Lets you set up the requirement that data *must* be entered into this field in every new record in the table. You might want to use this to compel the data entry person to include an important date—like a hire date, or a date of birth—in an employee record, for example.

Indexed Tells Access to keep a list of the fields in order—chronological order, if it's a Date/Time field. The results of this are a little abstract—they have to do with making things easier for Access. For example, indexing a field makes it easier for Access to use that field to link one table to another, and run the link faster. Too many indexes, though, will really slow things down.

See **Data Type; Data Types in Access; Text Data Type**

DBASE

See Part I (A Brief History of Databases); Attaching; Exporting; Importing; Importing from Other Database Programs

DBMS

DBMS is the cool way to say database management system, which is a program designed to allow you to organize and manipulate data for your own purposes. Access is a DBMS.

See Part I

DDE

DDE is the hip way to say dynamic data exchange, which is a method that allows Windows applications to send data back and forth.

See "Exporting" Data with DDE

DEFAULT

The setting for a device or function before you fiddle with it, *and* the setting it will go to if you don't say otherwise, is the *default*.

DELETE ACTION QUERY

A Delete action query deletes records from the table on which it is based. This is a

quick and easy way to purge a number of records from your table. Say, for example, you were working with a list of subscribers to your magazine, and that you'd sent out several renewal notices, gotten the results, and wanted to dump the names of those people who were not going to resubscribe. You could set up criteria to select all those records, then delete them as a group.

Once you've run a Delete action query, you cannot undo what you have done. Before you run a Delete action query, be absolutely, positively certain that the dynaset contains only records you want to delete from your table. It is a good idea to make a backup copy of the table on which your delete query is based, <u>before</u> you run a Delete action query. Then, if you find you've deleted something very important, you can restore the original records from the backup copy.

The first step in creating a Delete action query is to build a select query that creates a dynaset of those records that you want to purge from your table. Once you are certain that the select query selects only those records you want to delete, turn the select query into a Delete action query by following these steps:

1. Select Query ➤ Delete. This turns your current query into a Delete action query.

Just to trip you up, both the Edit menu and the Query menu have a Delete command. In this procedure, you must use the Delete command found in the Query menu.

2. Access adds a Delete row to the QBE grid (*See* QBE Grid). The new Delete row contains the word *Where* (because Access will delete records *where* the criteria is true). Click on the Execute icon on the toolbar.

3. Access displays the dialog box shown in Figure D.9, telling you how many records are about to be deleted. Click OK to go ahead and purge the records or click Cancel if you don't want to complete the procedure.

Tip

You can tell if a query listed in the Database window is a Delete action query because a special glyph (an x and an exclamation point) will appear to the left of its name.

✗!

Once you tell Access to go ahead and delete the records, you cannot get them back. Undo does not work on deleted records.

See   Queries; Action Queries; Query Wizards

DELETING

See   Database Window; Data Entry Shortcuts; Datasheet View: Deleting Records; Delete Action Query

DELIMITED TEXT

See   Exporting to a Text File; Importing from a Text File

DELETING OBJECTS

See   Database Window

DESCENDING ORDER

Descending order is from the highest number or value to the lowest (for example, from Z to A, or from 100 to 1).

Figure D.9

Click OK if you want to go ahead and purge the records or Cancel if you don't want to complete the procedure.

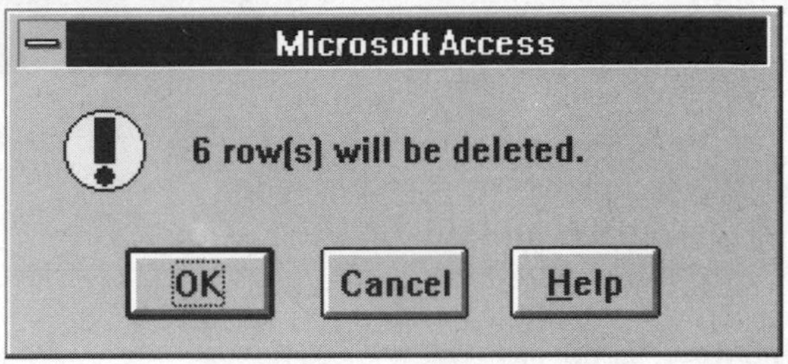

Microsoft Access

6 row(s) will be deleted.

OK   Cancel   Help

---

66 **Numbers come before letters in sorting.**

DESIGN VIEW

The view you use to modify (or to create) Access objects—like tables, forms, reports, and queries—is called Design View. In general, to get into Design View, you'll click on:

 Design   In the Database window

    In the toolbars

What happens in Design View varies depending on which object you're dealing with.

See **Database Window; Modifying Forms and Reports; Queries: Modifying Existing; Tables: Creating in Design View; Toolbar**

DIALOG BOX

A *dialog box* is a window in which you have a "dialogue" with your computer (it asks, you answer—that sort of thing).

DIRECTORIES

You (and all your computer-using pals) need a way to store files so you won't lose them. A very practical and orderly system exists for this; it involves keeping your files in *directories*. A directory—just a category under which files are grouped—is sometimes said to be similar to a drawer in a filing cabinet. In the same way you might name your filing cabinet drawers so you'll know what's in them, you name directories so you'll know what's in them. Each directory can contain other directories, known as *subdirectories*. Subdirectories can contain even more subdirectories.

The structure of directories and subdirectories is often described as similar to an upside-down tree. The top directory—the starting point—is called the *root*. Subdirectories are said to "grow" from the root directory.

A B C D E F G H I J KL M N O P Q R S T U V W XYZ

The root directory is usually marked by a backslash (\), which may appear after a *drive letter* (C:, for example) that indicates on which drive the directory is stored. The same backslash symbol may appear between the names of directories and subdirectories, to separate them, like this:

C:\ACCESS\SAMPAPPS

DISK SPACE

All Windows-based programs—including Access—need massive amounts of disk space. Not long ago, a 40 MB hard disk was considered huge—so much so that DOS was designed to work with drives up to only 32 MB in size. Now 120–220 MB drives are typical, and even they are easy to fill up fast. One way around the need for ever more hard-disk space is to use disk-compression software—software that reduces the amount of space files take up on your hard disk.

All forms of disk-compression come with a price—most notably, they slow down your computer and increase the risk of losing data. Maybe you think it's worth it to double your disk space, or maybe you don't. It's your call.

DOS

DOS stands for **D**isk **O**perating **S**ystem. This is the basic software that controls the disk drives and other basic parts of your computer.

See **Part I**

DPI

DPI is short for Dots Per Inch—in other words, how many itty-bitty dots of ink are crammed into a tiny space to make up printed characters.

See **Printing**

DRAFT MODE

The faster—but less attractive—way to print is called *draft mode*.

See **Printing**

DRIVE

A physical device on which you can store data files is called a *drive*. Each drive is identified by its own drive letter followed by a colon. For example, A:, B:, or C:.

DRIVER

A program that tells your computer what to do with things added to your computer—a printer, a mouse, that sort of stuff—is called a *driver*. In order for your printer to work, for example, you must have the correct *printer driver* installed along with your other software.

DROP-DOWN BOX

Also called a *combo box*, a drop-down box is one that, when you click on its control box, drops down, so you can type information into it or pick an item from a list it contains. You can add your own combo (drop-down) boxes to your forms.

> *See* **Control Wizards; Controls on Forms and Reports; Modifying Forms: Adding a Drop-Down Box**

DROP-DOWN MENU, DROP-DOWN LIST

A *drop-down menu* or *drop-down list* is what drops down when you click on a drop-down box.

DYNASET

Data that results from running a query appears in what looks like a table and is called a *dynaset*. You can do anything with a dynaset you can do with a table.

> *See* **Part I; Queries**

A
B
C
D
E
F
G
H
I
J
KL
M
N
O
P
Q
R
S
T
U
V
W
XYZ

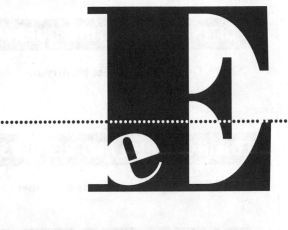

EDIT

To change data or objects is to *edit* them.

EDITING DATA IN DATASHEET VIEW

People make mistakes. We make mistakes, the president makes mistakes, and you will, too. If you flub something while you're entering data into a cell of the datasheet, you can do any number of things to correct the situation.

✪ As long as the little pen icon (the current record indicator) is still in the left margin, you can press Esc to back out of any changes you've made to the current record. (This restores the old contents of the record—the stuff that was already there before you began to change it—from the computer's hard disk.)

✪ Select File ➤ Undo to reverse the changes you have made to the current field. Watch out, though, because once Access commits your changes to the database file (you know this has happened when the little pen goes away) you cannot Undo what you have done.

✪ Once you have clicked on a cell and begun to enter data, you can use the ↑, ↓, ←, and → keys, along with the Backspace and Delete keys, to change what you have entered.

See **Current Record Indicator; Data Entry Shortcuts; Datasheet View; Datasheet View: Navigating; Entering Data**

EDITING DATA WITH A FORM

So there you are, looking at your data in a form, when you notice something you want to change—a spelling error, a number that needs to be updated, whatever. You can modify your data from within a form using techniques that are similar to those you use to modify data in Datasheet View.

Changing the Data

First, highlight the field you want to modify, making it the current field. Then, go ahead and type new data in there.

When you modify some data on a form, you'll see the current record indicator change to a little pen icon to tell you that the record was modified. When you either change to a new record or select Records ➤ Refresh from the menu bar, the little pen will go away, telling you that Access has saved the change in this record.

See **Current Record Indicator; Data Entry Shortcuts; Forms and Form Wizards; Forms: Moving from Record to Record**

EDITING DATA WITH JOINS

See **Joins and Relationships; Joins: Modifying Data With**

EDITING DATA WITH QUERIES

See **Action Queries; Queries; Query Wizards; Update Action Query**

EDITING AN EXISTING QUERY

See **Queries; Queries: Modifying Existing**

EDITING FORMS AND REPORTS

See **Modifying Forms and Reports**

EMBEDDED OBJECTS

See **OLE; OLE Object Data Type**

ENGINE

The part of an application (program) that drives or leads other applications is called an *engine*.

ENTERING DATA

You can enter data into tables in either of two convenient ways: using a *datasheet*, or using a *form*. The datasheet makes it easier to view a lot of records all at once (which may be a convenience in some circumstances), while the form makes entering data on a record-by-record basis especially easy. In either case, you'll always find an empty record at the end of your table, just waiting for you to type in new data.

> **Before you can enter data into a form, the form must be created (either manually or using the Form Wizard). A datasheet, on the other hand, exists and is available for data entry as soon as you create a table.**

See **Copy, Cut, and Paste; Data Entry Shortcuts; Datasheet View; Forms and Form Wizards; Joins and Relationships; Queries**

Entering Data Using a Datasheet

To enter data using a datasheet:

1. Open the Database window and select either the Table or Query button to see a list of tables and queries.

2. Highlight the name of the table or query you want to work with by pointing at it with the mouse pointer and clicking once.

3. Click on the Open button. The datasheet will appear. Each record of data is displayed in a single row on the datasheet. Each column contains data from a single field.

4. Enter a new record by going to the last record in the datasheet (the blank record) and typing in new data.
   or
   Enter data anywhere in the datasheet by clicking once on the cell into which you want to enter data (the cell will become highlighted) and then typing the new data.
   or
   Click once on the cell to highlight it, click again anywhere in the cell, and (when the cursor appears) edit the data as you like.

You can move along to the next field by pressing Tab or ↵, and you can use the arrow keys to move between fields in the datasheet. As you move from record to record, the data you entered or changed in the previous record will be saved.

> **Some queries produce <u>read-only</u> dynasets. You can't enter data into the datasheet for those dynasets, you can only read them.**

A
B
C
D
E
F
G
H
I
J
KL
M
N
O
P
Q
R
S
T
U
V
W
XYZ

See Copy, Cut, and Paste; Data
Entry Shortcuts; Datasheet View;
Datasheet View: Navigating

Entering Data Using a Form

To enter data using a form:

1. Open the Database window and click on the Form button to see a list of existing forms. (If no forms exist and you want to use a form, you'll have to create one.)

2. Highlight the name of the form you want to work with by pointing at it with the mouse pointer and clicking once.

3. Click on the Open button. The form will appear. The form's layout will vary depending on what type of form it is and how the form was created.

4. Enter data into a new record by selecting Records ➤ Go To ➤ New and typing in the new data.
or
Enter new data into an existing record by going to the new record (*See* Forms: Moving from Record to Record), clicking on the field into which you want to enter data (the cell will become highlighted) and then typing the new data.

You can use the Tab key to move between fields on the form, and when you're finished with the record you're working on, you can press the Page Down key to move to the next record and save the data you just entered.

See Copy, Cut, and Paste; Data
Entry Shortcuts; Forms and Form
Wizards; Forms: Moving from
Record to Record

EQUI-JOIN

An *equi-join* is a connection between two tables in which each record in the first table matches exactly one record in the second table.

See Joins and Relationships

EXECUTING A QUERY

See Queries: Running Existing

EXITING ACCESS

To exit Access, select Exit from the File menu. If you have changed any objects, a dialog box will appear asking if you want to save the changes. Click on Yes to save changes, No to go ahead and exit without saving changes, or Cancel to bail out of exiting.

See Part 1; Save/Save As

EXPORTING

Exporting is just what its name implies—sending data that was created in Access to other applications (in formats they can understand), to be used in whatever way that application uses data. You might want to export an Access table to a spreadsheet program like Excel, for example, so you can do more sophisticated number crunching than is allowed for in Access. Or you might want to take your Access mailing list and export it for use in a slick AmiPro form letter using fonts and styles that are beyond Access' capabilities. Maybe you've developed a nifty Access database for handicapping the ponies, and your dad wants to use it, but he's playing around in Paradox.

Whatever your reason for exporting, there is one important thing to keep in mind: to get information that was created in Access into another application, you must first convert that information into a file format the other application can understand.

66 Look through the sections on importing—along with this material on exporting—to get a good overview of the import/export business in Access.

Access gives you quite a list of applications to which you can export. We're going to tell you how to export to the most commonly used ones:

○ Microsoft Access (.MDB files)

○ dBASE III, dBASE IV, FoxPro 2.0, or FoxPro 2.5 (.DBF files)

○ Microsoft Excel or Lotus 1-2-3 (.WKS or .WK1 files)

○ Text (usually .TXT files)

○ Word for Windows (.TXT files)

············· Tip ·····················

Exporting from one Access database file to another is a convenient way to move your data within Access. Exporting to Word for Windows not only lets you use the file in Word for Windows, but also is handy for exporting to a number of other applications. In a later section, we'll tell you how to export to Word for Windows.

The DDE Connection

Another way to send data from Access to other applications is to form a link between the file in Access and the other application, so that when the data changes in Access, it will be changed in the other application automatically. In a number of different popular Windows programs—including Word for Windows and Excel—you can link data files using DDE (Dynamic Data Exchange), a powerful tool available in Access and some other Windows applications. (See "Exporting" Data with DDE)

A B C D E F G H I J KL M N O P Q R S T U V W XYZ

It's very important to note that you're limited in what you can export from Access to another program. When exporting to most programs you can export only tables and dynasets (the results of queries). When you are exporting to another Access file, you can export any of the objects (tables, queries, forms—*everything*) in the database file.

> *See* **Exporting to Another Access Database; "Exporting" Data with DDE; Exporting to dBASE or to Fox Pro; Exporting to Lotus 1-2-3 or to Excel; Exporting to a Text File; Exporting: The Word for Windows Trick; Importing Mail Merge to Microsoft Word**

EXPORTING TO ANOTHER ACCESS DATABASE

You can export any object in your current database into another Access database file.

If you want to use your data in two different database files, but want to store the data in just one file (to make it easier to edit and append the data) you might find it better to attach the two database files. (See Attaching)

To export an object in your current Access database to another Access database:

1. The database that holds the object you want to export must be open. Select File ➤ Export. The Export dialog box (Figure E.1) will appear.

Figure E.1

The Export dialog box

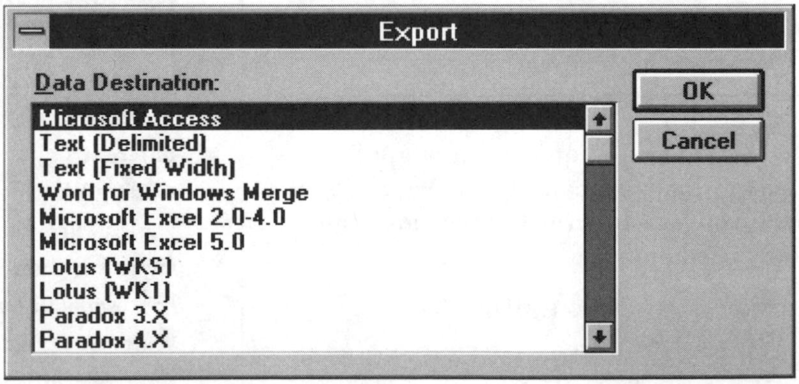

```
┌─────────────────────────────────────────────────────────┐
│ ─                        Export                          │
├─────────────────────────────────────────────────────────┤
│ Data Destination:                          ┌──────────┐  │
│ ┌────────────────────────────────────┐ ▲   │    OK    │  │
│ │ Microsoft Access                   │     └──────────┘  │
│ │ Text (Delimited)                   │     ┌──────────┐  │
│ │ Text (Fixed Width)                 │     │  Cancel  │  │
│ │ Word for Windows Merge             │     └──────────┘  │
│ │ Microsoft Excel 2.0-4.0            │                   │
│ │ Microsoft Excel 5.0                │                   │
│ │ Lotus (WKS)                        │                   │
│ │ Lotus (WK1)                        │                   │
│ │ Paradox 3.X                        │                   │
│ │ Paradox 4.X                        │ ▼                 │
│ └────────────────────────────────────┘                  │
└─────────────────────────────────────────────────────────┘
```

2. From the list that appears in the Export dialog box, select Microsoft Access. Access will display the Select Microsoft Access Object dialog box.

3. Select the type of object you want to export—Tables, Queries, Forms, Reports, Macros, or Modules—from the Object Type drop-down list. Access will display a list of all the objects of that type that are in the current database (see Figure E.2).

4. Select the name of the object you want to export from the Objects list. (You might want to export the structure of a table, but not the data contained in the table. If so, you can tell Access to export only the structure by clicking on the Structure Only button.)

5. Once you have specified what it is you want Access to export, click on OK. Access will display the Export to File dialog box.

6. In the Export to File dialog box (Figure E.3), click on the name of the existing file into which you want Access to copy the object. (This is known as the *target* file.) If the target file is on another drive or in another directory, you won't see it in the list. In that case, you'll have to select the drive from the Drives list, and the directory from the Directories list before you can select the target file.

> (66) **You can export only to an existing Access database file.**

7. Click on OK. Access will display the Export dialog box, asking you what name the object should have in the target file.

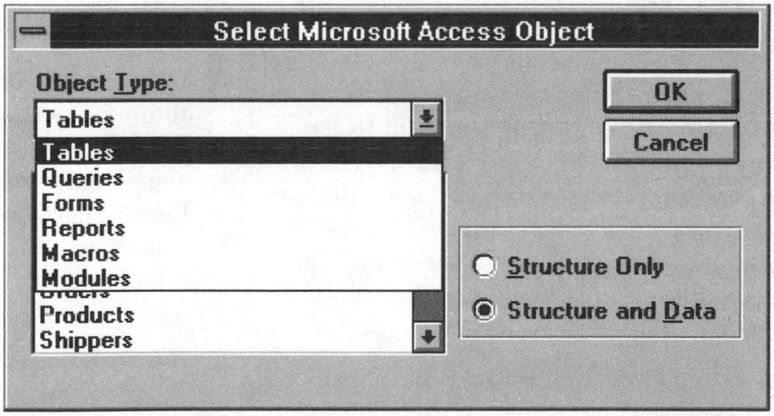

Figure E.2
··

The Select Microsoft Access Object dialog box, showing the Object Type drop-down list

A
B
C
D
E
F
G
H
I
J
KL
M
N
O
P
Q
R
S
T
U
V
W
XYZ

Figure E.3

The Export to File dialog box, showing a target filename

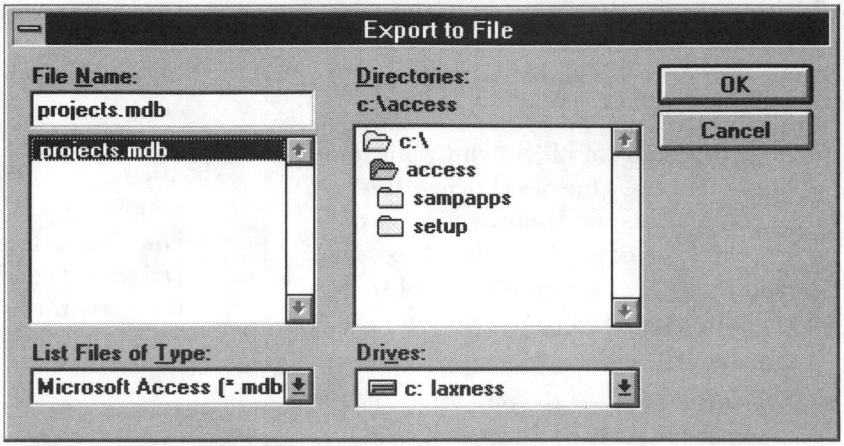

Export to File

File **N**ame:
`projects.mdb`

projects.mdb

Directories:
c:\access

- c:\
- access
- sampapps
- setup

OK

Cancel

List Files of **T**ype:
Microsoft Access [*.mdb]

Dri**v**es:
c: laxness

---

8. Type a new name for the object in the Export dialog box, or accept the default name (by doing nothing to change it). Click on OK when you're ready to continue.

9. If the target file already has an object of the same type and with the same name, Access will warn you and ask if it should overwrite the object. Select OK to replace the existing object with the new one, or Cancel to forget it.

You'll be returned without fanfare to the Database window. If you want to see whether your export was successful, close the current database file, and open the target database file by clicking on it in the Database window. When you open up the target database file you'll see the object's name listed in the Database window.

See **Exporting; Import Database (Add-In)**

"EXPORTING" DATA WITH DDE

Wouldn't it be just great if you could use Access to organize your numeric data, and Excel or another spreadsheet to analyze that same data—without having to keep two files that have to be updated and maintained separately when things change? That's what *DDE* is meant to do.

DDE (Dynamic Data Exchange) is very similar to OLE except that, while OLE allows you to *embed* one file in another, DDE allows you to *link* data in different files. With DDE, you can paste a link from an Access table into another application. Then, when data changes in your Access table, it will change in the other application as well.

DDE is a very powerful conceptual tool. When it works you're going to love it, but for now, it's still kind of raw. You'll find that between Access and some applications DDE works just fine, while between Access and other applications it simply doesn't work. Until the kinks are worked out, you may find the more traditional ways of using your Access data in other applications more successful.

Using DDE: An Example

Throughout this book, we describe procedures in terms that cover the broadest range of possibilities. For example, we don't tell you how to create a database for a certain kind of business, we tell you how to create a database, period. That way, you can apply the principles of setting up a database to your particular project.

Here, we're going to take a different approach. Because DDE is not always smooth sailing, we're going to describe setting up a DDE link between Access and just one other program—the Microsoft spreadsheet program, Excel. (Not surprisingly, it's easiest to make DDE links between Access and another Microsoft program.)

Most of what we say here *should* hold true for Windows spreadsheet programs other than Excel. But some of the particulars—menu names and the like—may change from program to program.

To create a DDE link between two applications, you should have both applications—Access and Excel, in our example—running. Open both programs by double-clicking on their icons in the Windows Program Manager. To switch back and forth between the two programs' windows, you can hold down the Alt key and press the Tab key.

Copy a table or dynaset to the clipboard. Start in Access. First, you must copy the Access data you're going to want to use in Excel onto the Windows Clipboard. To do this, in the Access Database window, highlight the table or query you want to use and select Edit ➤ Copy. This places a copy of the table or query on the Clipboard. (You won't *see* the copy or the Clipboard, but trust us, they're there.)

Place the data into excel. Now switch to Excel. Make the current cell the one in which you want the top-left corner of your data to appear—A1 is a good choice if you're pasting your data onto an empty spreadsheet. Select Edit ➤ Paste Link. This tells Excel to paste a link to the data on the Clipboard.

Now and forever after you have done this, when you reopen this Excel file, Excel

A B C D E F G H I J KL M N O P Q R S T U V W XYZ

will display a message asking if you want it
to update the linked information.

Select Yes if you want Excel to get the
updated information from Access. You
must have Access running for the update to
take place. If Access is not running at the
time you open the Excel spreadsheet file,
Excel will start up Access and even open
the Access database file to get the needed
information. Incredible, isn't it?

**Once you've created a DDE link
between an Access database and an
Excel spreadsheet (or any other two
application files), if you move one of
the linked files to a different drive
or directory, the whole link will
break down. The two linked applications will complain through error
messages that they can't find each
other.**

See **Exporting; OLE**

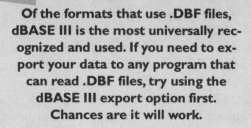

······Tip······

**Your best bet to avoid trouble with
your DDE link is to be sure to place
the Access database file in its final
home before you create DDE links to
it. If you must move the database file
later, you'll find it easiest to use (from
the Access menu bar) Edit ➤ Copy,
then Edit ➤ Paste Link to reestablish
the link to the database file in its new
location.**

EXPORTING TO DBASE
OR TO FOXPRO

Many database programs use the .DBF file
format, which came first from dBASE. Access allows you to export your tables to a
number of applications that use .DBF files.

······Tip······

**Of the formats that use .DBF files,
dBASE III is the most universally rec-
ognized and used. If you need to export your data to any program that
can read .DBF files, try using the
dBASE III export option first.
Chances are it will work.**

To export an Access table to a .DBF file:

1. Open the database file that contains the data you want to export.

2. Select File ➤ Export from the menu bar. The Export dialog box will appear.

3. From the list of choices that appear in the Export dialog box, select the program to which you're going to export the data. The options for .DBF files include: FoxPro 2.5, FoxPro 2.0, dBASE IV, and dBASE III.

4. Click on OK. Access will display the Select Microsoft Access Object dialog box.

5. From the list of tables in the Select Microsoft Access Object dialog box, select the table you want to export. If you wish to export the contents of a query, click on the Queries button near the bottom of the dialog box. Then select the name of the query from the list of queries. Click on OK, and Access will display the Export to File dialog box.

6. In the Export to File dialog box, Access will display a suggested filename for the file into which Access will copy the table. (This is known as the *target* file.) You can either accept the filename or type in a new one. If you want the target file to be stored on a drive or directory other than the ones displayed in this dialog box, you'll have to select the drive from the Drives list, and the directory from the Directories list.

7. Once you have specified a name for the target file, click on OK to continue. Access will warn you if a file with that name already exists. (See Figure E.4.) If this happens, click on No to return to the Export to File dialog box and type in a different filename, or click on Yes to replace the existing file with the one you are exporting.

You'll be returned to the Access Database window. If you want to see the exported file, you can open it in the .DBF file application you specified. The file can now be used as if it were created in that application rather than in Access.

See **Exporting**

Figure E.4

Access will warn you if a file already exists with the same name as your target file.

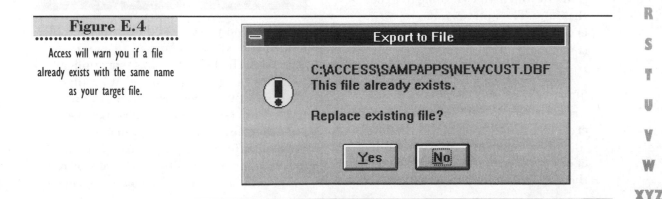

EXPORTING TO LOTUS 1-2-3 OR TO EXCEL

The Lotus 1-2-3 and Excel export options are so similar, we'll cover both here.

The Excel options export Access data to files formatted for either Excel versions 2 through 4, or Excel 5. Some other spreadsheet applications can also read Excel files, so try this option if you need to export your data into another program.

When you export to a Lotus 1-2-3 file, you can choose either the .WKS and .WK1 format. .WKS is an early Lotus 1-2-3 format, and is still widely used. The .WK1 format is used by Lotus 1-2-3 Release 2. Most other spreadsheet applications can read .WKS format files.

To export to either an Excel or Lotus formatted file:

1. You must open the database file that contains the data you want to export.

2. Select File ➤ Export from the menu bar. The Export dialog box will appear.

3. From the list of choices that appear in the Export dialog box, select the program to which you're going to export the data. The options include: Microsoft Excel 2–4, Excel 5, and Lotus (.WKS and .WK1 formats.)

4. Click on OK. Access will display the Select Microsoft Access Object dialog box.

5. From the list of tables in the Select Microsoft Access Object dialog box, select the table you want to export. Then click on OK, and Access will display the Export to File dialog box.

6. In the Export to File dialog box, Access will display a suggested filename for the file into which Access will copy the table. You can either accept the filename, or type in a new one. If you want the target file to be stored on a drive or directory other than those displayed in this dialog box, select the drive from the Drives list, and the directory from the Directories list.

7. Once you have specified a name for the target file, click on OK to continue. Access will warn you if a file with that name already exists. If this happens, click on No to return to the Export to File dialog box and type in a different filename, or click on Yes to replace the existing file with the one you are exporting.

You'll be returned to the Database window. You can open and use the exported file in the spreadsheet application you specified.

See **Exporting; Output To**

EXPORTING TO A TEXT FILE

Usually when you export data into a text file, it is because you are planning to import the data from the text file into some application that can't read .DBF or .WK1 files. This doesn't happen very often, but when it does, the text file acts as a go-between for Access and the other application.

Now, different applications like their text files formatted differently, so you're going to have to make some choices when you're exporting the data from Access into the text file, to anticipate the needs of the target application. The two choices are:

- Delimited Text
- Fixed-Width Text

The difference between these types of text has to do with how fields are indicated. We'll tell you about this more specifically in just a second. Meanwhile, remember that to figure out which one you need, you'll have to check the documentation for the application into which you'll be importing the data from the text file.

To export data to a text file:

1. You must have the database open that contains the table you want to convert into a text file.

2. Select File ➤ Export. The Export dialog box will appear.

3. In the Export dialog box, select Text (Delimited) to indicate the type of text file you're targeting, and click on OK. The Select Microsoft Access Object dialog box will appear.

4. In the Select Microsoft Access Object dialog box, you can choose to have Tables, Queries, or Both listed by clicking on the buttons by those names. From the list that appears, select the object you want to export by clicking on its name in the list. Click on OK. The Export to File dialog box will appear.

5. In the File Name text box of the Export to File dialog box, Access will suggest a filename for the text file to which you're going to export the table. You can

Delimited Text versus Fixed-Width Text

There are two ways to represent data from Access in a text file. The difference between these has to do with how fields are indicated in the text file. Text files just run text together, without any formatting, but data stored in Access is organized into fields. To make any sense of that data in a text file, there must be some way to indicate where one field ends and another begins. In Delimited text, a special character is placed between the data in each field, to separate one field from another. Fixed-Width text makes each field the same size and pads the fields with blank characters.

Delimited text is easier to work with and is used in most applications. You should use it unless you are exporting to an application that, in its documentation, indicates a preference for Fixed-Width text.

In our description of exporting to a text file, we'll assume that you're using the more popular format, Delimited text.

either accept the suggested name or type in a new one. (Note that text files usually end with the extension .TXT.) If you want the target file to be stored on a drive or directory other than those displayed in this dialog box, you'll have to select the drive from the Drives list, and the directory from the Directories list.

6. Once you have specified a name for the target file, click on OK to continue. Access will warn you if a file with that name already exists. If this happens, click on No to return to the Export to File dialog box and type in a different filename, or click on Yes to replace the existing file with the one you are exporting. Click on OK. The Export Text Options dialog box will appear.

7. In the Export Text Options dialog box, click on the Options button. The dialog box will expand, as shown in Figure E.5, to show all the options, which you can then set as needed, and as described in the documentation for the target application.

8. When you are finished, click on OK to go ahead and export the data.

You'll be returned to the Access Database window. You can open and use the exported text file in any application that reads Delimited text files.

See   **Exporting; Output To**

EXPORTING: THE WORD FOR WINDOWS TRICK

Those tricky people at Microsoft included an Export option they called "Word for Windows Merge" even though it can be used to export data to many different applications. This export option creates a text file—very similar to the text file created by the Text (Delimited) export option—that is specially designed to work as a Word for Windows Print Merge document.

The Word for Windows Merge export option neatly converts Access field names to field names that Word for Windows—*and many other programs*—will recognize. It

Figure E.5
....
The Export Text Options dialog box

Export Text Options - CATEGORI.TXT

☐ Store Field Names in First Row

Specification Name:

File Type: Windows (ANSI)

Text Delimiter: "   Field Separator: ,

Dates, Times, and Numbers

Date Order: MDY   ☐ Leading Zeros in Dates   Time Delimiter: :

Date Delimiter: /   ☐ Four Digit Years   Decimal Separator: .

OK
Cancel
Options >>
Save As...

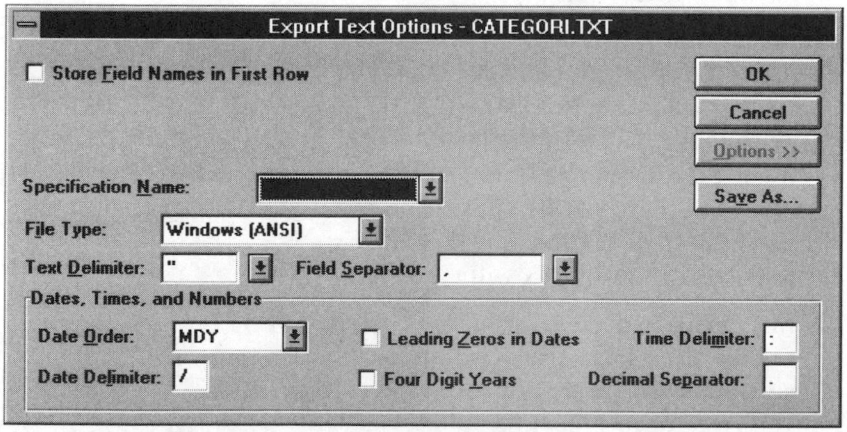

removes blank spaces and any special or strange characters, leaving only the characters that are actually in field names.

The beauty of this is that many applications other than Word for Windows don't like all the same gobbledygook that Word for Windows doesn't like. This means that you can use data exported using this option not only in Word for Windows merges, but also in Ami Pro, for example.

How to Do It

To export data using the Word for Windows Merge export option:

1. You must have the database open that contains the table you want to convert into a text file.

2. Select File ➤ Export. The Export dialog box will appear.

3. In the Export dialog box, select Word for Windows Merge from the Destination list and click on OK. Access will display the Select Microsoft Access Object dialog box.

4. In the Select Microsoft Access Object dialog box, you can choose to have Tables, Queries, or Both listed by clicking on the buttons by those names. From the list that appears, select the object you want to export by clicking on its name in the list. Click on OK. The Export to File dialog box will appear.

5. In the File Name text box of the Export to File dialog box, Access will suggest a filename for the file to which you're going to export the table. You can either

accept the suggested name or type in a new one. If you want the target file to be stored on a drive or directory other than those displayed in this dialog box, select the drive from the Drives list, and the directory from the Directories list.

6. Once you have specified a name for the target file, click on OK to continue. Access will display the Export Word Merge Options dialog box.

7. Access will warn you if a file of the same name already exists. If this happens, click on No to return to the Export to File dialog box and type in a different filename, or click on Yes to replace the existing file with the one you are exporting. Click on OK.

8. In the Export Word Merge Options dialog box, you can tell Access how to format the data as it is exported. The default settings shown in Figure E.6 should be fine, so just click on OK to continue.

You will be returned to the Access Database window. You can open and use the exported Word for Windows text file in any application in Word... or in just about any other application that deals with text files.

Using the Exported Data

So you've got your data converted into a text file specially designed for Word for Windows. Now what?

In Word for Windows In Word you can create a Print Merge document to combine the contents of your Word

Figure E.6
....

The Export Word Merge Options
dialog box

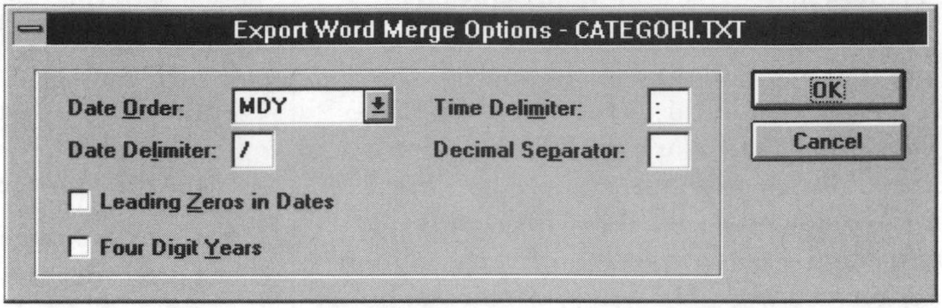

Export Word Merge Options - CATEGORI.TXT		
Date Order: MDY ⬇	Time Delimiter: :	OK
Date Delimiter: /	Decimal Separator: .	Cancel
☐ Leading Zeros in Dates		
☐ Four Digit Years		

document with the data you just exported. Using this technique, you can make really handsome form letters that combine the power of an Access database with the text formatting capabilities of Word for Windows.

In Other Programs Most word processors have a print merge function that can use the file you just exported. Check your word processor's documentation—under "print merge"—to find out how to do this.

See **Exporting; Mail Merge to Microsoft Word**

EXPRESSION BUILDER

The Expression Builder, a new feature in Access 2, allows you to create expressions in a cinch. When you find yourself needing an expression—say you're designing a query, and you want to enter an expression into the criteria cell of the QBE grid—you can just call up the Expression Builder,

and select operators and fields from a handy dialog box. A great advantage of the Expression Builder is that it provides you with a list of the fields in your queries and tables from which you can choose as you build your expression. You don't have to remember the names of fields, you can just click on them. You can use the Expression Builder anytime you want to enter an expression, for example:

✪ In a field cell of the QBE grid

✪ In a criteria cell of the QBE grid

✪ In a property value cell in Form Design View

✪ In a property value cell in Table Design View

To use the Expression Builder in an example, start with an open database file, open a query in Design View, click on a criteria cell to make it active, then:

1. Click on the Builder tool

on the toolbar (or, if you are entering properties in Design View, click on the Build button to the right of the highlighted properties box). A window will appear like the one in Figure E.7.

66 **If you've already entered part of an expression before you call up the Expression Builder, whatever you've already entered will appear in the Expression box.**

When the Expression Builder window appears, the cursor will be in the Expression box. You can type an expression there if you want, or you can use the features of the Expression Builder window to make building an expression even more convenient. A list of objects appears along the left side of the window, under the expression box. The objects include:

Tables   All the tables in the current database

Queries   All the queries in the current database

Forms   All the forms in the current database

Figure E.7

The Expression Builder window makes entering expressions more convenient.

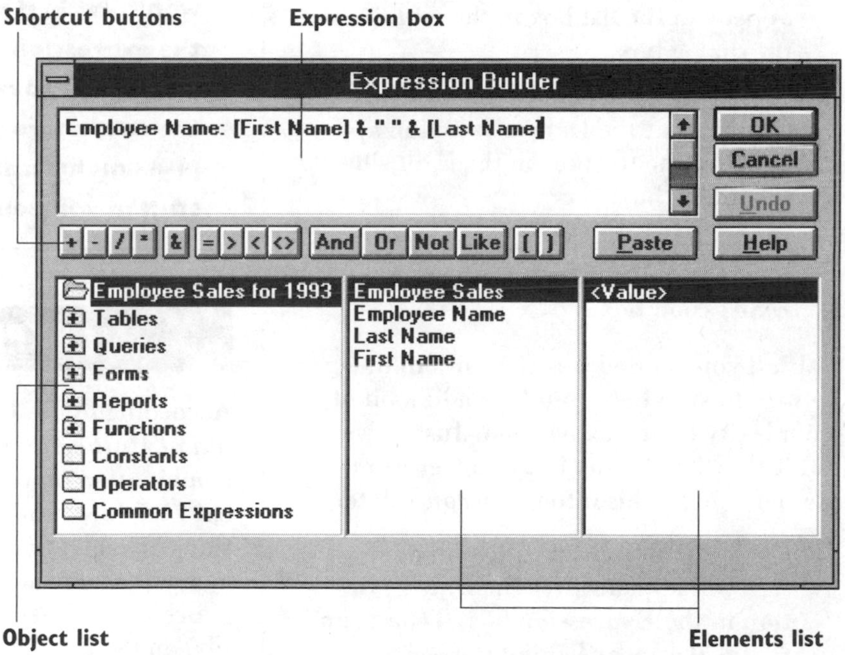

Shortcut buttons   Expression box

Expression Builder

Employee Name: [First Name] & " " & [Last Name]   OK Cancel Undo

+ - / * & = > < <> And Or Not Like [ ] Paste Help

Employee Sales for 1993 | Employee Sales | <Value>
Tables | Employee Name
Queries | Last Name
Forms | First Name
Reports
Functions
Constants
Operators
Common Expressions

Object list   Elements list

Reports All the reports in the current database

Functions Both built-in Access functions and functions defined in modules

Constants Predefined Access constants

Operators Access operators

Common Expressions Commonly used expressions (in the estimation of Microsoft)

Let's use one of Microsoft's "common expressions" and then expand on it as an example of how to use the Expression Builder.

2. To select one of the common expressions, first click on Common Expressions. A list of common expressions will appear in the list box in the middle of the dialog box.

3. Select Current Date by clicking on it. (Notice that the Date ( ) function appears in the list box on the right side of the dialog box.)

4. Click on the Paste button and the Date ( ) function will appear in the Expression box.

If all you wanted was the current date, you could stop here, but let's add a bit of complexity to our expression. Just as we did it the "hard" way in an earlier example, let's make this into *tomorrow's* date.

5. Click on the button with + on it. A + sign will appear after the Date ( ) function in the Expression box. Type 1, and that will appear behind the + sign.

6. Click on OK. You will be returned to the QBE grid and the expression will appear in the cell that was active when you began using the Expression Builder.

See **Expressions; Expressions: Components; Expressions: Using**

66 **If you change your mind about the last thing you did using the Expression Builder, you can click on the Undo button to undo it. Once you click on OK to accept the expression you've created, however, you're committed—the undo option won't work. If you want to remove the expression after you've OK'd it, you'll have to remember what was in the cell before you created an expression in it, and type that original stuff in yourself.**

EXPRESSIONS

According to the *VNR Concise Encyclopedia of Mathematics*, "an *expression* is a combination of numerical symbols, numerical variables, and (meaningful) juxtapositions of such symbols with operational symbols and brackets." In other words, an expression is just a calculation. More simply, an expression is a kind of mathematical sentence, which can be as simple as

1 + 1 or as complicated as you want to make it, written to get a result.

Expressions also have *values* (a value can be a number, like 1 or 2, or, in Access, it can be the text contained in a field, like the name of a business associate). Values are both the pieces of the expression—what goes into it—and the results of the expression. You get the value of an expression by *evaluating* it. When Access evaluates an expression, it just figures out what value it should use in the expression's place. The expression 1 + 1, for example, evaluates to 2.

Luckily for us, Access follows these definitions pretty closely. You use an expression any time you want Access to calculate a value for you. The one oddity Access adds to the mix is that it has the ability to include fields in expressions.

That means that when you're putting together a mathematical sentence, you can use an Access field where you might have used a number. Let's say you have a field called "Amount" with a number in it. You can write an expression—a mathematical sentence—to add together 1 + the number *contained in the field called Amount.*

When you add a field name to an expression, the field acts much like it's a variable in the expression. (A *variable* is a symbol that represents a value. In $x + 1 = 2$, for example, x is a variable that represents the number 1.) When you run a query or open a form that is based on a query, the value of the field is used in the expression as if it were a variable.

Access lets you use expressions in the designing of just about every type of object.

Some of the more useful places to use expressions are:

- As the value of a calculated field in a query
- As part of a criteria used to select records in a query
- As a value to display on a form or report
- As part of a validation rule

With an Access expression, you can calculate a value of any datatype that Access knows about. For example, the expression

```
Date( )+1
```

calculates a date one day after today's date (*tomorrow*, that is), and

```
[First Name] & " " & [Last Name]
```

calculates a text string that winds up being a full name, with the first name and last name separated by a space.

See **Expression Builder; Expressions: Components; Expressions: Using**

EXPRESSIONS: COMPONENTS

In Access, an expression is made up of a combination of the following bits and pieces:

- Field and variable names. (Usually you should surround these in square brackets like this: [Last Name] so Access can distinguish between one field or variable name and the next.)

- Literal values—numbers, dates, or text strings that you want to use "as is."

- Operators, such as + and −.

- Function calls. These can call either the functions that come with Access BASIC or your own Access BASIC functions.

- Parentheses, which you use to group together terms, just as you did in high school algebra.

You get to write expressions in Access by putting together these bits and pieces into a meaningful combination. Then you can use your expression anywhere Access wants a value:

- In a calculated field

- In the Validation Rule property box

- On forms and reports

You'll often use expressions in queries. In a query you can use an expression to make a <u>calculated field</u>—a field that displays information calculated from data that's in other fields of your table. You also can use expressions when you are writing criteria to determine which records will become part of the dynaset. Adding expressions to your queries unleashes a lot of power.

Fields

When you include field names in an expression, you are actually telling Access to take data that is stored in a field in one of your tables, and *do* something to it—add a number to it, run it through some Access function, whatever. You are telling Access to *calculate a new value* based on your data.

Operators

Operators are mathematical symbols like plus (+) and minus (−) that, in Access, as in math class, indicate that some kind of arithmetic should be done. Access knows what to do with these operators:

Operator	Meaning
^	Raise one number to the power of another
*	Multiply one number by another
/	Divide one number by another
\	Divide one number by another, resulting in an integer
mod	Modulus (or Remainder)
+	Add one number to another

Operator	Meaning
–	Subtract one number from another
&	Combine two strings into one

---

66 An <u>integer</u> is a number that does not include a fractional part. 3 is an integer, 3.1 is not. Neither is 3.00.

---

66 Access follows the standard order of mathematical precedence. It first evaluates whatever's in brackets or parentheses, then works its way out—in the example ((2+2)-3)×4, first 2 is added to 2, then 3 is subtracted from that, and then the result is multiplied by 4.

You can also use *comparison* operators (sometimes called relational operators), if you like, that will *compare* two values. Access can relate to the following comparison operators:

Operator	Meaning
<	Less than
< =	Less than or equal to
>	Greater than

Operator	Meaning
> =	Greater than or equal to
=	Equal to
<>	Not equal to

When you are using an expression in a criteria or a validation rule, and you want to compare the result of the expression to the field for which you are setting the criteria or rule, add the comparison operator *before* the expression, like this:

```
<20
```

to ensure that the values entered into a number field are less than 20.

You can also add comparison operators inside expressions to create expressions that evaluate the Yes/No datatype. For example, the value of

```
Left$([Name],1) = "A"
```

will be "Yes" if the left-most character in the name field is an A.

Literals

A *literal* is literally anything you want to show up as you literally entered it. A literal is a value that you want to use in an expression "as is." Examples include the number "4" if you entered the number 4, the text "Hey, you!" if that's what you typed, and the date "1/1/95" if you entered #1/1/95# in a date field.

A
B
C
D
E
F
G
H
I
J
KL
M
N
O
P
Q
R
S
T
U
V
W
XYZ

When you want to enter a literal date into an expression, you must surround the date with pound signs (like this: #05/22/50#). Text literals are surrounded by double quotes (as in "yadda-yadda").

Functions: For the Stout-Hearted Few

In your expressions, you can call upon any of the hundreds of built-in Access BASIC functions. A complete list with descriptions of these functions could entirely fill up a book of this size, so we're going to skip lightly through the topic.

To enter a function name into an expression, use the name of the function followed by an opening parenthesis, any arguments, and a closing parenthesis.

Some of the more useful functions are in Table E.1. Access includes many more functions for specialized and arcane purposes. Search the on-line Help for "Functions: Reference" or put on your hip boots and wade through the Access Language Reference to find out more about Access' built-in functions.

Table E.1 shows some of Access' most useful functions.

EXPRESSIONS: USING

Access accepts expressions any place it wants a value, though you have to do some tricky things depending on where you're using the expression.

Here are the most common ways to use expressions in Access:

In a criteria When you use an expression as part of a query's criteria, you must add a comparison operator before the expression. The operator tells Access how to compare the *result* of the expression with the *value* of the field while it's evaluating the criteria.

In a validation rule An expression in a validation rule should return a Yes/No value. You can do this either by using functions that return this type of value or by including comparison operators in your expression.

In calculated fields Access will calculate a value and use it as a read-only field in the dynaset of the query.

In an action query You can use expressions in action queries to calculate new values to store in your tables. The most useful method is to enter an expression based on the field you are changing in the Update To: row.

Table E.1

Some Useful Functions in Access

Function	Data Type	Description
Choose	Yes/No	Allows you to determine a value based on an index number.
IsNull	Yes/No	Returns either Yes or No based on whether the named field is null. Access considers null any field that has not had any data assigned to it.
Date	Date/Time	Returns today's date.
Now	Date/Time	Gets the current date and time.
LCase	Text	Returns a text string in all lowercase letters.
Trim	Text	Removes the ending white space from a text string.
LTrim	Text	Removes leading space from a text field.
UCase	Text	Returns a text string in all uppercase letters.

If by some chance you leave out the comparison operator, Access will assume that you want to use equal (=) as the comparison operator. That's because if you don't tell Access how the two things it's comparing are supposed to be different, Access will very sensibly assume that they're going to be the same (=). You can also enter two expressions separated by a comparison operator into a criteria cell if you like.

As Calculated Fields in Queries

You can create calculated fields in a query to combine two fields into a new field. This new value will then appear in every record of the dynaset.

You can also use calculated fields on forms and reports. (See Forms; Reports)

In the calculations you set up to produce a calculated field, you can even use data from another field that's in the same record. For example, to create a calculated field called Total Compensation that is the sum of the Salary field and the Bonus field,

A B C D E F G H I J KL M N O P Q R S T U V W XYZ

you can enter the following expression into a query's QBE grid:

```
Total Compensation: [Salary] +
[Bonus]
```

Another example of a calculated field is:

```
Full Name: [Last Name] & ", " &
[First Name]
```

This example uses the & operator to combine three text strings together into a new field that contains the last name of a person (presumably an employee), followed by a comma and a space, then the first name of the same person.

In the two examples above, a new name is given for the new field. The new field name is whatever comes before the colon (:). In our examples, Total Compensation: and Full Name: indicate that the new fields will be named Total Compensation and Full Name.

See **Queries; Queries: Fields Combined With**

In Criteria

You can use an expression in the criteria field to give Access something against which to compare the field. In the sections on queries, we show you how to compare a Bonus field against a number that was calculated using a Salary field.

To do this, in the Criteria row for the Bonus field, enter:

```
>[Salary] *0.2
```

In this example, the > is not actually part of the expression. Rather it tells Access that you want the Bonus field to be <u>greater than</u> the expression that follows. You can use any of the comparison operators before your expression when you are entering a criteria. If you do not enter a comparison operator, Access will cleverly guess that you want the field to <u>equal</u> the expression. After all, you aren't saying that you want it to be <u>different</u>.

See **Criteria**

In Validation Rules

To enter validation rules, you must be in the Table Design View window. Every field in a table can have its own validation rule, which you establish when you set up the properties for the field.

Once you have set a validation rule for a field, Access will see to it that any data entered into that field meets the rule. Every time you or your learned associates enter data into a table, Access checks the data.

If it does violate the validation rule, Access displays the text that you entered into the Validation Text property and simply refuses to store the value.

A validation rule consists of a comparison operator followed by an expression. If you omit the comparison operator, Access will, as usual, assume that you want the field to equal the expression you enter. For example, if you want to ensure that a field called Category always starts with "AA," you would use the validation rule:

```
left$([Category], 2) = "AA"
```

You can also enter a message in the Validation Text property box, and Access will display that message any time the validation rule is violated.

Tip

You can say anything you like in the message that's displayed when the validation rule is violated. But "That's wrong, Bonzo!" probably won't be much help to the user. It's a good idea to compose a message (of up to 255 characters) that tells the user how to enter the data correctly—something along the lines of "You must enter the horse's full name, beginning with a capital letter," or "Enter the purse for this race."

To set a validation rule, you must be viewing the table in Table Design View. Then follow these steps:

1. Select the field to which you want to add a validation rule.

2. Click in the Validation Rule property box (along the bottom part of the window) and type in a validation rule. The rule should begin with a comparison operator and be followed by an expression. If you want the field to equal the value of the expression you can omit the comparison operator.

3. Press the Tab key to move to the next property box.

4. Enter some text for Access to display when the rule is violated.

5. Close the Table Design window, and the validation rule will be saved. From now on, whenever you enter data into the field, Access will check that data against the validation rule.

See **Data Type; Data Type: Specifying and Modifying**

A B C D E F G H I J KL M N O P Q R S T U V W XYZ

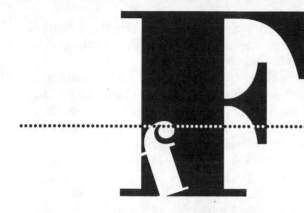

FIELD

In Access, a *field* is the space in a table or dynaset that stores or displays data.

See Part 1; Field Name; Tables: Creating Fields In

FIELD: CREATING

See Tables: Creating Fields In

FIELD NAME

The name you give to a field to describe the data contained in the field is the *field name*. Phone Number, for example, is a good name for a field that contains (you guessed it) phone numbers.

Access allows you to use field names up to 64 characters long. You can't use some special characters in field names—periods, exclamation points, single quote marks, and square brackets won't work. You could call a field *supercalifragilisticexpialidocious* if you wanted, or just +. But you're going to have to use field names when you create forms, reports, and so on, and while you want to minimize typing and potential spelling errors, you also want to know what the field name means. It's a better idea to keep your field names short but descriptive. You don't want to call a field "Subscriber's Last Name." *Last Name* will do.

You name fields when you set them up, which you do when you're creating a table.

See Brackets: Using; Tables: Creating Fields In

FILE

See Database File

A B C D E F G H I J KL M N O P Q R S T U V W XYZ

FILTERS AND SORTS

You can use Filter/Sort whenever you are displaying a table as a datasheet or a form. (You cannot use Filter/Sort when you are displaying the results of a query as a datasheet.) To display the Filter window, click on the Edit Filter/Sort button on the toolbar.

In the Filter and Sort window, you can specify just about every criteria and sorting option you could have entered while creating a query. A *filter* allows you to filter out unimportant records so you can concentrate on the records you want. A *sort* determines in what order records will appear on the form or datasheet. Filters and sorts allow you to search or arrange data quickly, without the trouble of modifying a query.

Filter/Sort is controlled by three buttons along the toolbar. Each of the buttons also has a menu equivalent.

To create a filter and sort while you are viewing a form or a table in Datasheet View, click on the Edit Filter/Sort button or select Records ➤ Edit Filter/Sort to display the Filter window, as shown in Figure F.1.

The Filter window looks a lot like the Query Design View window, and it works in a similar way. You will find using the Edit/Sort property much quicker than setting up queries when you are displaying your data. You enter criteria and sorting orders in the QBE grid along the bottom of the Filter window, just as you do in the Query Design View window.

The Field List box along the top of the window shows you all of the fields that are part of the table or dynaset on which the form is based. Either you can drag field names from the table to the QBE grid or you can select the field names from the drop-down list in the Field row cell of the grid, just as you do in the Query Design View window.

Figure F.1
....
The Filter window

Filter: EmployeesFilter1

Employees
×
Employee ID
Last Name
First Name
Title
Birth Date

Field:
Sort:
Criteria:
or:

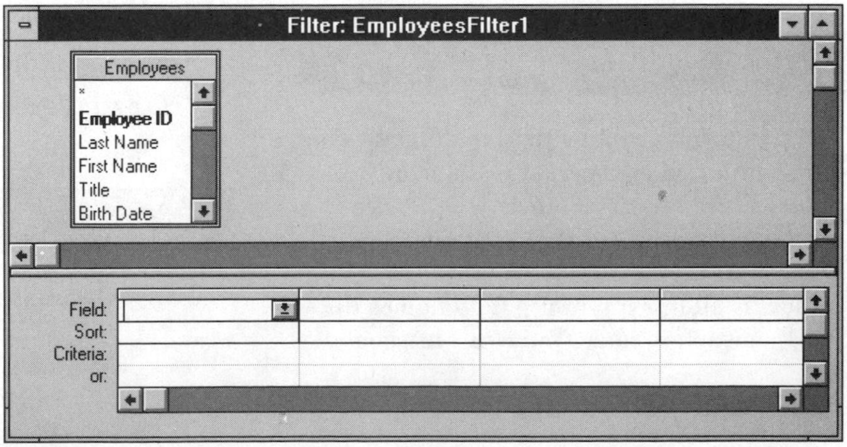

Table F.1

The Toolbar Filter/Sort Buttons

Toolbar Button	The Button's Name	The Menu Bar Commands	What They Both Do
	The Edit Filter/Sort button	Records ➤ Edit Filter/Sort	Allows you to enter filtering and sorting information into a QBE grid much like the grid used for creating queries
	The Apply Filter/Sort button	Records ➤ Apply Filter/Sort	Starts the filtering and sorting of your data, based on the information you entered into the filter/sort
	The Show All Records button	Records ➤ Show All Records	Stops filtering and sorting your data and shows all records regardless of what you entered into the filter/sort criteria

You need to place fields in the QBE grid only if you want to use them in the criteria or the sort order. It is not necessary to include all the fields that appear on the form or datasheet.

Once you have entered criteria and sorting information for your table, click on the Apply Filter/Sort button to make your filter and/or sort take effect.

As soon as you apply your Filter/Sort, Access will redisplay the form or datasheet and you will see your data, filtered and sorted for your purposes.

If you want to modify the filter/sort, you can do so by selecting the Edit Filter/Sort button again. To stop the filter/sort and see all the records that resulted from it, click on the Show All Records button.

See **Datasheet View; Expression Builder; Expressions; Forms and Form Wizards; Queries; Queries: Sorting Data on a Field; Quick Sort**

FINDING AND REPLACING TEXT

See **Datasheet View: Finding and Replacing Text**

FONT

A *font* is the style of type in which text appears. Fonts have names, like Courier,

Helvetica, and Times New Roman. Fonts also have sizes, like 8-point, 10-point, and 12-point.

See **Controls: Selecting a Font and Point Size; Options Dialog Box: Changing Options; Printing Datasheets; Text: Toolbar Shortcuts for Changing**

FORMATTING

You can control the manner in which Access displays your data on datasheets, forms, and reports by setting the Format property. The format property tells Access how data should look when it is displayed. You can control whether the day or just the month and year appear in date/time data, whether cents appear and how they look in currency data, whether negative numbers appear in red with brackets around them in number data, and more.

See **Counter Data Type; Currency Data Type; Date/Time Data Type; Memo Data Type; Number Data Type; Text Data Type; Yes/No Data Type**

FORM LETTERS: CREATING BY USING A REPORT

One way you can do a form letter is to export your Access data into a word processor. This has an advantage in that, even

with Access' extensive report writing capabilities, a word processor can create much more polished documents with tools like the spelling checker, grammar checker, and on-line thesaurus. A word processor also gives you much greater control over the use of fonts and the placement of fields that were imported from your database.

See **Export; Mail Merge to Microsoft Word; Output To**

Creating a Blank Report

Sometimes, however, getting your data out of Access and into a word processor may be a hassle. So in this section we're going to explain how you can create a one-page form letter using a report.

To create a form letter with Access, you must first create a blank report by following these steps:

1. Open the Database window and click on the Report button to display a list of existing reports.

2. Click on the New button.

3. Select the table or query that contains the information you want to use in your form letter. This information will probably come from a mailing list or some similar table.

4. Since we are not using the Report Wizard this time, click on the Blank Report button.

You'll see an empty report in Design View. On that report, below the band labeled "Detail," we're going to place everything we want to have printed on our form letter.

But first we have to make the report wider—we want to be able to fill up an entire $8\frac{1}{2}'' \times 11''$ letter-size page.

1. The white area in Report Design View represents the area where you can place controls. Move the mouse pointer to the right edge of the white area of the report. The mouse pointer should change to a two-headed arrow as you pass it over the edge.

2. Click and drag the two-headed arrow to the right until the report is about $6\frac{1}{2}''$ wide, as shown in Figure F.2. (You'll see the width of the report by looking at the ruler along the top of the Design window.)

3. Now increase the length of the form letter. Move the pointer to the band *above* the words "Page Footer." Again the pointer should turn into a two-headed arrow.

4. Now click and drag the two-headed arrow down the report until the report is about 6" long. This should be enough space for your letter.

See **Bands; Reports and Report Wizards**

Figure F.2

When you widen your report, the two-headed arrow should be below the 6" mark, as shown here.

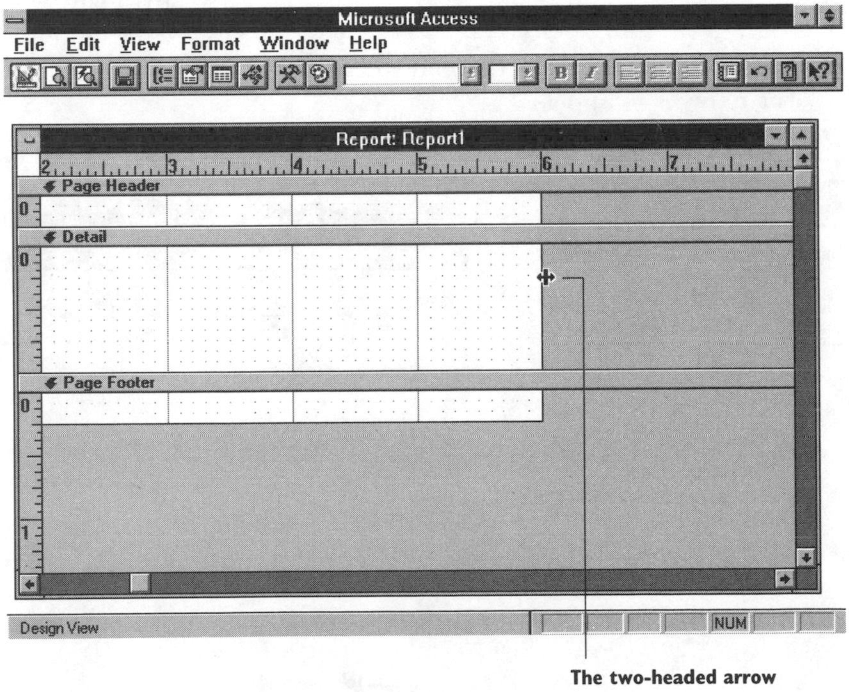

The two-headed arrow

Starting Your Form Letter

Now you're ready to insert information from the table or query on which you're basing the form letter. To do this, you'll drag those fields that contain the person's name and address from the Field List box to the report. Since you are going to place items in the upper-left corner of the report, scroll around a bit (using the vertical and horizontal scroll bars along the sides of the Report Design window) to make this area visible.

1. You'll have to combine two fields—the First Name field and Last Name field— to use a full name on your form letter. To do this:

○ Click on the Text Box tool in the toolbox. (*See* Toolbox)

○ Click on the report, in the spot where the name is to appear.

○ Type an expression into the Control Source property. (*See* Expressions) A typical expression to combine a First Name Field with a Last Name field might be:

```
=[First Name] & " " & [Last Name]
```

If the Property Box is not visible on your screen, select View ➤ Properties from the menu.

2. Get rid of the label control that appears next to the text control for the full name. Click on the label control, which appears to the left of the control for the full name, and press the Delete key. Figure F.3 shows the Report Design window after removing the label control.

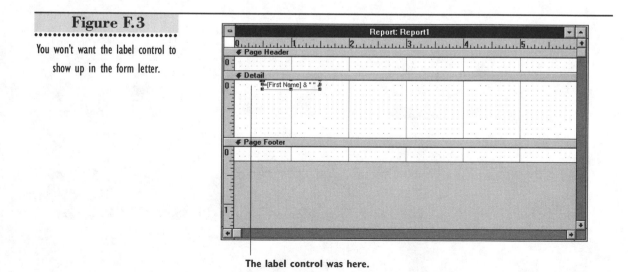

The label control was here.

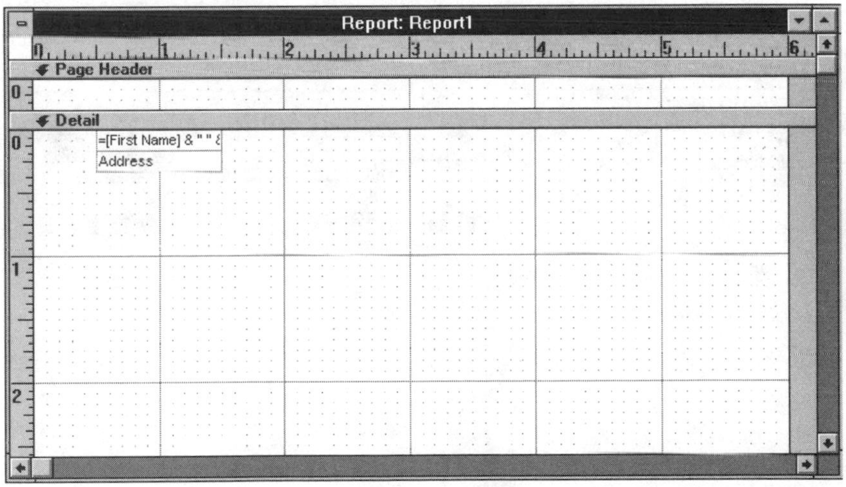

A
B
C
D
E
F
G
H
I
J
KL
M
N
O
P
Q
R
S
T
U
V
W
XYZ

Tip

Access doesn't create the extra label control if you place the control real close to the left edge of a report or form.

3. To place the street address on the report, click on the Address field in the Field List box, and drag the field over to the report, placing it just under the spot where you placed the name, as shown in Figure F.4.

4. Again, get rid of the label control (this time for the Address field), by clicking on it and pressing Delete.

5. Using the same techniques described in steps 1 and 2, place the fields that make up the City, State, and ZIP code. The expression you'll use in this case will look something like this:

```
=[City] & ", " & [State] & " " &
[ZIP]
```

66 Take the time to arrange fields nicely, so they'll look good when the report (your form letter) is printed.

See **Controls on Form and Reports; Expressions; Toolbox**

Figure F.4

Place the Address field just under the name.

Adding a Date to Your Form Letter

1. Select the Text Box tool from the toolbox. The Text Box tool looks like this:

2. Click on the place in your report where you want the date to appear. (You won't see the date just yet, we're just creating a place for it right now. You'll see the word "Unbound" instead.) You will probably want the date to appear below the address block. When you're finished with this step, the report will look like Figure F.5.

3. Click on the label control to the left of the empty field you've just created, and press Delete to delete the label.

4. Click on the control that contains the word "Unbound."

5. In the Control Source property, type the expression

    =Date()

as the property.

6. Go To the Format property, and click on the little box with the down arrow in it. Select Short Date from the drop-down list that appears. This will format the date as mm/dd/yy.

7. If you want to move the date control to the right side of the page, just click on it and drag it over there.

8. You can change the width of the date control by clicking and dragging on the sizing handle along the left side of the control. Make the control wide enough to display the widest date you anticipate, based on the date format you

Figure F.5

The address block and date are in place.

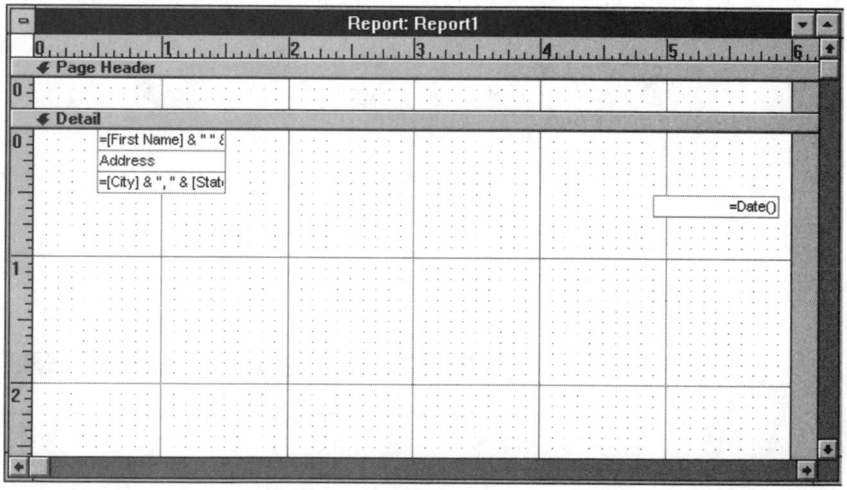

Report: Report1
Page Header
Detail
=[First Name] & " " &
Address
=[City] & ", " & [State]
=Date()

have selected. (For the Short Date format, this will be eight characters wide.)

9. You'll always want the date to be right justified (assuming it's on the right side of the page), so click on the Right Align button on the toolbar. It looks like this:

![Right Align toolbar button]

See **Controls on Forms and Reports; Expressions; Text: Toolbar Shortcuts for Changing; Toolbox**

Adding a Personalized Greeting to Your Form Letter

You probably want your letter to start out with some kind of greeting. Something as generic as "Dear Human Resources Professional" might do, but the great advantage of computers is that you can personalize just this sort of detail, adding pizzazz to your communications. Here's how to do it:

1. Select the Text Box tool from the toolbox.

2. Click on the report, where you want the greeting to appear.

3. Delete the label control as usual, by clicking on it and pressing the Delete key.

4. Select the Text control you just placed on your report.

5. In the Control Source property, type the following expression:

```
="Dear " & [First Name] & " " &
[Last Name] & ":"
```

You can make adjustments in this expression to suit your preferences. For example, if you prefer to end your greeting in a comma, just replace the colon (:) with a comma(,).

See **Controls on Forms and Reports; Expressions; Toolbox**

Creating a Block of Text for Your Form Letter

Now that you've got the address, date, and greeting in place (as shown in Figure F.5), the next step in building your form letter is to create a block of text that contains the body of your letter. You don't have a field that contains this information, and you don't want it to be part of any table or query. Instead, you'll trick Access by making a big *label* that Access will then display as the body of your letter.

1. Select the Label tool, shown here:

2. Click along the left side of the report, below where you placed the name and

address controls.

3. Start typing your letter. Don't press ↵ when you get to the end of a line; Access will wrap your text down to the next line for you. You can place blank lines in your letter by using Shift-↵. Enter all of the text you want to appear in your letter into this one label control.

A
B
C
D
E
F
G
H
I
J
KL
M
N
O
P
Q
R
S
T
U
V
W
XYZ

4. When you get to the end of the body text, add a blank line by pressing Shift-↵, then type in a closing like "Sincerely," or "Best Regards." Then press Shift-↵ four times to make a place for your signature. Finally, type in your name (or the name of whoever's actually sending the letter).

You may have to move the label control that contains the body of your letter up and down on the page a bit, until it looks nice. Take a look at Figure F.6 to see an attractively arranged form letter report.

See **Controls on Forms and Reports; Expressions; Toolbox**

Adding a Page Break

You'll have to add a page break at the end of your report, so Access will know to start a new page after each letter.

> **If you don't add a page break at the end of the report that will be your form letter, Access will print one letter after another on the same page. You'll have to cut them apart with scissors before you stuff them into envelopes, and that's no fun.**

Figure F.6
· · · · · · · · · · · · · · · · · · · ·
The form letter report with all of its parts in place.

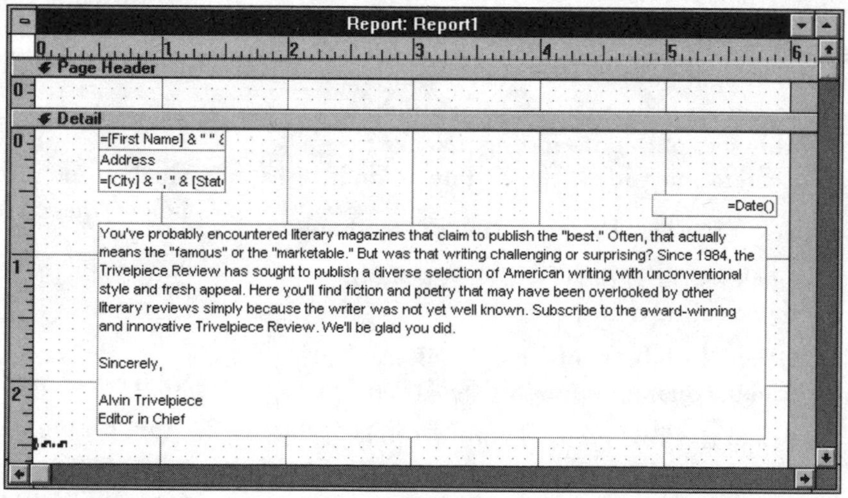

Report: Report1

Page Header

Detail

=[First Name] & " " &
Address
=[City] & ", " & [State]

=Date()

You've probably encountered literary magazines that claim to publish the "best." Often, that actually means the "famous" or the "marketable." But was that writing challenging or surprising? Since 1984, the Trivelpiece Review has sought to publish a diverse selection of American writing with unconventional style and fresh appeal. Here you'll find fiction and poetry that may have been overlooked by other literary reviews simply because the writer was not yet well known. Subscribe to the award-winning and innovative Trivelpiece Review. We'll be glad you did.

Sincerely,

Alvin Trivelpiece
Editor in Chief

1. Select the Page Break tool from the toolbox. (*See* Toolbox)

2. On your report, click just below the control that contains the body of your letter.

After you've placed a page break, your report (your form letter) is finished.

> **66** Don't place anything on the report below the page break. If you do, Access will create extra pages when you print.

To see what it's going to look like, select File ➤ Print Preview, or click on the Print Preview button. When you do this, you'll see the form letter as it's actually going to appear, with data (the name, address, and date) in its proper place on the letter, as shown in Figure F.7. You'll ordinarily see the first record first, and if you want to look at others, you can use the VCR-type buttons at the bottom of the window to change pages.

When you close your form letter report, you'll be asked if you want to save it. If you do, select Yes and type in a name for the form letter. Access will save it, and when you want to use this form letter either as is or as the basis of a new one, you'll find it listed with the other reports in the Database window when you click on the Report button.

Figure F.7

You can take a look at how your form letter is actually going to appear by clicking on the Print Preview button.

```
Report: Report1

Howard Snyder
2732 Baker Blvd.
Eugene, OR  97403
                                                          4/22/94

You've probably encountered literary magazines that claim to publish the "best." Often, that actually means the
"famous" or the "marketable." But was that writing challenging or surprising? Since 1984, the Trivelpiece
Review has sought to publish a diverse selection of American writing with unconventional style and fresh
appeal. Here you'll find fiction and poetry that may have been overlooked by other literary reviews simply
because the writer was not yet well known. Subscribe to the award-winning and innovative Trivelpiece Review.
We'll be glad you did.

Sincerely,

Alvin Trivelpiece
Editor in Chief

Page: 1
```

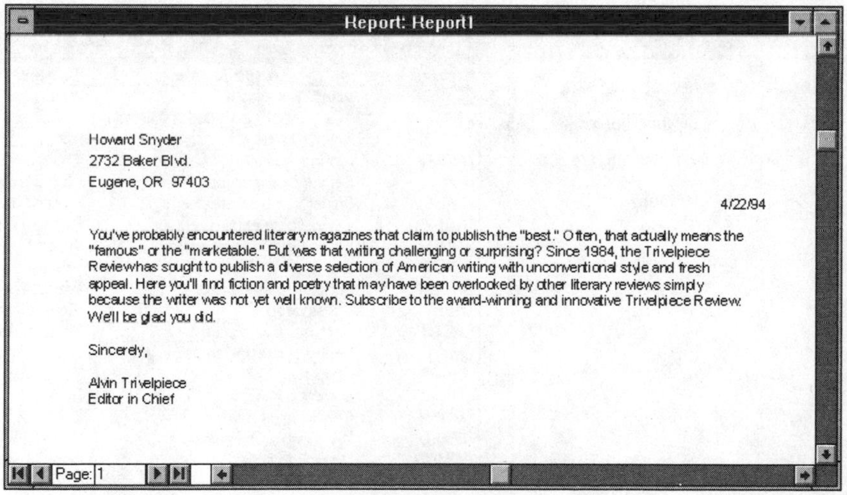

To address envelopes for your form letter, use the Report Wizard's Mailing Label Wizard to create mailing labels.

See Printing; Reports and Report Wizards

FORMS AND FORM WIZARDS

Wouldn't it be lovely if you could design a handy, professional-looking *form* to make data entry easier? And what if you could have your data displayed on-screen in the form of that attractive, easy-to-read form? ...*What* could be better?

Looking at Data in the Form of a Form

With the Access Form Wizard, you can create forms quickly and easily, in a number of sleek styles. Just compare the data shown in Datasheet View in Figure F.8 to the same data shown in the form of a form in Figure F.9.

What's Behind the Form Wizard

A form is nothing more than an on-screen layout of your data, designed to make it easy to enter data or to look at it. The Form Wizard starts by laying out fields from a table or dynaset in a window for

Figure F.8

The Datasheet View of your data shows you a lot of stuff, but makes it hard to concentrate on any single record.

Customer ID:	Company Name:	Contact Name:	Title:	
ALFKI	Alfreds Futterkiste	Maria Anders	Sales Representative	Obere Str
ANATR	Ana Trujillo Emparedados y helados	Ana Trujillo	Owner	Avda. de
ANTON	Antonio Moreno Taquería	Antonio Moreno	Owner	Matadero
AROUT	Around the Horn	Thomas Hardy	Sales Representative	120 Hand
BERGS	Berglunds snabbköp	Christina Berglund	Order Administrator	Berguvsv
BLAUS	Blauer See Delikatessen	Hanna Moos	Sales Representative	Forsterstr.
BLONP	Blondel père et fils	Frédérique Citeaux	Marketing Manager	24, place
BOLID	Bólido Comidas preparadas	Martín Sommer	Owner	C/ Araqui
BONAP	Bon app'	Laurence Lebihan	Owner	12, rue de
BOTTM	Bottom-Dollar Markets	Elizabeth Lincoln	Accounting Manager	23 Tsawa
BSBEV	B's Beverages	Victoria Ashworth	Sales Representative	Fauntlero
CACTU	Cactus Comidas para llevar	Patricio Simpson	Sales Agent	Cerrito 33
CENTC	Centro comercial Moctezuma	Francisco Chang	Marketing Manager	Sierras de
CHOPS	Chop-suey Chinese	Yang Wang	Owner	Hauptstr.
COMMI	Comércio Mineiro	Pedro Afonso	Sales Associate	Av. dos L
CONSH	Consolidated Holdings	Elizabeth Brown	Sales Representative	Berkeley
DRACD	Drachenblut Delikatessen	Sven Ottlieb	Order Administrator	Walserwe
DUMON	Du monde entier	Janine Labrune	Owner	67, rue de
EASTC	Eastern Connection	Ann Devon	Sales Agent	35 King G
ERNSH	Ernst Handel	Roland Mendel	Sales Manager	Kirchgass
FAMIA	Familia Arquibaldo	Aria Cruz	Marketing Assistant	Rua Orós
FISSA	FISSA Fabrica Inter. Salchichas S.A.	Diego Roel	Accounting Manager	C/ Moralz

Record: 1 of 91

Figure F.9

You can display the same data in an attractive, easy-to-use form that displays one record at a time.

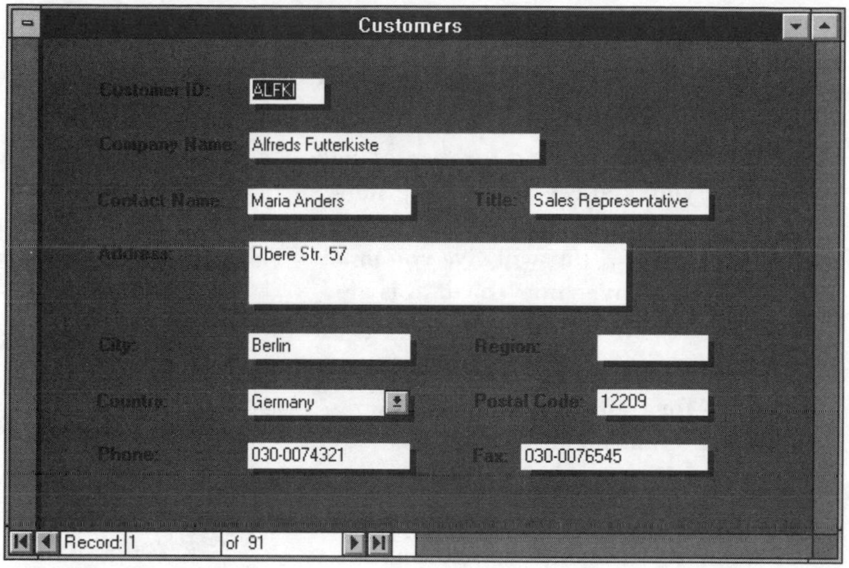

In Access, forms are meant for viewing and editing, and reports are for printing. But you can also print your forms. If you want to print a graph, for example, you'll find it a lot easier to create a form for the graph and print it out than to print the graph in the form of a report. In general, forms are much more versatile than reports.

you. Then the Form Wizard asks you a few questions—just simple things it needs to know to create your form, like what table or query you want to use to create the form, what fields you want to include on

the form, and what the general look of the form should be. You answer the questions, and the Form Wizard does the design work.

Tip

This wizardry stuff is all well and good, and often you'll find that a form created with the Form Wizard is exactly right for you. If it's not quite what you're looking for, however, you can modify the form. Changing a form that was created by the Form Wizard instead of designing a brand new form from scratch will save you lots of time. *See Modifying Forms and Reports.*

A
B
C
D
E
F
G
H
I
J
KL
M
N
O
P
Q
R
S
T
U
V
W
XYZ

The Form Wizard can create these forms:

A **Single-Column** form is good for looking at one record at a time.

A **Tabular** form is good for displaying a table of your data, which will be similar to the table you've seen before in Datasheet View, but will give you much more control over how the data is arranged and presented.

A **Graph** form is good for displaying a graph—for example, a graphic summary of numeric data.

A **Main/Sub** form is good for displaying data from two tables (related by a one-to-many relationship) at one time.

AutoForm is good for displaying all the data from the table or query the form is based upon in a single-column format similar to a Single-Column form.

> 66 **Just as the Form Wizards help you design on-screen formats in which to view your data, the Report Wizards help you design useful and attractive printed reports that will communicate to others the information contained in your tables, and its meaning.**

Forms Are Based on a Table or Dynaset

When you create a form you tell Access what table or dynaset to base it on. This is how Access knows what data to display in the form. You can base a form on any table or dynaset, though some queries will produce dynasets that you can't modify.

See **Forms: Choosing; Forms: Creating with the Form Wizard; Modifying Forms and Reports**

> 66 **You can do some funky things with forms and reports—such as building forms from Crosstab queries to summarize your data. You can also modify the forms you've created with the Form Wizard. The processes for modifying forms and reports are so similar that we've combined that information.**

FORMS: CHOOSING

Let's look at the various kinds of forms you can create with the Wizards and what they're good for.

Single-Column Form

The Single-Column form, the simplest form available in Access, displays one record at a time, with the fields lined up in a single column on the form. This is just great for entering new data, because you can zip from field to field in a snap. A Single-Column form is shown in Figure F.10.

Tabular Form

A Tabular form displays your data in a column-and-row layout that is similar to the layout in Datasheet View, but the Tabular form is a silk purse compared to that sow's ear, the datasheet. When you display your data in a Tabular form instead of a in a datasheet, you have exact control over the width of each field, the font in which each

field will be displayed, and whether the field will appear in **bold**, *italics*, or ***bold-italics***. You can even create 3-D-looking boxes around each field. A Tabular form is shown in Figure F.11.

Graph Form

To make complicated numeric information easy to see and understand, you can create a graph. The graph will appear in the form of a form, and will give you a pictorial representation of your data. Looking at a graph, you'll know the answer to a question about your data almost before you can ask the question. Graphs are great any time you have a sequence of numbers that reflect some change, like the price of bananas or the time it takes Worker X to change the widget once you've installed the new widget-changing gadget. A Graph form is shown in Figure F.12.

Figure F.10
....

A Single-Column form

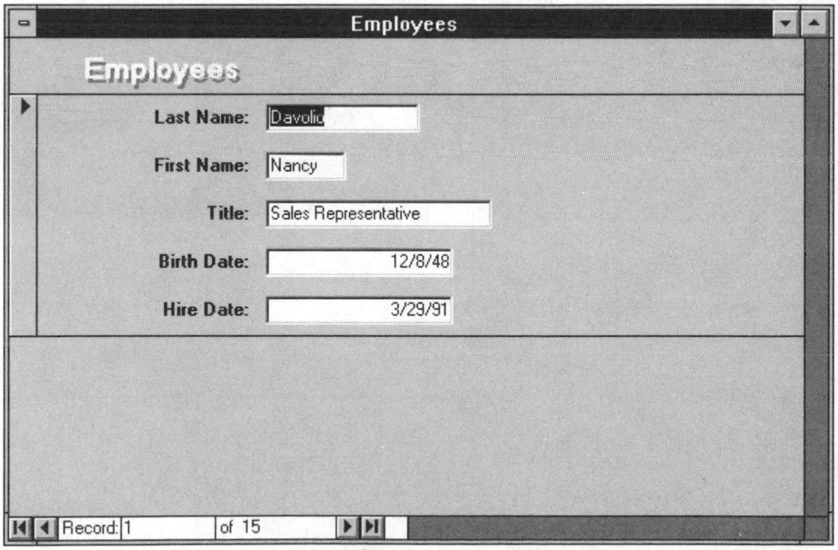

Figure F.11
....
A Tabular form

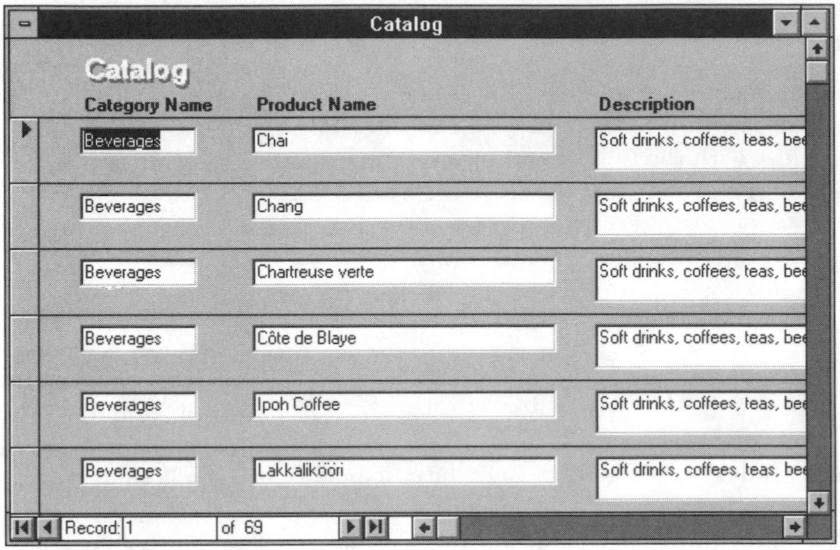

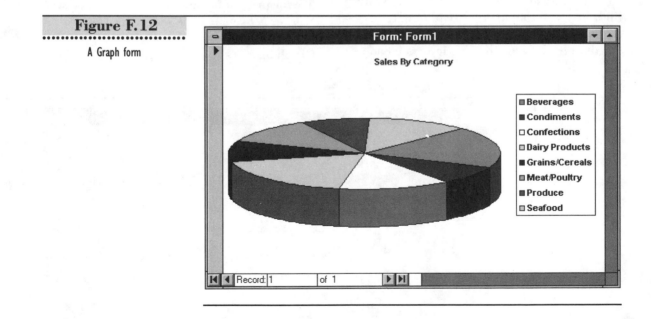

Figure F.12
....
A Graph form

About the Graph Wizard
. . . .

The Graph Wizard is one of the Form Wizards. Like the other Wizards, the Graph Wizard asks about your data. Then it asks what you want to graph, and how you want it to appear. Finally, the Graph Wizard creates a form to display the graph.

In the Graph Wizard's dialog boxes, it will ask you: <u>Which fields contain the data you want to graph?</u> You should specify Number fields here, because those are what the Graph Wizard can graph. You can also specify one field that does not contain a number. The Graph Wizard will use this field as a label running along the bottom or side of the graph, or if it's a pie graph, around the edge.

<u>What type of a graph do you want?</u> The Graph Wizard can create a number of different styles of graphs, including line graphs, pie graphs, and bar graphs.

Main/Sub Form

The Main/Sub form—the most complicated form the Form Wizard can create—allows you to view data contained in two related tables at one time.

66 **We cover how tables are related with joins, and the three types of relationships (one-to-one, one-to-many, many-to-many) in Joins and Relationships.**

With a Main/Sub form, you can see the results of a one-to-many join on-screen. You can use this type of form any time you have related information you want to view. In a database for a nonprofit arts organization, for example, you can create a Main/Sub form to display each person's name from the Mailing List table along with a list of the dates and amounts of that person's contributions from the Contributions table. Take a look at the Main/Sub form in Figure F.13.

See **Forms: Creating with the Form Wizard**

FORMS: CREATING WITH THE FORM WIZARD

A
B
C
D
E
F
G
H
I
J
KL
M
N
O
P
Q
R
S
T
U
V
W
XYZ

To create a form using the Form Wizard:

1. Display the list of Forms (if any) in the Database window by clicking on the Forms icon.

2. Select the New button.

3. Access will display a dialog box like the one shown in Figure F.14, asking you to pick a source for your new form.

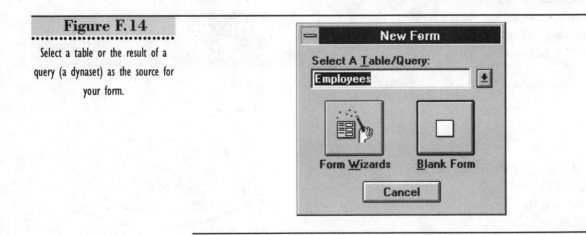

Figure F.13

A Main/Sub form

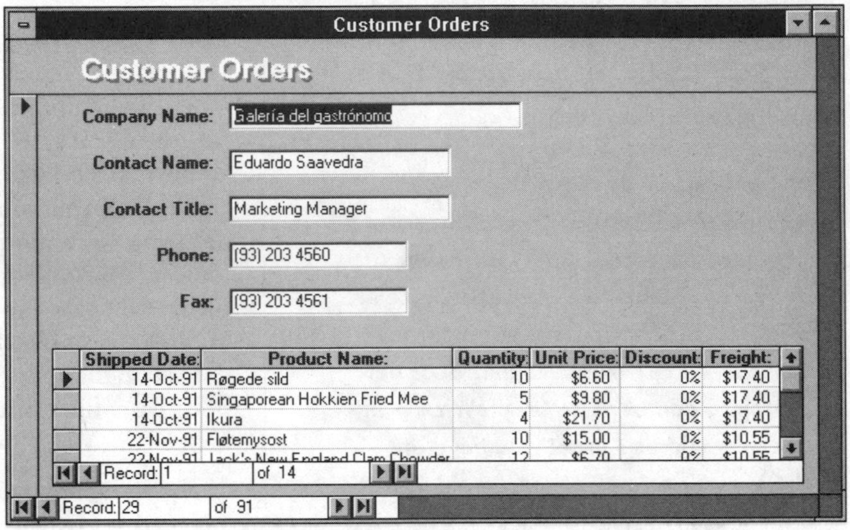

Figure F.14

Select a table or the result of a query (a dynaset) as the source for your form.

4. Enter the name of the table or dynaset on which you want to base your form. You can type the name in the text box provided or you can click on the little box with the down-arrow in it and select the name from the list that appears.

Tip

Later you'll tell the Form Wizard which of the table or dynaset's fields you want to include in the form itself, so don't worry if the table or dynaset you've chosen contains a lot more fields than you want in the form.

5. Click on the Form Wizard button to start the Form Wizard.

Tip

You cannot add more tables or dynasets to your form as you design it. If you want to display information from multiple tables on a single form, you must first create a query that pulls together all the data you want to display, then use the dynaset from that query as the basis for your form.

6. Access displays the dialog box shown in Figure F.15 asking you to pick the type of form you want to create.

You can choose any of the types of forms we've been talking about. The process for each is a little different, so let's go over all of them, one at a time.

Figure F.15

Choose the type of form you want, then click on OK.

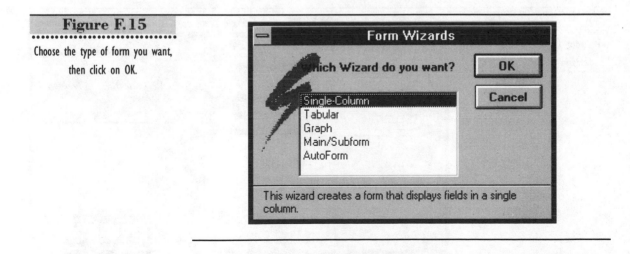

A
B
C
D
E
F
G
H
I
J
KL
M
N
O
P
Q
R
S
T
U
V
W
XYZ

If you're following these directions to create a form now, look over the types of forms listed below, and choose the type of form you want. Then you can proceed with the directions under the name of that form.

Creating a Single-Column Form or a Tabular Form

The processes for creating a Single-Column form or a Tabular form are identical:

1. When you get to step 6 (as described previously), select either Single-Column or Tabular.

2. A dialog box (shown in Figure F.16) will appear, asking which fields you want to include from the table or dynaset on which you're basing the form.

Place fields on the form by moving them from the Available Fields list box on the left to the Field Order on Form list box on the right. Only those fields that are in the box on the right will be included in the form you are building. You move a field from the list on the left to the list on the right by selecting the field name and clicking the add-one-field icon:

Figure F.16

The Form Wizard displays all the fields in the table or query.

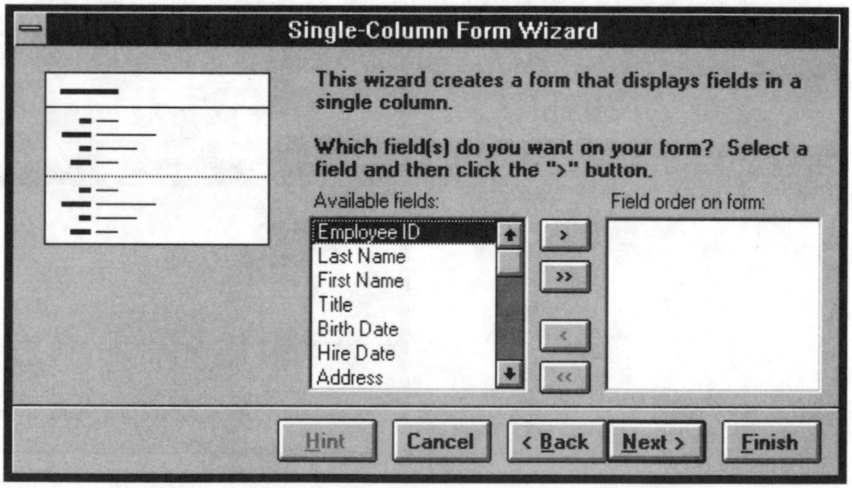

Single-Column Form Wizard

This wizard creates a form that displays fields in a single column.

Which field(s) do you want on your form? Select a field and then click the ">" button.

Available fields:

- Employee ID
- Last Name
- First Name
- Title
- Birth Date
- Hire Date
- Address

Field order on form:

| > |
| >> |
| < |
| << |

Hint   Cancel   < Back   Next >   Finish

Or, you can add all the fields by clicking on the add-all-fields icon:

Conversely, if you wish to remove a field, you just select the field and click the remove-one-field icon:

Or you can remove all fields you have added by clicking the remove-all-fields icon:

3. When you have moved all of those fields you want to include to the Field Order on Form list box, click the Next button at the bottom of the window.

4. The Form Wizard will display a dialog box (Figure F.17) asking what look you want the form to have. Choose from these possibilities:

Standard This is the plain-Jane version.

Chiseled Fields are indicated by a chiseled underline.

Shadowed Fields appear in shadowed boxes, giving the form a 3-D look.

Boxed Fields and their names are surrounded by boxes.

Embossed Fields have raised gray borders that make them seem to pop off the form.

5. Once you've made your choice of style, click the Next button.

Figure F.17

Select the look you want for your form.

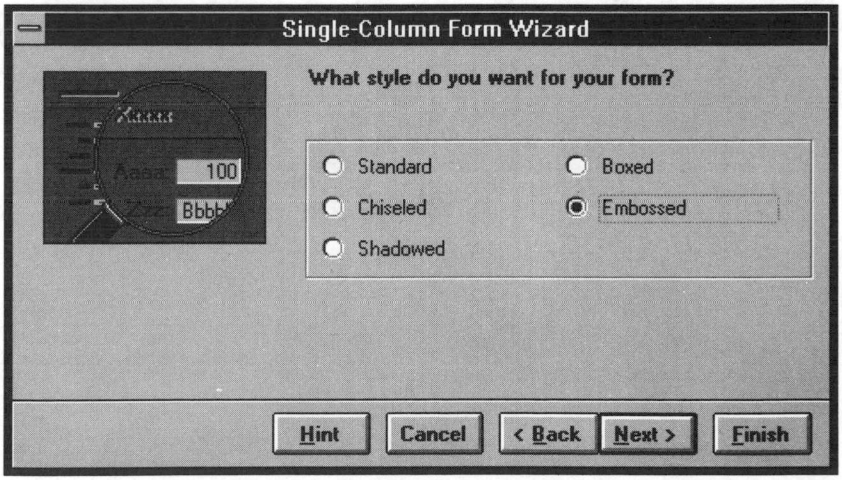

Single-Column Form Wizard
What style do you want for your form?

○ Standard   ○ Boxed
○ Chiseled   ● Embossed
○ Shadowed

[Hint] [Cancel] [< Back] [Next >] [Finish]

A
B
C
D
E
F
G
H
I
J
KL
M
N
O
P
Q
R
S
T
U
V
W
XYZ

Tip

The Form Wizard displays a sample form in the graphic along the left side of the window. The graphic (which shows a generic form) will change to reflect your choice of style. You can always backtrack to the last question the Wizard asked by clicking on the Back button.

6. Now you must tell the Form Wizard what you want to title your form. Type a nifty title in the Form Title box (see Figure F.18). Remember, this title will appear on the top of your form.

7. Click on the Finish button to open up your form. The Form Wizard will work for a few seconds—putting together what you've requested—and then you will see your form on-screen.

Creating a Graph Form

To use the Graph Wizard to create a graph:

1. Complete the steps outlined above in the section titled Forms: Creating with the Form Wizard and select Graph for your form type. This will tell Access you want to use the Graph Wizard.

2. The Graph Wizard will now display a dialog box asking you which fields you want to include in your graph. Pick as many Number fields as you want. You are limited, however, to a single Text field. The Wizard will use whichever Text field you select as a label along the bottom edge of the graph and will display each Number field as its own line (or slice of a pie).

Figure F.18

Give your Single-Column form a meaningful title.

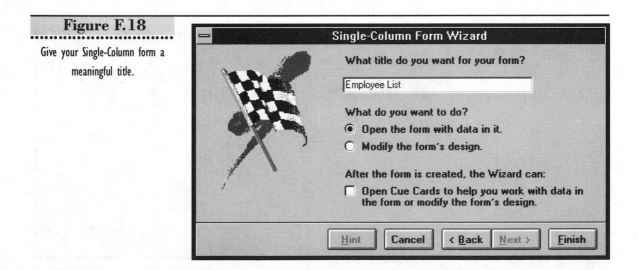

3. In the next dialog box you'll tell Access what to do with data in the same *category* (data that has the same label is placed in the same category when Access creates your graph). Select one of the following options (by clicking on the corresponding button):

Add (sum) the numbers Adds all the numbers in the category

Average the numbers Uses the average value of all the numbers in the category

Count the number of records in each category Uses the number of entries in each category

Once you have picked one of the options, click on the Next button to continue.

4. In the next dialog box, shown in Figure F.19, select the type of graph you want to create. As you click on graph types along the right side of the window, the Sample area will update to give you an idea of what your graph will look like. When you are satisfied that you have picked the appropriate type of graph, click on the Next button to continue.

5. The Wizard will display a window asking for a title for your graph. Type a title into the text box, and Access will later display that title whenever it displays your graph. You can select whether a legend is displayed on the graph by selecting either the Yes or No option button below the question about the legend. Once you are done with this dialog box, click on the Next button to move on.

6. You can either view your graph in Form View or Design View by selecting the appropriate option button in this dialog box. Once you have selected one of the buttons, click on the Finish button. Your graph will appear in the view you selected.

Figure F.19

Select the style of graph you want the Graph Wizard to create.

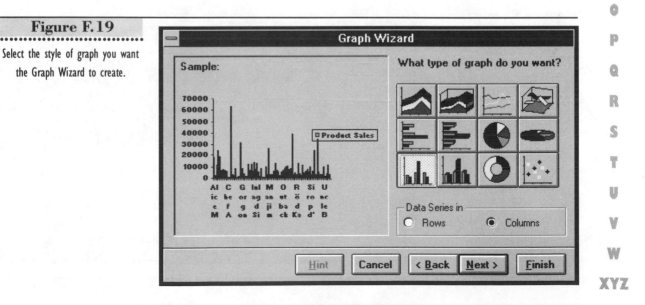

Choosing among Types of Graphs

· · · · · · · · · · · ·

Pick the type of graph that will best represent the data you are displaying. Maybe you're graphing year-to-date sales for this year and last. In that case, you probably want a bar graph. If you're graphing a change—such as in stock prices, for example—a line graph will give you the best results. To show how the whole of something (your paycheck, for example) is divvied up, use a pie graph. Various types of graphs are shown in Figure F.20.

Creating a Main/Sub Form

Remember that when you create a Main/Sub form, you are dealing with *two* forms:

⊗ The *Main* form

⊗ The *Sub* form

To create a Main/Sub form:

1. Complete steps 1–6 as they are outlined earlier in Forms: Creating with the Form Wizard and select Main/Sub as your form type.

2. In the dialog box that appears (Figure F.20), select the source of the Sub form. The source can be either a table or a dynaset. Once you have selected the table or query that contains data to display on the sub from, click on the Next button to continue.

Figure F.20
· ·

The Main/Sub Form Wizard dialog box

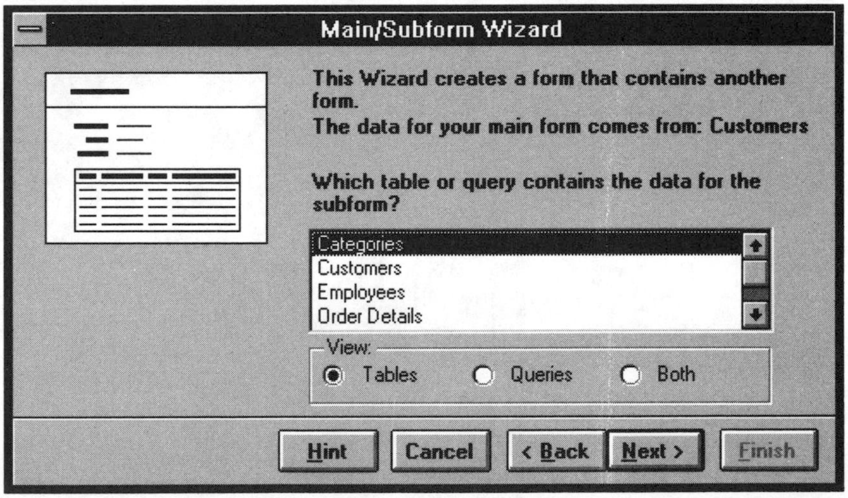

66 Access will figure out how the two tables or dynasets are related, based on the relationships you have created. If you haven't created a relationship between the two tables or dynasets, Access will try to <u>guess</u> at how the tables are related. Sometimes Access will guess right, sometimes it will guess wrong or not be able to guess at all. For best results, you should define the relationship between the two tables <u>beforehand</u>.

3. Next, select those fields from the main table or dynaset that you want to include in the *Main* form by moving the

fields from the Available Fields list box to the Fields on Main Form list box. Once you have selected the fields, click the Next button.

4. A dialog box will appear (Figure F.21) in which you can select the fields to include on the *Sub* form. Select fields by moving them from the Available Fields list box to the Fields on Sub form list. You do this by clicking on the same buttons you used in the last step. Click the Next button when you are done.

5. Now you get to tell the Form Wizard what style you want for your form. As you select the style, the Wizard will show you a sample in the graphic along the left side of the window. Once you have selected a style that you are happy with, click on the Next button.

Figure F.21

Select the fields you want to include in the Sub form.

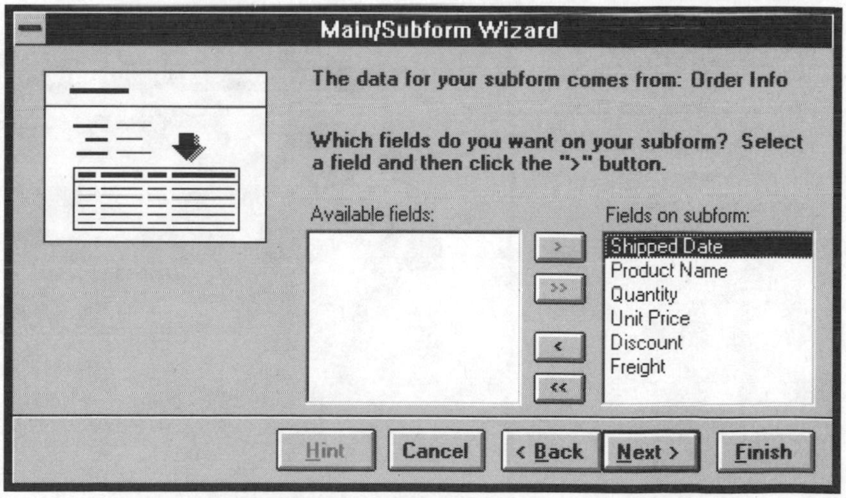

Main/Subform Wizard

The data for your subform comes from: Order Info

Which fields do you want on your subform? Select a field and then click the ">" button.

Available fields:

Fields on subform:
Shipped Date
Product Name
Quantity
Unit Price
Discount
Freight

Hint   Cancel   < Back   Next >   Finish

66 If the Form Wizard can't figure out on which field your two tables are joined, it will display a dialog box asking for help. It will display all the fields it thinks the two tables are joined on in a list box. Click on the name of the field the two tables share in common and click on the Next button to continue to step 5.

6. Yet another dialog box will appear (Figure F.22) in which you give your form a title and choose either to view your new form (by selecting "Open the form with data in it") or to review the form in Design View (by selecting "Modify the form's design").

7. Enter a title for the form in the Form Title box, then click on the Finish button. The form will appear.

66 The first time you open a Main/Sub form you've created with the Wizard, you will be prompted to save the Sub form. Just click OK, then type in a name for the Sub form in the Save As dialog box. Once you have typed a name, click on OK to save the Sub form.

See Forms: Moving from Record to Record; Forms: Saving; Forms: Viewing Data With; Printing Forms; Save/Save As

Figure F.22

We gave this form the name "Orders by Categories."

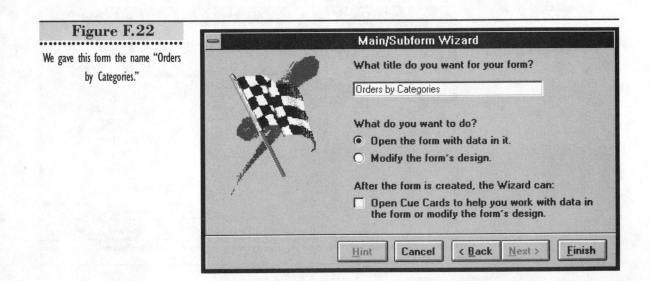

Main/Subform Wizard

What title do you want for your form?

Orders by Categories

What do you want to do?

● Open the form with data in it.
○ Modify the form's design.

After the form is created, the Wizard can:

☐ Open Cue Cards to help you work with data in the form or modify the form's design.

Hint   Cancel   < Back   Next >   Finish

Navigating in a Main/Sub Form

The Main/Sub form feature is very cool, and it's not available in many databases other than Access. In a Main/Sub form, you're actually looking at a one-to-many relationship between two tables or dynasets on-screen. The Main form displays data from the "one" side of the relationship, while the Sub form displays all the related records from the second table or dynaset. See Joins and Relationships.

This means you can be-bop around in the Main form, changing data as you need to, and as you change the record displayed in the Main form, the data will be changed automatically in the Sub form to reflect what you've done. Using the example of Mailing List and Contributions tables, in the Main form you can move between records in the Mailing List table, and the related records from the Contributions table will appear in the Sub form.

You can link data one-to-many using joins, but often you'll find that using a Main/Sub form provides more freedom—for one thing, it doesn't restrict which tables you can modify.

You can use the VCR-type buttons along the bottom of the Main form, or the options under Records ➤ Go To in the menu bar, to go from one record to another record in the Main form. Of course, as you switch from one record to another in the Main form, the related data in the Sub form will change, too. For example, when you switch from Lydia Artsmatron's record to Starr Wannabee's record in the Main form, you'll see the Contributions information in the Sub form change to show Starr's gifts instead of Lydia's.

You can also add new records to a table or add data to records using the Main form, just as you would using any other type of form. And (this is really special) you can even add data to the table displayed in the Sub form. You do this in the same way you add data to a datasheet. Just go to the blank record that's always at the end of a table (whether you're viewing the table as a datasheet or form), and start typing in your new data.

You will see the Main form on screen in its entirety. The Sub form, though, is…well, a sub form, so Access treats it like it's secondary, and gives the Main form first dibs on screen space. If all the Sub form data can't be displayed in the screen space allowed, vertical scroll bars appear along its right side. You can scroll around in the Sub form by clicking on the scroll bars in the usual ways.

A
B
C
D
E
F
G
H
I
J
KL
M
N
O
P
Q
R
S
T
U
V
W
XYZ

FORMS: MOVING FROM RECORD TO RECORD

Once you have your data displayed in a form, you can zip around in your table or dynaset, viewing all your data with ease. If you select the Edit ➤ Find, and Edit ➤ Replace commands from the menu bar, they'll act just the same here as they did in Datasheet View. (Edit ➤ Find lets you search for data, and Edit ➤ Replace lets you search for and replace data.)

You can move around (while you're in a form) by any of these methods:

○ From the menu bar, use these commands (in the obvious ways):

Records ➤ Go To ➤ First
Records ➤ Go To ➤ Last
Records ➤ Go To ➤ Next
Records ➤ Go To ➤ Previous
Records ➤ Go To ➤ New

○ Click on the VCR-type buttons that appear along the bottom of the form's window, as shown in Figure F.23.

Moving to a New Record

To move to a new, empty record (presumably so you can fill it with new data, creating a new record), you can use either of two techniques:

○ Select Records ➤ Go To ➤ New from the menu bar. (If you're viewing a Main/Sub form, make sure first that the Main form is active.)

○ Click on the Last Record button, which appears at the bottom of the window:

Figure F.23
. . . .
You can move to different records by clicking on the VCR-type buttons along the bottom of the form's window.

```
┌─────────────────────────────────────────────┐
│ ⊟              Employee List            ▼ ▲ │
├─────────────────────────────────────────────┤
│   Employee List                             │
│ ▶                                           │
│                    Title: Sales Representative│
│                                             │
│               Hire Date:         3/29/91    │
│                                             │
│               Birth Date:        12/8/48    │
│ ◄◀│◀ Record:1      of 15     ▶│▶│           │
└─────────────────────────────────────────────┘
```

Previous record   **Last record**

First record   **Next record**

Either of these techniques will move you to an empty record, into which you can enter new data.

Moving from Field to Field

You can move around the form, changing the current field from one field to another, for example, by using the following keys.

What It Is	What It Does
↑	Moves up one field
↓	Moves down one field
→	Moves to the right one field
←	Moves to the left one field

Tip

The Tab and Shift-Tab keys also move you forward or backward one field. The Tab key also moves you into the Sub form, once you have tabbed to the last field in a Main form.

FORMS: SAVING

Whenever you close the Form Design View or Form window for a form that you have changed, Access will prompt you with a dialog box that asks oh-so-politely if you want to save the changes. If you want to use the form again, click Yes (Figure F.24).

If you have not yet named the form, Access will then display the dialog box asking for a form name. Type in a name for your form—one that's easy to remember and tells you what the form is all about—and click OK to continue (Figure F.25).

Once your form is saved, it will appear in the Forms list in the Database window, as shown in Figure F.26. You can open the form up again any time you want by selecting its name from the list and clicking on Open. To view the form in Design View, select the form name from the Database window as usual and click on the Design button.

See Save/Save As

Figure F.24

Click Yes to save the changes to the form.

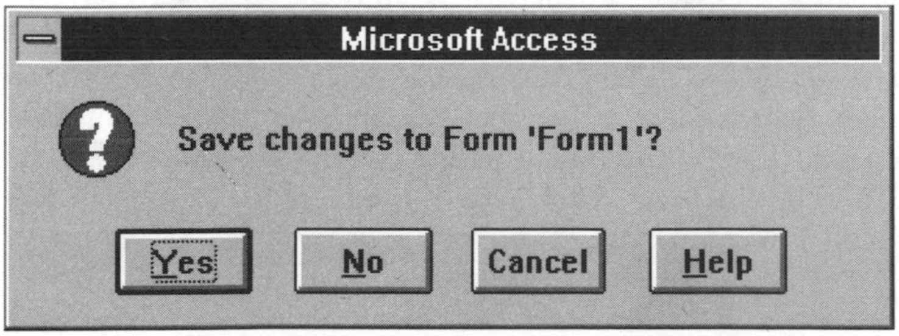

Microsoft Access

Save changes to Form 'Form1'?

Yes   No   Cancel   Help

Figure F.25

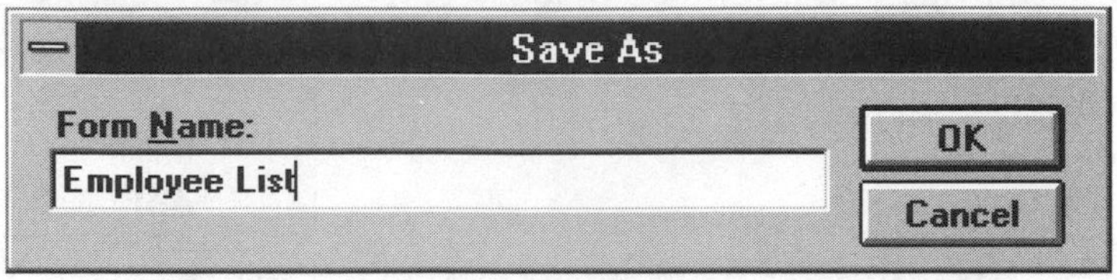

The Save As dialog box

Save As

Form **N**ame:

Employee List

OK

Cancel

Figure F.26

Once you have saved a form, it will appear in a list of forms in the Database window.

FORMS: VIEWING DATA WITH

To view your data in the form of an existing form, click on the Forms button in the Database window, and when the list of forms appears, highlight the name of the form you want. Then either click on Open or double-click on the form's name. Access will open up the form, and there, incredibly, you'll see your data.

Switching Views

You can switch quickly between Form View and Datasheet View by using the buttons provided for that purpose. The buttons, shown below, are on the toolbar at the top of the screen. To switch from Form View to Datasheet View, click on the Datasheet View button:

To switch back to Form View from
Datasheet View, click on the Form View
button:

You can switch back and forth, back
and forth, as much as you like.

**If you are viewing a Main/Sub form,
you can switch to Datasheet View
only when the Main form is active.**

See   **Datasheet View; Viewing Data**

A
B
C
D
E
F
G
H
I
J
KL
M
N
O
P
Q
R
S
T
U
V
W
XYZ

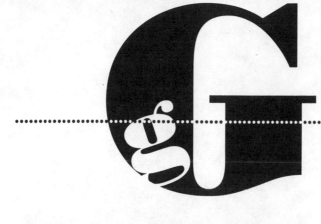

GRAPHS

Using graphs, you can communicate simple or complex information in the instant it takes to see the graph. Graphs are so effective they often answer questions before the viewer even asks them. In Access, graphs are displayed as forms (on-screen) or as reports (on paper).

Among the Forms Wizards is a special Graphs Wizard that lets you create on-screen graphs (in a form) in a jiffy. (To print that graph, you'd print the form.)

You can also place a graph on a report and print it, but there's no Wizard for this, and it's really pretty complicated. In this book, we're going to stick with what you can do with the Graphs Wizard.

See **Forms and Form Wizards**

GUI

GUI (pronounced *gooey*) stands for Graphical User Interface. A GUI is a systematic way to interact with your computer by manipulating graphical images on the screen rather than typing in commands at the C: prompt. Windows is a GUI, and all Windows-based applications, including Access, allow you to use a mouse to click on icons, buttons, and pull-down lists of commands, and select from among other graphical elements.

See **Part I**

AB CD EF GH IJ KL M N O P Q R S T U V W XYZ

HANDLE

The area at the corners of controls in Form Design View and Report Design View that gives you something to grab onto so you can manipulate the control is called a *handle*.

> *See* **Controls; Forms and Form Wizards; Modifying Forms and Reports**

HARD-DISK DRIVE

The *hard-disk drive*, *hard disk*, or just plain *hard drive* is a storage device in your machine. It is on the hard disk that your program and data files are stored. When we say "save to disk" we mean "save to the hard-disk drive"—the place where you store things for future use.

> *See* **Disk Space**

HELP

Everybody needs Help once in a while. Access includes a very powerful and complete on-line Help system. Most of the information included in the Microsoft Access manuals is also available on-screen at the stroke of the F1 key. The Access Help system is *context-sensitive*, which means that Access notices what you're doing and tells you all about that particular task or feature when you tap the F1 key. You don't have to search through a long index of Help topics.

To search the Help system, select Search from the Help menu and type in the topic you want to find.

Another trick is to press Shift-F1 and, when the mouse pointer changes to a little question mark, click on the screen element you want to find out about. (You can get rid of the question mark and out of this Help mode by pressing the Escape key.) Above all, remember that context-sensitive Help is there on the menu bar, waiting for you to need it.

Getting Around in Help

The Access Help system is written in a Windows Help style, which means it includes not just printed text but also "hot spots." Hot spots are words you can click on to jump from a Help topic window to other related Help topics and subtopics. Hot spot words appear in green.

You can also click on the Contents button in the menu bar at the top of the Help window to get a complete list of major topics covered in the Help system.

Adding Your Own Notes to Access Help

You can add your own notes to any topic in the Help system. While the topic that interests you is displayed on-screen, select Annotate from the Edit menu. Type in your notes as shown in Figure H.1.

Once you have added your own notes to a Help topic, that topic will be marked with a paper clip icon to remind you that you've included your two cents on the subject.

See **Cue Cards**

Setting Bookmarks in the Help File

You can set bookmarks in the Help file to help you quickly locate those topics you use all the time. Once you have the topic on screen, select Define from the Bookmark menu. A dialog box appears, into which you can type a name for the bookmark. When a bookmark is defined in this way, its name appears in the Bookmark menu in the Help system.

Figure H.1

You can add your own notes to the Help file text any time you want.

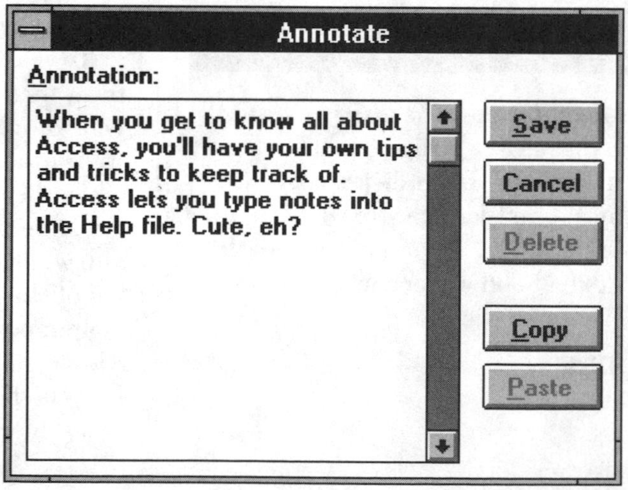

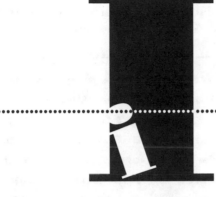

ICON

Tiny pictures on screen that are meant to represent some function or option are called *icons*. You click or double-click on the icon to get or do whatever the icon represents. For example, if you click on the icon on the toolbar that has a picture of a printer in it, you'll print the open object (or document.)

See **Windows Basics**

IMPORT DATABASE (ADD-IN)

The Import Database add-in allows you to quickly import all the objects (including tables, queries, forms, reports, and more) from any other Access database into your current Access database.

To use the Import Database add-in, select File ➤ Add-Ins ➤ Import Database. The Import Database window will appear. Select the name of the database you wish to import in the File Name box and click on

the OK button. Access will import all the objects from the selected database into your current database.

When the import is done, Access displays a dialog box saying that the database was successfully imported. If any object in the database you are importing has the same name as an object in your current database, Access will change the name of the imported object by adding a number to the end of the name to make it unique.

See **Importing**

IMPORT ERRORS

If Access encounters errors while importing data, it will log the errors into a special "Import Errors" table. You can view the log of errors by opening the Import Errors table in Datasheet View. Correct the errors, if you like, by going back to the original data and making changes.

See **Importing**

IMPORTING

Lots of data was stored in different database formats before Access came along, and you might find yourself having to work with some of it. Maybe you've inherited a dBASE file from the person who did your job before you. Maybe someone wants to share data with you—and maybe this someone stores it in a Lotus 1-2-3 *spreadsheet*, no less. The problem with this is that each database or other type of program formats data differently, to fit in with that program's own inner workings. When you try to use a file from another program, it will seem to Access like gobbledygook unless you first pass the file through a process that translates one file format into another.

We're going to show you how to bring information *into* Access that was first stored in another format.

You'll be able to import data from:

☼ Other database programs, such as dBASE III, dBASE IV, FoxPro, and Paradox

☼ Spreadsheet programs, such as Lotus 1-2-3 and Excel

☼ Text files, if they are formatted in a way Access can understand

What Importing Is

Importing is the process of bringing data into Access from other programs. Once you import data into Access, it becomes an Access table, which you can use just as if you had created it in Access. That table is then stored in Access' own file format.

66 Many database programs—dBASE, FoxPro, and some others—use similar file formats (their files end in the extension .DBF). Paradox uses a different file format (its files end in the extension .DB). Access 2 handles the importing of .DBF files similarly to .DB files. Access files (in case you've forgotten) have the extension .MDB.

If, however, you need to use that data in Access, but want to keep the file in its original format—perhaps because someone else (who is using a .DBF file) also needs to use the data—you should not *import*, but instead *attach* to the data file.

To Import or to Attach

While you are working in Access with data that has been imported or attached, you can do almost anything you can do with a file you've created in Access. There will seem, then, to be little difference between importing and attaching. There is, however, a very big difference—importing changes the data into an Access format forever, while attaching changes it only temporarily. You can (as we've said) do almost everything with it that you can do with an Access table, and the data will change as you modify it. But the file format hasn't been changed and the data is still available for use (as-is) in the other application.

Let's say you need to work in Access on your machine with data that has been created in dBASE on a co-worker's machine. If your co-worker is never going to need that file again, you should import the file. If, however, you are going to make changes to the file and then have to pass it back (either on disk or through a network), your best bet is to attach it.

> **Many other database programs can do importing. It is possible, when you are working in some other programs, to import Access files into that program. But (and this is an important but) Access is still fairly new, and you will be able to import Access files only into other programs that actually recognize Access. You'll have to find out from the maker of the program you're using whether that program can import from Access.**

See Attaching; Importing from Other Database Programs; Importing from a Spreadsheet Program; Importing from a Text File

IMPORTING FROM OTHER DATABASE PROGRAMS

The most common importing you might do is from other database programs. Often, this will be because your company is switching programs, or because you've purchased a mailing list in a format other than Access, or because you're sharing files with someone who uses a different program.

There are important differences between .DBF programs like dBASE and Fox Pro, and .DB programs like Paradox. Nevertheless, Access handles the importing of data from these programs in essentially the same way.

Importing .DBF or .DB Files

You are most likely to be importing data from dBASE III, dBASE IV, FoxPro 2.5, FoxPro 2, Paradox 3.X, or Paradox 4.X—some of the most popular database programs.

dBASE was one of the first PC-based database programs—it was developed long before IBM even dreamed of becoming a personal computer company, back when databases were run on room-sized machines serviced by specially trained, full-time operators. The influence of dBASE is still felt throughout database programs in general. Many database programs use the .DBF file format, which came first from dBASE. This means that you'll very commonly find yourself importing .DBF files. dBASE III, dBASE IV, FoxPro 2.5, and FoxPro 2 all use the .DBF format.

A
B
C
D
E
F
G
H
I
J
KL
M
N
O
P
Q
R
S
T
U
V
W
XYZ

Paradox, another popular relational database program, comes in both DOS and Windows versions. Like Access, Paradox stores records in tables. Access can import data from Paradox tables into its own tables. Paradox files end with the extension .DB.

To import a .DBF or .DB file into Access:

I. You must open a Database window into which you will import the data. Either you can use an existing Access database file, or you can create a new one by selecting File ➤ New from the menu bar. (Remember that you can't create a new database in this way while you have an existing one open.) (*See* Database File: Creating)

2. Select File ➤ Import from the menu bar. The Import dialog box will appear.

3. In the Import Dialog box's Data Source list box, select the application with which the .DBF or .DB file was created. Then click on the OK button. The Select File dialog box (Figure I.1) will appear.

················Tip················

If you don't know exactly what application was used to create a .DBF file, try selecting dBASE III. dBASE III files are the most common .DBF files.

4. In the Select File dialog box, select the name of the .DBF or .DB file you want to import into Access. Then click the Import button.

5. Access will import the data into a table and display a dialog box telling you everything is done. Close the dialog box by clicking OK.

6. You'll be returned to the Select File dialog box. If you want to import more files, go back to step 4.

7. When you're done, click the Close button.

Figure I.1
··························

The Select File dialog box

Select File		
File Name:	**Directories:**	Import
newcust.dbf	c:\access\sampapps	Close
newcust.dbf	c:\	
	access	
	sampapps	
List Files of Type:	**Drives:**	
dBASE III [*.dbf]	c: laxness	

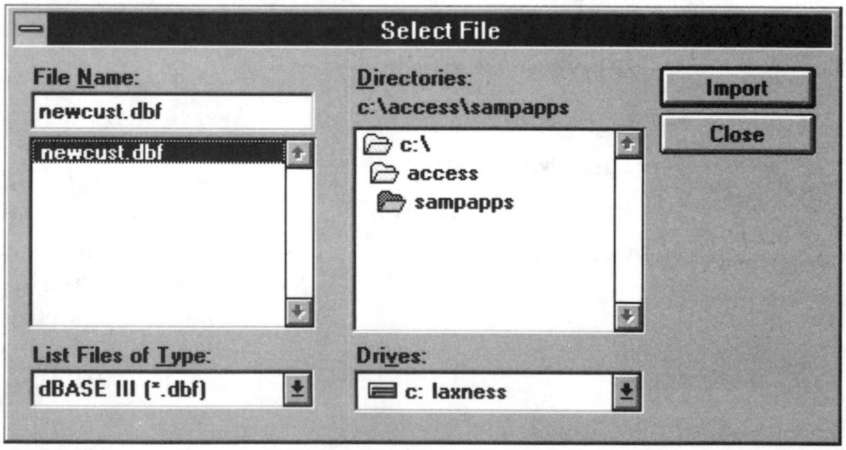

66 If your database already has a table with the same name as the table you are importing, Access will change the new one's name into something unique by adding a number at the end.

You'll see the new table appear in the list of tables in the Database window. Access will have named the new table with a name similar to the original file's name.

You may want to give the table a more meaningful name. To do this, first select the table's name from the list and then select File ➤ Rename from the menu bar. A dialog box will appear and you can type in the new table name. Press ↵ to close the dialog box, and the new table name will appear in the list of tables in the Database window.

See **Attaching to a Paradox Table; Importing**

IMPORTING FROM A SPREADSHEET PROGRAM

In a spreadsheet program—like Lotus 1-2-3 or Microsoft Excel—data is laid out in a column-and-row format, which at first glance seems very similar to Access' datasheet. A spreadsheet, however, allows the users to use much more complex math calculations, and often presents numeric data in a way that's more useful for bookkeeping, accounting, or mathematical analysis. A database allows you to do math calculations *and* manipulate text and other kinds of data. A database really excels in areas where the spreadsheet is weaker— like searching, sorting, querying, and summarizing.

Access can import data from both Excel and Lotus 1-2-3 spreadsheet files, as long as the data is laid out with each column representing a different field and each row a new record. (See Figure I.2)

In Excel and 1-2-3, it is possible to assign a name to a *range* of cells. (A range is a rectangular block of cells.) You might, for example, want to call a block of cells that hold bookkeeping data for June 1995 "June95." Then, when referring to the cells in that range—to print them, or to copy them to another block of cells, for example—you'd just call them "June95" instead of having to select and highlight all of them.

When you are importing data from Excel or Lotus 1-2-3 into Access, you must know the *range* or the range *name* of the cells that contain the data.

Tip

Just about every other spreadsheet program can save data in Lotus 1-2-3 format. If you're using a spreadsheet other than 1-2-3 or Excel, read your program's documentation to find out how to save your data in 1-2-3 format.

Figure I.2

In this spreadsheet, each column represents a field and each row is a new record, just as it would be in Access' Datasheet View.

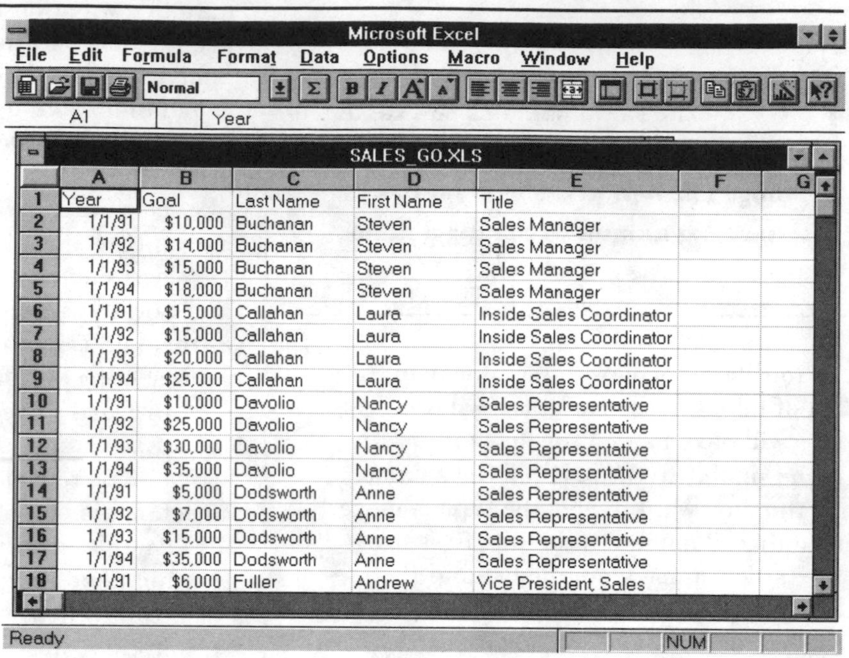

To import a spreadsheet into Access:

1. You must open a Database window into which you will import the spreadsheet data. You can either use an existing Access database file, or create a new one using File ➤ New from the menu bar. (*See* Database File: Creating)

2. Select File ➤ Import from the menu bar. The Import dialog box will appear.

3. Select the type of spreadsheet containing your data from the list of Data Sources in the Import dialog box. The types of spreadsheets are:

✪ Microsoft Excel 2.0–4.0

✪ Microsoft Excel 5.0

✪ Lotus (.WKS)

✪ Lotus (.WK1)

✪ Lotus (.WK3)

4. Click on OK. The Select dialog box will appear.

5. In the Select File dialog box, select the name of the spreadsheet file that contains the data you want to import into Access.

6. Click on the Import button. The Import Spreadsheet dialog box will appear.

7. In the Import Spreadsheet Options dialog box (shown in Figure I.3), you need to specify information about the data you are importing.

Figure I.3
....
The Import Spreadsheet Options
dialog box

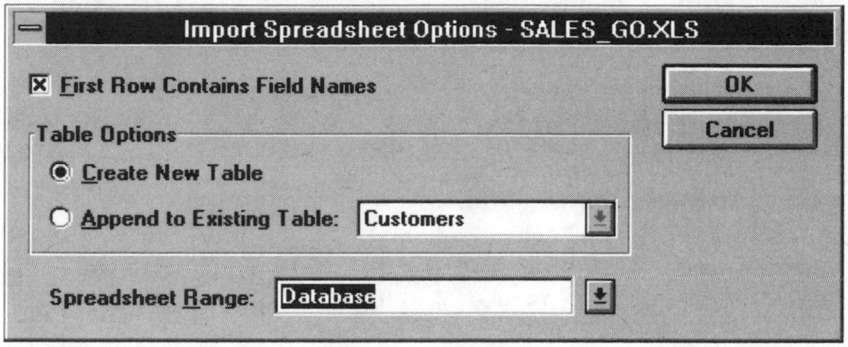

Import Spreadsheet Options - SALES_GO.XLS

☒ First Row Contains Field Names

OK

Cancel

Table Options
◉ Create New Table
○ Append to Existing Table: Customers ▮⬥

Spreadsheet Range: Database ▮⬥

○ If the first row of the spreadsheet contains column headings that you want Access to use as field names, select the First Row Contains Field Names box.

○ In the Table Options section, tell Access if it should append the data from this spreadsheet to an existing table or create a new table to hold the data.

○ If you want to import only a named range from the spreadsheet into Access, enter the range name in the Spreadsheet Range box. (If you leave this box blank, Access will import the entire spreadsheet.)

8. Click on the Import button to begin importing. A dialog box will appear, telling you how many records were successfully imported.

9. Close the dialog box, and you'll be returned to the Select dialog box, asking you if you want to import another file. If you do, repeat steps 5 through 9.

10. When you are finished, click on Close.

The new table will appear in the list of tables in the Database window. Access will have named the file using a name that is similar to that of the original file.

To give the table a more meaningful name, first select the table's name from the list and then select File ➤ Rename from the menu bar. A dialog box will appear, where you can type in the new table name. Press ↵ to close the dialog box, and the new table name will appear in the list of tables in the Database window.

If Access encounters any errors while importing your spreadsheet data it will log the error messages into its own table. You can view the log of errors by opening up the Import Errors table in Datasheet View. Then, if you want, you can go back to the original spreadsheet and fix the errors.

See **Import Errors; Importing**

IMPORTING FROM A TEXT FILE

The developers of PCs thought we'd need one file format that could be understood by any program, and they gave us text files. Text files are actually plain text, without all the coding and formatting that makes the text into a file suited to a particular program. Text files usually end in the extension .TXT (though people sometimes give them other extensions).

If you want to "see" what's in a text file, you can, at the DOS prompt (C:\) type type and the name of the text file. Like this:

```
C:\Type WHATSIS.TXT
```

then press ↵, and the text file will flit by on your screen too quickly to actually be read.

If a text file is set up so that it contains one record per line, and if each field is to be separated on the line by a *delimiter*— a Tab character, comma, or space—you can import straight text files into Access. For example, you can import the following text into an Access table:

```
First Name, Last Name, Phone Number
"Floss", "Dailey", "215-555-1212"
"Nita", "Vacation", "707-555-1212"
```

Notice that you must place quotation marks around anything that Access should take literally—in this case, the names and phone numbers.

To import a text file into an Access table:

1. You must open a Database window into which you will import the text file. You can either use an existing Access database file, or create a new one using File ➤ New from the menu bar. (*See* Database File: Creating)

2. Select File ➤ Import from the menu bar. The Import dialog box will appear.

3. In the Import dialog box, select Text (Delimited) and click on OK. The Select File dialog box will appear.

4. In the Select File dialog box, select the name of the file that contains the data you want to bring into Access.

5. Click on Import. The Import Text Options dialog box will appear.

6. If the text file you are importing contains field names in its first line of text, select the First Row Contains Field Names box.

7. If the file you are importing does not have double quotes around the text and commas between the fields (as described above) click on the Options button. Access will expand the Import Text dialog box to include more options (see Figure I.4). Usually, though, you won't have to change any of these special settings.

If you do have to change the settings, you can specify these options:

- ✪ In the Text Delimiter drop-down list, select the delimiter symbol (usually quotation marks) that surrounds the text in your text file.

- ✪ From the Fields Separator drop-down list, pick the field separator (usually a comma).

- ✪ In the Dates, Times, and Numbers section you can change the way Access expects dates, times, and numbers to be formatted.

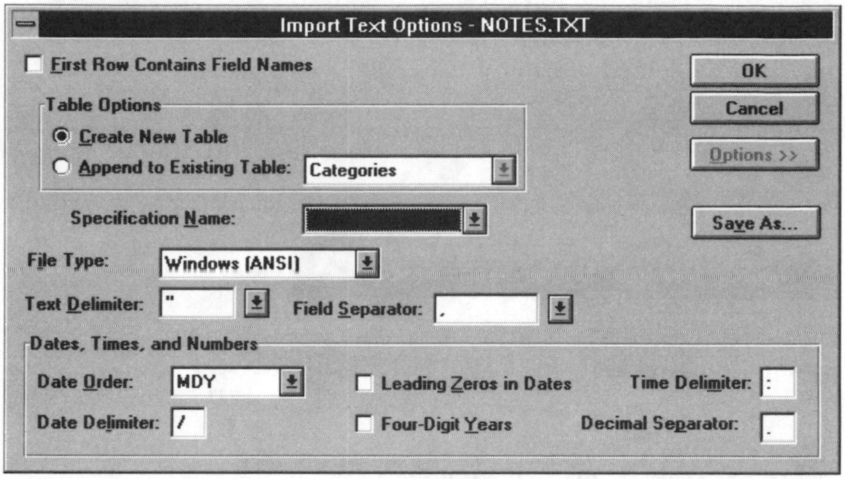

Figure I.4

The Import Text dialog box after clicking on Options

Import Text Options - NOTES.TXT

☐ First Row Contains Field Names

OK

Cancel

Options >>

Table Options
- ◉ Create New Table
- ○ Append to Existing Table: Categories

Specification Name: [   ]

Save As...

File Type: Windows (ANSI)

Text Delimiter: "   Field Separator: .

Dates, Times, and Numbers

Date Order: MDY   ☐ Leading Zeros in Dates   Time Delimiter: :

Date Delimiter: /   ☐ Four-Digit Years   Decimal Separator: .

---

8. Click on the OK button to begin importing. A dialog box will appear, telling you how many records were successfully imported.

9. Close the dialog box. You'll next see the Select File Dialog box, asking you if you want to import another file. If you do, start with step 4 and repeat what you've done.

10. When you are finished, click on Close.

The new table will appear in the list of tables in the Database window, and Access will have named the file using a name that is similar to that of the original file.

To give the table a name that's more helpful and memorable, first select the table's name from the list and then select File ➤ Rename from the menu bar. A dialog box will appear, where you can type in the new table name. Press ↵ to close the dialog box, and the new table name will appear in the list of tables in the Database window.

Using SQL Database Servers

Many companies that rely on databases for doing their business will have a SQL database server on their network. A SQL database server is like a file server, except it serves data instead of files to workstations. Access can access data stored on a database server by using a method called Open Database Connectivity (ODBC). To access data on the database server, you must have the ODBC drivers so Access will know how to access the data. Access comes with drivers for a number of database servers. You should contact your network or database administrator if you need to access data stored on a server.

If Access encounters any errors while importing your data it will log the error messages into a special table. You can view the log of

A
B
C
D
E
F
G
H
I
J
KL
M
N
O
P
Q
R
S
T
U
V
W
XYZ

errors by opening up Import Errors table in Datasheet View. Change the errors, if you like, by going back to the original text file.

See **Importing**

INPUT MASK WIZARD

Using the Input Mask Wizard, you can select an *input mask* (a set of characters that will impose a format on an empty field) from a handy list of possibilities.

Let's say you've opened a database file, opened a table, and you're looking at it in Design View. (Or maybe you're creating a new table, either way, you're in Design View.) You want to control the type of information that will appear in that field in a very specific way—perhaps you want a field of the Text data type to hold only phone numbers, for example. To do this, you make the field of the Text data type, of course, and then you click in the box for the Input Mask. Now it occurs to you that you're going to use a very common set up for a phone number field. You can click on the Builder button (the one with three dots on it) on the toolbar, and the Input Mask Wizard dialog box will appear.

Here, you'll be presented with a list of popular and convenient input masks.

66 **The Input Mask Wizard provides help only with the Text and Date/Time data types.**

Your choices for text data are:

- Phone Number
- Extension
- Social Security Number
- ZIP Code
- Password
- Medium Date
- Short Date
- Long Time
- Medium Time
- Short Time

Your choices for date/time data are:

- Medium Date
- Short Date
- Long Time
- Medium Time
- Short Time

Click on the input mask you want to use (Phone Number in our example). You can then test the input mask you've chosen by clicking in the text box labeled "Try it" and entering some sample data. The sample data you type in will appear just as it would if you were typing it into your table (with the input mask imposed). If you click on Finish, the input mask will be entered as the Input Mask property.

Before you click Finish, you can click on Next to move into another dialog box, if you like, that will let you set more options (the options vary for each input mask listed in the Input Mask Wizard dialog box).

When you're finished setting these additional options, click on Finish and the input mask you've specified will become the Input Mask property.

See   **Date/Time Data Type; Text Data Type**

INSERT MODE

Insert mode is a typing mode in which whatever you type shoves its way in between whatever's already there. You can toggle Insert mode on and off in most applications by tapping the Insert key on your keyboard.

INSTALLING ACCESS

Like most Windows programs, Access pretty much installs itself. Just follow the easy instructions here, and Access will take care of getting itself in the right place in the right way.

What You Need

First, let's make sure you have everything you need. To run Access, you need:

- ✪ An IBM-compatible computer with at least an 80386 processor. (An 80386SX or 80386SL is okay. An 80286 is not.)

- ✪ At least 6 megabytes (MB)—but preferably more than 8 MB—of random access memory (RAM).

- ✪ A hard-disk drive with more than 19 MB of free disk space for a typical install (you can get away with only 5 MB if you elect a laptop install.) The Access installation program will tell you whether you have enough disk space.

- ✪ DOS in a version later than 3.1 (preferably 5.0 or later), and Windows version 3.0 or later—the later the better.

- ✪ A mouse, or a trackball, or some other pointing device that does the work of a mouse. (While you can, technically, work in Access without a mouse, it's clumsy and weird. Get a mouse.)

- ✪ An EGA, VGA, or SVGA screen. Old monochrome and amber monitors won't work. Anyway, you want to save your eyesight, and what's the fun of a color program if you don't have a decent monitor?

- ✪ A printer, if you're going to print anything. If your printer works with Windows (most do), it will work with Access. It's up to you whether you want the high-quality output of a laser or ink-jet printer, or whether that old workhorse dot matrix will do.

Access Diskettes

Access comes on either $5\frac{1}{4}''$ or $3\frac{1}{2}''$ diskettes. When you're handling the $5\frac{1}{4}''$ type, be careful not to get your fingers (or coffee or cigarette smoke) on the soft material showing through the oval hole in the plastic diskette cover. That'll wreck the diskette. The $3\frac{1}{2}''$ type is a lot more sturdy, but even so, you don't want to abuse your diskettes. Keep them out of the sun, and away from magnets.

Types of Installation

Access offers you three basic choices for how to install the program:

Typical   Installs the most useful parts of Access. This includes not only the program files, but sample files, the Cue Cards, Help, Microsoft Graph, and file translators that allow you to use data from dBASE, Paradox, and other database programs.

66   We recommend the Typical installation, and in the rest of this book we assume you have performed a Typical installation. Access is jam-packed with Help, and the Cue Cards are really great—not just for beginners but also for people who don't want to have to go find the manual—and how can anybody do without those translators?

Complete/Custom   Lets you specify which files you do or do not want included, and tells you how much space you'll need on your hard disk to do that. This option is useful when you know what you're up to and which files you need.

Laptop (Minimum)   Installs only those files that are most basic to running Access in a bare-bones way. This does not include the Cue Cards, Help, Microsoft Graph, or the file translators. Use this option only when you have no other choice—probably because you don't have enough disk space to run all of Access, but you need the basic program.

66   You can use Access on a network (a lot of PCs cabled together so they can share printers and programs), but we're going to stick to talking about single-user installation—that's installation on one computer for use by one person sitting at the computer at a time. If you want to find out about using Access on a network, check out Understanding Microsoft Access 2 by Alan Simpson (Sybex, 1994), or refer to the Access manuals. You'll also have to get your network administrator involved to get Access to run smoothly on a network.

Actually Installing Access

This is going to be short and sweet because Access does all the work for you. You need to have all the diskettes sitting there with you, but you don't have to be fussy even about having them stacked up in order. Access will tell you which diskette to insert next; if you pop in the wrong one, Access will tell you so, and prompt you for the correct one.

For the sake of convenience, we're going to assume you're installing Access by inserting diskettes into floppy-disk drive A:. If you're actually using drive B:, just substitute B: for A: in the instructions below.

To install Access:

1. Start Windows.
2. Insert the Access Setup disk—Disk 1—in drive A:.
3. If the Windows Program Manager window is not open, double-click on the Program Manager icon.
4. Choose File ➤ Run from the Program Manager's menu bar. The Run dialog box will appear.
5. Type a:setup in the Command Line text box.
6. Press ↵, or click on OK.
7. Follow the setup instructions as they appear on the screen.

When you are asked for your name and your company's name, type in that information. It will be written to disk and will permanently identify your copy of Access. Keep an eye on this as you do it. You will get a chance to confirm, but after that,

your name and company name are carved in granite, so if you glide through this, you'll be looking at your misspelled name every time you start the program.

The upgrade version of Access 2 is only available to people who have previously purchased a copy of Access 1.X (or certain other competing database products). When you install the upgrade version, its Setup program checks your hard disk for one of those products that make you eligible to purchase it. If it does not find evidence of the product, Setup will display a dialog box reminding you of the conditions under which you purchased the software (meaning that Microsoft expects you to have previously purchased a copy of Access or a competing product). You can continue to install Access by selecting the Continue button in this dialog box.

When you are asked where you want to install the program (in which drive and directory), Access will suggest C:\ACCESS as the default option. That's a fine choice, and we recommend you go with it. If you have some reason to put Access in another directory, type in the name of that directory. Either way, Access will create the directory automatically for you if it doesn't already exist. If you want Access placed on a drive other than C:, type in the drive letter to be used instead of C:, like this: E:\Access.

When Access asks you what type of installation you want—Typical, Complete/ Custom, or Laptop (Minimum) (described earlier in this section)—we recommend that you choose Typical. (See Figure I.5.)

Each time you make a selection, you'll have to press ↵ or click on OK to move along.

8. Access will prompt you to "Insert Disk 1," then "Insert Disk 2," then "Insert Disk 3," and so on. Just keep doing what you're told. Again, you'll have to press ↵

or click on OK each time you pop in a new disk. As Access installs files from each disk, you'll see a kind of "thermometer" graphic, which will tell you how things are progressing. The whole business takes less than 20 minutes.

66 If you're trying to install a copy of Access that's been installed by someone else before (even by you), a message will appear telling you that this copy of Access has already been installed.

Figure I.5

Choose Typical to get the benefit of Cue Cards, Help, MS Graph, and the file translators.

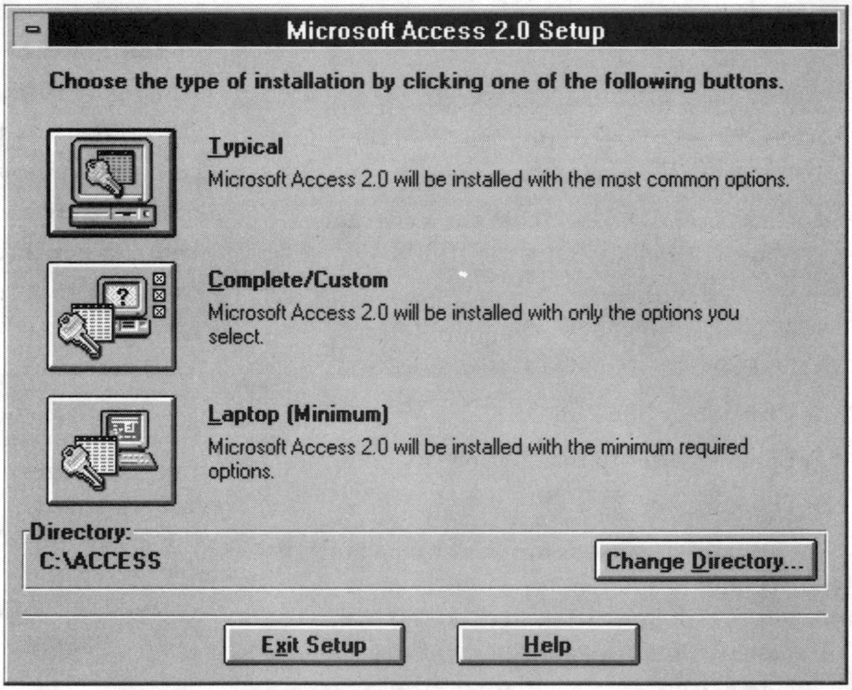

Microsoft Access 2.0 Setup

Choose the type of installation by clicking one of the following buttons.

Typical
Microsoft Access 2.0 will be installed with the most common options.

Complete/Custom
Microsoft Access 2.0 will be installed with only the options you select.

Laptop (Minimum)
Microsoft Access 2.0 will be installed with the minimum required options.

Directory:
C:\ACCESS   Change Directory...

Exit Setup   Help

9. After installing all the files, Access will create a window for itself—the Microsoft Office Program Group in Windows—and will place its own icons in the window.

When you're finished, store your original Access disks safely away, and you're ready to start working with Access.

See **Part 1; Starting Access; Windows Basics**

INTEGER

An *integer* is a number without a fractional part. 5 is an integer; 5.2 is not, and 5.0 isn't either.

See **Number Data Type**

Make sure you're installing Access into <u>its own</u> directory, whether or not that directory is named C:\ACCESS. Don't install Access into the root directory—C:\. If you do, Access' files will get mixed up with other, more basic files that are supposed to be in the root directory, and it will be a big mess for whoever maintains your computer.

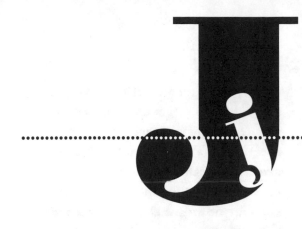

JOIN

A *join* is a relationship between two tables. A join combines data in two tables into a single dynaset. Some people call joins *links*.

See   **Joins and Relationships**

JOINS: CREATING

If you understand a few concepts and know some buzzwords about joins, you'll be better able to use joins in your own databases.

Basic Principles

You join two tables by creating a query that includes at least two tables as its basis. Then you tell Access how the two tables are related, by telling it what field they have in common. (They should not have more than one field in common.)

Keep in mind these principles:

✪ The two fields that join two tables must be of the same data type, and must hold the same value. They do not, however, have to have the same field name.

✪ Every rule has an exception and relating tables is no exception. It is not strictly true that you can join tables only on fields that have the same data type. You join tables on fields that have *compatible* data types, and all data types are compatible with themselves.

66 **The Counter data type is also compatible with the Long Integer data type. This is very handy, since you will often be joining tables based on a counter field and a long integer field.**

Most commonly, when you join tables the following will be true:

- One table will have a field of the counter data type that contains a value to uniquely identify each record in the table. In our example in the other Joins sections, this is the Customers table.

- You will want to bring information from two tables into one dynaset. In our example, the second table is the Orders table.

- You create a query that is based on both tables and that links them on their common field. In our example, this is how you get an Invoice out of the two tables.

Before you join two tables, you should think about how the data in the two tables are related. The most important thing to know is that if the tables are related:

One-to-one, each record in one table has a shared field with exactly one record in the other table.

One-to-many, a single record in the first table has a shared field with many (or no) records in the second table.

Many-to-many, each record in the first table has a shared field with zero or more records in the second table, and the same field in the second table is shared with one or more records in the first table.

When you have the first type of relationship between tables, you use a one-to-one join (also called an *equi-join*). The other two types of relationships call for *outer* joins.

66 Remember, a one-to-one join (equi-join) is a connection between two tables in which each record in the first table matches exactly one record in the second table. When you are creating the Invoice query, each order is placed by only one customer. This means that each record in the Orders table matches only one record in the Customers table.

Creating a One-to-One Join

To join two tables together with an equi-join, you need to create a query that includes both tables. You can do this by joining two existing tables (or dynasets), or by adding a second table to an existing query.

To create a new query to join two existing tables or dynasets together, do the following:

1. Create a new query. (*See* Queries: Creating)

2. A dialog box will appear. Select each of the tables you want to join from the list, and click Add in turn.

3. Click Close.

If you create a **global relationship** between fields in the two tables you just added to the query, Access goes ahead and creates the join for you without any further work. This is because once you tell Access that two tables are related, it assumes you want to use that relationship in any queries that contain both tables or queries. See Joins: Referential Integrity In for information on how to define global relationships.

If you already have a query that includes one table and you want to add a join to it, do the following:

1. Open the query up in Design View.
2. Select Query ➤ Add Table. A dialog box will appear.
3. From the list in the dialog box, select the new table or query you want to use in the join, and click Add.
4. Click Close.

Having done either of the procedures described above, you'll now see the Query Design View window—just as you did when you set up your first query, but with one difference. This time, you will have two Field List windows instead of one above the QBE grid.

Each table that you add to a query adds a new Field List box to the Query Design View window.

To create an equi-join between these two tables you must do the following:

1. Arrange the two Field List windows so they both display the field on which you want to create a join.
2. Select the field in the master table.

The master table is the one you want to control the join. The table that **controls** the join is the table on the "one" side of a one-to-many join. In our Orders and Invoices examples (in the other Joins section) you would want all of the orders to show up, whether or not an invoice has been created, so you would make the Orders table the master table and Invoice table the slave table.

3. With your mouse, click and drag the field you want to join from the master table. Drop it on top of the field in the other table (the field to which you want to join).

Access will now display a simple line between the two fields to show you that they are joined. This is how Access represents an equi-join. Left- and right-outer-joins create lines with little arrow heads on the ends. If you switch now to the query's Datasheet View, you'll see the results of joining the two tables—a datasheet from both tables.

Creating a One-to-Many Join

When a one-to-many relationship exists between tables, you should use a left- or right-outer-join, depending on which table holds the "one" record and which table holds the "many" records. To create a query that includes a one-to-many relationship, do the following:

1. Create an equi-join between the fields you want to join, as described above.

2. Double-click on the line representing the join. You will see the Join Properties dialog box, as shown in Figure J.1.

3. The Join Properties dialog box will appear with join type 1—an equi-join—selected. Select type 2 if all of the records from the first table should be displayed along with matching records from the second table. Select type 3 if all records from the second table should be displayed along with matching records from the first table.

Congratulations. You have just created either a left- or right-outer-join.

See **Joins and Relationships**

JOINS: MODIFYING DATA WITH

Joins allow you a very powerful window through which to look at your data. And—if you aren't doing anything terribly tricky—they give you a way to modify multiple tables all at once. But when you create a query with a join, you are limited in the ways you can update your information.

- When you create a one-to-one join, you are usually free to modify data in either table on which the join is based.

- If you have a one-to-many relationship, such as our Invoice query example (in which many orders may be placed by one customer), you are limited to modifying the "many" side of the join. You can modify data in the Orders table but not the Customers table. This is a pain, but it's true.

See **Joins and Relationships**

JOINS: MULTIPLE

Once you have mastered joining two tables together in a single query, nothing is stopping you from creating *multiple* joins in a single query. You may have a query that includes three tables, each joined to the next one. Your Invoice query, for example, may have an equi-join to the Customers table and a right-outer-join to a Point-of-Purchase table.

We don't have to tell you how to do this, you can just experiment with different kinds of joins that you now know how to do. It's always a good idea, though, when

Figure J.1

The Join Properties dialog box

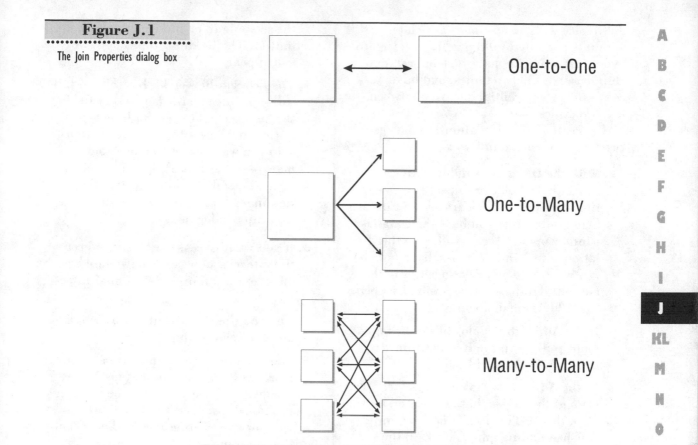

One-to-One

One-to-Many

Many-to-Many

A B C D E F G H I J KL M N O P Q R S T U V W XYZ

you're fooling with new techniques, to have a back-up copy of your database file. That way, if something goes wrong, you'll be covered. You won't lose your important data.

See **Joins and Relationships**

JOINS: REFERENTIAL INTEGRITY IN

When you have a database that contains relationships whose integrity you want main-

tained, you should create *global* relationships. When you create a global relationship between two tables, you can have Access enforce *referential integrity*.

Referential integrity is a condition that ensures that relationships between records are sound and that you don't delete related data accidentally.

A good example of this is in an Orders database. You wouldn't want anyone to delete a customer from the Customers table while that customer has a record in the Invoices table, right? Then you would have an invoice with no customer associated with it, so no one would pay the invoice! To avoid this, you can make a global relationship between the two tables, and have Access enforce referential integrity between the two tables.

To create a global relationship between two tables in your database:

1. With the Database window active, select Edit ➤ Relationships. (The Relationships option appears on the Edit menu only while you have the Database window open.) Access will open the Relationships window. If you have not already created any relationships in the current database, Access will also open the Add Table dialog box.

2. If the Add Table dialog box didn't appear, pull down the Relationships menu and select Add Table.

3. In the Add Table dialog box, select each of the tables that are related and click the Add button. When you have finished adding tables, click on the Close button.

4. Now click on the related field in one of the tables, drag to its related field in

the second table, and release the mouse button. The Relationships dialog box will appear.

5. The Relationships dialog box (Figure J.2) will show the two fields you selected in the last step. Click on the Join Type button and select the type of relationship you want—one-to-one or one-to-many—in the Join Properties dialog box. Click OK to close the Join Properties dialog box and return to the Relationships dialog box.

6. If you want Access to enforce referential integrity between the two tables, click on the Enforce Referential Integrity check box.

7. Click on the Create button to actually add the relationship.

8. You can create relationships between more tables by repeating steps 2 through 7. Once you are done creating relationships, close the Relationships window by selecting File ➤ Close from the menu bar.

See **Joins and Relationships**

Figure J.2

In this dialog box, you can establish a relationship between tables and tell Access not to let anyone mess with it.

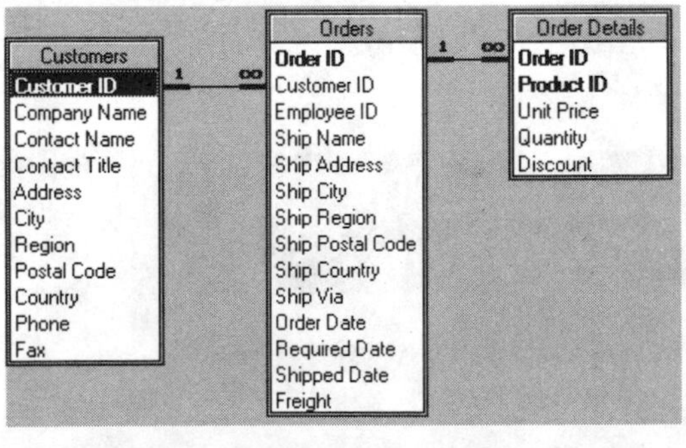

JOINS AND RELATIONSHIPS

A *relational* database is one that lets you set up and work with the shared data in two or more tables.

As an example of this, think about your checkbook, your checks, and your bills. Your checkbook is like a table that shows what checks you've written, when, and for what amounts. You could arrange your phone bills in a stack, with some marked paid and some still unpaid, and that would be like another table. On the paid phone bills, you will (if you're a conscientious record-keeper) have written the number of the check with which you paid the bill. Your checkbook and your phone bill are related through the check they have in common.

Of course, in a relational database program like Access, that check's number would appear as a field in each of two tables—the Checkbook table and the Phone Bill table—and would create a relationship between the two tables.

There are three kinds of database table relationships:

- One-to-one
- One-to-many
- Many-to-many

We'll cover each of these, as well as some more sophisticated types of *joins* (ways to connect tables so you can view or modify data all at once) in these sections.

Types of Relationships

A **one-to-one** relationship occurs when each record in one table is related through a shared field to exactly on record in the other table. A perfect example of this is your checkbook and telephone bill. You pay each phone bill with a single check and you pay only one bill with that single check.

A **one-to-many** relationship exists when each record in the first table is related through a shared field to many records in the second table. In an example involving two tables—Customers and Orders—one customer can place many orders, so a one-to-many relationship exists.

A **many-to-many** relationship is one in which each record in the first table shares a field with zero or more records in the second table and the same record in the second table shares a field with one or more records in the first table. In the Customers and Orders

A
B
C
D
E
F
G
H
I
J
KL
M
N
O
P
Q
R
S
T
U
V
W
XYZ

example, you'd toss into the equation an-other table—for Products. The Orders ta-ble might include many orders for many products from the Products table.

Figure J.3 illustrates these three types of relationships.

A one-to-many relationship may occur even if a record in the table on the "one" side has no matching rec-ords in the "many" side. For example, One customer may place no orders, but if that customer did place orders there could be many—thus, a one-to-many relationship exists, even if there are no actual records appearing on the "many" side.

················Tip····················

The least common relationship be-tween database tables is one-to-one. When database developers find a one-to-one relationship, they usually just combine those tables, because they have so much in common. The most complicated relationship is many-to-many, which poses special challenges to developers. To deal with a many-to-many relationship in Access, a third ta-ble has to be created, so that instead of a many-to-many relationship be-tween two tables, you have two one-to-many relationships. In that case, the two one-to-many relationships are between the third table and the two original tables. (See Figure J.4)

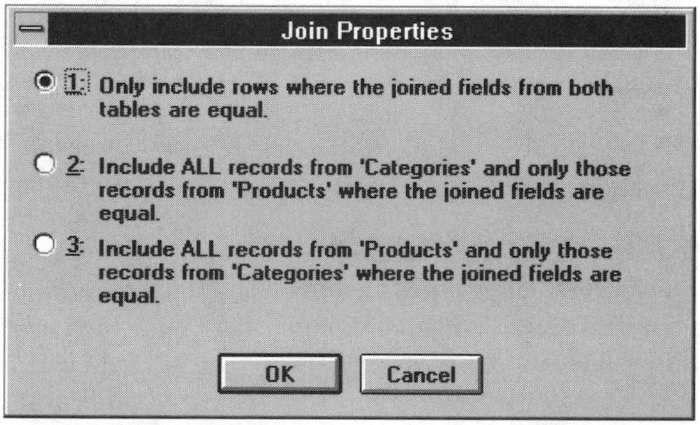

Figure J.3
···························

There are three possible types of relationships in Access.

Join Properties
⦿ **1:** Only include rows where the joined fields from both tables are equal.
○ **2:** Include ALL records from 'Categories' and only those records from 'Products' where the joined fields are equal.
○ **3:** Include ALL records from 'Products' and only those records from 'Categories' where the joined fields are equal.
[OK] [Cancel]

Figure J.4

To deal with the complexity of a one-to-many relationship, set up a third table and break the more complicated relationships into two one-to-many relationships.

A B C D E F G H I **J** KL M N O P Q R S T U V W XYZ

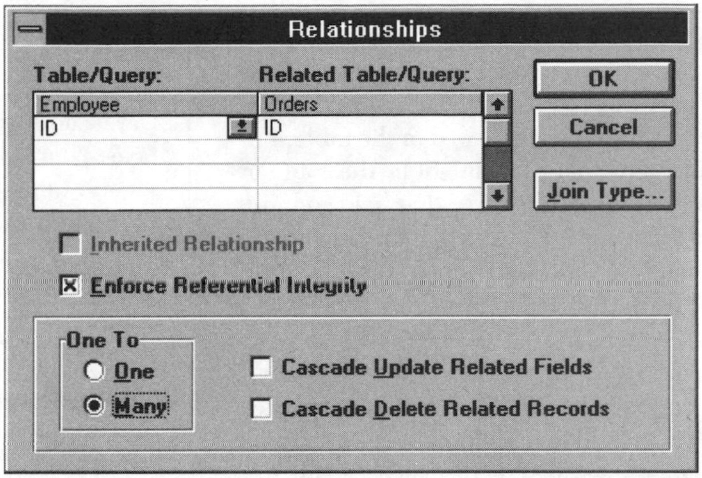

Joins: The Real Power of Access

In a business database, the customers' names and addresses are stored in a Customers table. Data for each purchase is stored in a second table—the Orders table. You can create an invoice that brings together related information from these two tables and presents it all at once. Furthermore, you can have a third table—an Inventory table—from which the items that were purchased are automatically deducted. Joins are the stuff that makes this possible—the stuff that makes a relational database relational, and the stuff that gives Access its real power.

In Part 1, we told you how to design a database. We said you should break your data down into its most basic pieces, organized logically and arranged into tidy, related tables. Now we'll talk about why.

You join tables on a common field, one that holds the same values in both tables. Each order in your Orders table contains a unique customer ID number. That number identifies which record in the Orders table belongs to the customer making the order. Joining the Orders table to the Customers table on this field, you can create a query that displays all the information you need to bill your customer.

Remember the Primary Key

A *primary key* is a field that contains a unique value in every record in the table. For example, a primary key might be the counter field in the record, because that field contains a number, assigned by Access, that increases incrementally with each new record, and that cannot be duplicated in any other record in that table. This makes it perfect for joining together tables. Because most of the joins you do will be one-to-many, you'll need a unique value in the field on the "one" side of the join. The primary key field is just such a field.

The primary key has other uses in Access, but the one we're going to talk about here is that it provides an efficient way to *join* records in two tables. The *join* is a link between two tables, based on a shared field.

There are different kinds of joins available to use. Each has its advantages, depending on the relationships between your tables.

Types of Joins

Access supports four types of joins. Let's go over all of them:

Equi-Join   Also known as a *one-to-one* join, this is a join in which each record that matches in both tables is displayed.

Left-Outer-Join   Also known as a *one-to-many* join, this displays all records in the first table regardless of whether they match records in the second table. Fields from the second table, in records that have no match, are considered empty.

Right-Outer-Join   Also known as a one-to-many join (though many-to-one is a better description), this displays all records from the second table, along with matching records from the first table. In records in the second table that do not match the records in the first table, empty fields are displayed.

Self-Join   The fourth type of join is called a *self-join*. One use of a self-join might be in an Employees table that includes a Managed By field for each employee, showing the name of his or her supervisor. Of course, the supervisor, who is also an employee, also has a record in the Employees table, so the table would have to be linked to itself.

We're going to dwell a bit on equi-joins, because they're simplest and make a handy reference point. Then we'll cover the other common joins: left- and right-outer-joins. (Besides, the first step in making either a left- or right-outer-join is to create an equi-join and then modify its properties.)

You can have Access _enforce_ relationships, to keep your data consistent. Access does this with a feature called _referential integrity_. You can have Access enforce referential integrity on your related tables to stop someone from deleting a customer who has orders still on file, for example.

See   **Joins: Creating; Joins: Referential Integrity In**

JOINS: VIEWING JOINED DATA

Once you have joined the tables that are related in a query and added the fields you want to view to the QBE grid, you can view the results (as usual) by clicking on the Datasheet View button on the button bar. You will see the datasheet you've seen so much of already.

See   **Database Window;**
Datasheet View

A
B
C
D
E
F
G
H
I
J
KL
M
N
O
P
Q
R
S
T
U
V
W
XYZ

KEYBOARD OPTIONS: CHANGING

See **Options Dialog Box: Changing Options**

KEY FIELD

See **Primary Key**

KILOBYTE

See **Byte Sizes**

LANDSCAPE

When you're looking at a piece of paper sideways, that's known as *landscape orientation.*

See **Portrait; Printing**

LETTER-QUALITY MODE

Letter quality is the mode in some printers that produces high-quality print that won't embarrass you if you use it for your resume or letters to your clients.

See **Printing**

LINK

To *link* two tables together is to join the tables on a field.

See **Joins and Relationships**

LOGICAL OPERATORS

Logical operators compare two values. The result in a Yes or No value—less-than (<), for example.

See **Criteria; Expression Builder; Expressions: Components**

LOGO

See **Modifying Forms/Reports: Adding a Logo**

MACRO

A *macro* is a group of instructions auto-mated to run together to accomplish those tasks that you do most often. We don't cover macros in this book, because it's such a big subject that it would make the book twice as thick.

MAIL MERGE TO MICROSOFT WORD

With Access and a little quick mouse work, you can easily create a Microsoft Word mail merge document. This can make sending out slick, professional-looking form letters a real breeze. To use this feature, you must have both Access and Word for Windows (version 6) installed on your computer.

Here's the really great advantage of this feature: you don't have to reestablish a link or pull data from your mailing list into the letter every time you want to send the letter out. Once you've set things up with the Mail

Merge to Microsoft Word Wizard, you are guaranteed that when you perform the Mail Merge in Word, you will be using your most current Access data.

To use the Mail Merge to Microsoft Word Wizard, follow these steps:

1. Open the Database window and high-light the name of the table or query that contains the data you want to use in your mail merge.

2. Click on the Merge It button on the toolbar.

3. The Microsoft Word Mail Merge Wizard dialog box will appear (Figure M.1). In the dialog box, you can click on either of two options to link your Access data to an existing Word document or to create a new Word Print Merge document in which to use the Access data.

> 🛣️ **To see helpful information in Access about using Word's Print Merge feature, select the check box labeled "Open Microsoft Word Help on how to complete your mail merge" in the Microsoft Word Mail Merge Wizard dialog box.**

4. Click on the OK button.

5. If you selected to use your Access data in an *existing* Word document in step 3, Access will display the Select Microsoft Word Document dialog box. The names of Word documents will be listed on the left side of the dialog box; select the one you want by highlighting it and then click the OK button.

6. Access will switch you to the Word window. (If Word is not already running, Access takes care of starting it.)

7. In Word, you can use the Mail Merge toolbar and all the power of Word to create your document. Click on the Insert Merge Field button on the Mail Merge toolbar, and a list of field names (from the table or query you picked in step 1) will appear. (For details on this, refer to your Word user's manual or Sybex's *Mastering Word 6 for Windows*.)

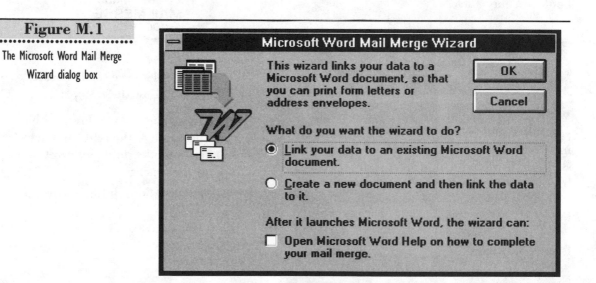

Figure M.1

The Microsoft Word Mail Merge Wizard dialog box

Your Word 6 Mail Merge document will draw its data (names, addresses, or whatever you specify) from Access.

See **Exporting: The Word for Windows Trick; Form Letters: Creating by Using a Report; Output To; Reports: Creating with Report Wizards**

MAIN FORM

A *Main* form is one that contains another (Sub) form.

See **Forms and Form Wizards**

MAKE TABLE ACTION QUERIES

A Make Table action query will create a whole new table based on the results of your query. To design the Make Table query:

1. Create a new query, as described in the Queries section.

2. Add those fields you want to copy to your new table to the query's QBE grid, again by using either the click-and-drag or the pull-down menu method.

66 **You can also specify criteria to determine which records from the table you want to copy. Do this using the methods described in the sections on Queries and Select Queries.**

3. Test your query by entering it first as a select query. (This part is only a test. We'll tell you how to make it into a Make Table action query in a moment.) Click on the Datasheet View icon on the toolbar to take a look at the dynaset that results from your query. Go back to Query Design View (by clicking on the Query Design View icon) to make any adjustments in the way your query is set up. Then go back to Datasheet View to inspect your new table one more time. Once you are convinced that your query selects all the data you want to copy into your new table, click on the Query Design View icon to go back to Query Design View.

66 **If you want to use certain fields as criteria, but don't want those fields to appear in the QBE grid, you can make them hidden fields. (See Queries: Showing and Hiding Fields)**

4. Back in the Query Design View window, select Query ➤ Make Table to turn your query into a Make Table action query. Access will now display the Query Properties dialog box shown in Figure M.2.

5. If you want to create a table in another database file, select the Another Database check box, then enter the path and filename for the database file in the File Name text box.

A
B
C
D
E
F
G
H
I
J
KL
M
N
O
P
Q
R
S
T
U
V
W
XYZ

Figure M.2

The Query Properties dialog box asks for information about your Make Table action query.

Query Properties

Make New Table

Table **N**ame: `Active Customers` ▼

● **C**urrent Database
○ **A**nother Database:
　File Name: `_____`

[**OK**]
[**Cancel**]

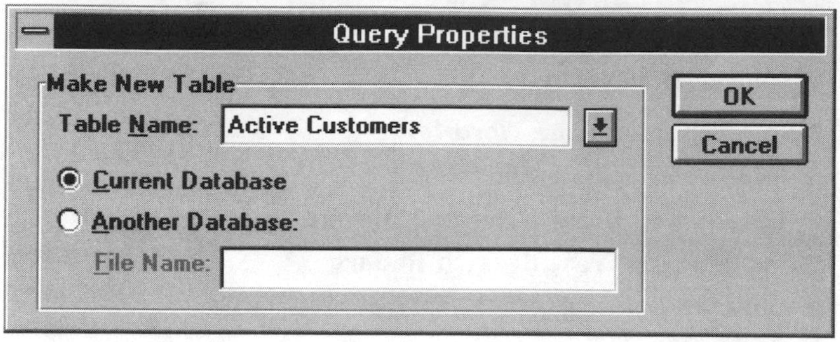

To enter information into the File Name text box, you'll need to know the exact database filename and its location. For example, for the Northwind Traders database (the sample that comes with Access) you would type:

```
C:\ACCESS\SAMPAPPS\NWIND.MDB
```

to indicate that the file named NWIND.MDB is located in the ACCESS directory on the C: drive. You have to do this because, unfortunately, Access does not let you browse for a file on your disk.

6. In the Table Name box, enter a name for your new table.

7. When you are done, select OK to indicate that your query is all set up.

8. Now you're ready to execute your query, by clicking on the Execute icon on the toolbar:

9. If a table with the same name as your new table already exists, Access will display the dialog box shown in Figure M.3, warning you that the action query is about to replace an existing table. If that's okay with you and you want to go ahead, click on Yes to continue with the query. If you want to bail out, click on No to cancel.

10. Access now displays the dialog box shown in Figure M.4, telling you just how many records it's copying into the new table. If you're satisfied with the whole deal and you click OK, Access will now—finally—copy the records to the new table. If, for any reason, you don't want to go ahead, you can click Cancel to stop the Make Table action query from finishing its business.

Figure M.3

If a Make Table action query is about to replace an existing table, Access warns you when you run the query and gives you a chance to bail out on the procedure.

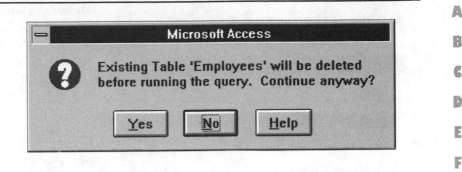

Microsoft Access

? Existing Table 'Employees' will be deleted before running the query. Continue anyway?

Yes   No   Help

Figure M.4

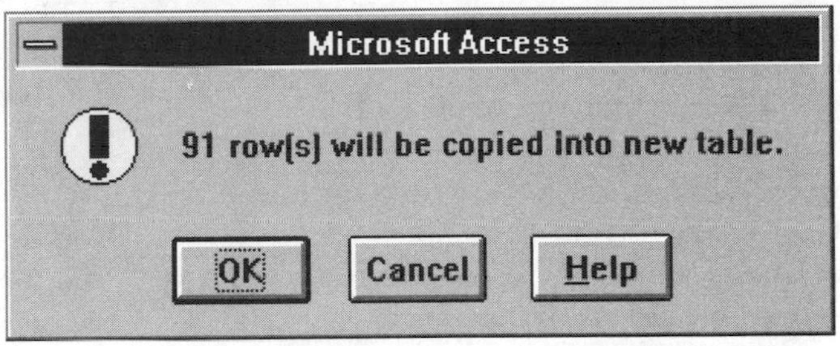

After Access creates the dynaset from the Make Table action query, it tells you how many records it will copy to the new table. Click OK to tell Access to go ahead or click Cancel to stop the process.

Microsoft Access

! 91 row(s) will be copied into new table.

OK   Cancel   Help

66 **Once Access has created the new table, that table will appear in the Database window's list of tables. You can double-click on the table's name to view its contents.**

See **Action Queries; Queries**

MEMO DATA TYPE

When you want to yack on extensively, it's best to do that in a memo field. Memo fields stretch to fit what's stored in them. You can store up to 64,000 characters in a memo field (that's about 64 double-spaced pages of textual information).

A
B
C
D
E
F
G
H
I
J
KL
M
N
O
P
Q
R
S
T
U
V
W
XYZ

Memo Data Type Properties

When you assign properties to a memo field, you can choose from these properties:

- Format
- Caption
- Default Value
- Validation Rule
- Validation Text
- Required
- Allow Zero Length

Because these properties of memo fields are so similar to the properties for text fields, we're going to ask you to turn to the sections on Text Data Type for more information.

Note these special considerations:

Format determines how the field looks when it is displayed. Since memo fields usually hold longer pieces of data than text fields, most of the Format properties that apply to text fields don't make sense here and aren't useful. You may, however, find that you want to specify all uppercase letters (>), or all lowercase (<).

Caption is text that Access will display along the bottom status bar while data is being entered into the field. In the case of a memo field, you might want to suggest to the person doing data entry that they "Keep the memo to less than 25 words," or "Include your initials," or whatever.

DefaultValue is something Access will put into the field every time it creates a new record. Now, it's unlikely you'll want to make the same note for every record, but if you do, set that up here. If you want to make the same note for *most* of the records, you can save some typing time by making that commonly used note the Default Value. Watch out, though, it may wind up in some records inappropriately.

Validation Rule is a rule that determines what data is valid—the free-form information that should be stored in a memo field does not lend itself to the strict sort of tests Access can perform to determine whether a piece of data is acceptable.

Required is a rule that determines whether Access will force the data entry person to enter data into this particular field while entering new records.

Allow Zero Length controls whether Access allows the field to be empty (hold nothing).

See **Data Type; Text Data Type**

MEMO FIELD

A memo field is of a data type that can contain thousands of characters. Basically, you can babble on as long as you like in a Memo field.

See **Memo Data Type**

MEMORY

Memory is where information that your computer is processing is stored and acted upon.

See **Random Access Memory**

MODIFYING CONTROLS ON FORMS AND REPORTS

Tables and fields are fine, and the Wizards are wonderful, but what you really want to know is how to do all that nifty stuff that impresses your boss and customers, right? Well, you can easily do these quick tricks:

- Place a drop-down box on your form, just like the ones you see so often in Windows programs. You can then simply click on the box, and a list of options will appear from which you can choose. (This sure beats trying to *remember* the options.)

- Add a *logo* (an image that uniquely represents your company) or even a picture of Oliver North or Mahatma Ghandi to your report or form.

- Use a report to do a letter, combining information from your tables into the text of the letter so that even the FBI won't guess it's a form letter.

And *guess what*. As you master these tricks, you'll also increase your skills in modifying forms and reports and you'll learn more about them.

See **Controls; Control Wizards; Form Letters: Creating by Using a Report; Modifying Forms: Adding a Drop-Down Box; Modifying Forms/Reports: Adding a Logo**

MODIFYING FORMS AND REPORTS

When it comes to creating forms and reports in a snap, you can't beat those Wizards. Wizards make things happen fast, with flash and dazzle. But they can't guess your every tiny desire, and so the Wizards of Access have limited power. When you work with a Wizard in Access, the Wizard decides where to place fields on the form or report. You don't get to actually *design* your form or report. The Wizard may put things in places you don't like. That can be the price you pay for the services of the Wizard, unless you know how to change what the Wizard has created.

You Can Change What the Wizard Has Created

When you need a form or report quick and easy, the Wizard is miraculous. But if you want to change something—if, for example, you may want one field to appear in italics instead of plain type—you can take what the Wizard has done for you, and change it.

Forms and reports, like tables and queries, have a Design View. In their Design View, tables show up as column-and-row grids, and queries show up as column-and-row grids with list boxes above them. Forms and reports in Design View look quite different from that. Take a look at Figure M.5 to see a typical Design View window for a form.

In Design View, forms and reports look very similar to each other, and the techniques for changing them are so much alike that we've combined the information into one section. Just about everything we say in this section holds true for both forms and reports. When that's not true—when there's some difference in how you'd treat a form or report while you're changing it—we'll let you know what to do about it.

How to Modify Forms and Reports

The easiest way to start building a form or report is with the Wizard. If you want to

follow the procedures here, and you don't already have a form or report to modify, create one. We're going to tell you how to change a form or report that already exists.

Let's tour Design View for forms and reports.

Viewing a Form or Report in Design View

To modify a form or report, you must first view it in Design View. To do this:

1. Select File ➤ Open from the menu bar.

2. In the dialog box that appears, select the name of the database file that contains the form or report you want to modify. Click OK. Access opens the Database window.

Figure M.5
....

A form shown in Design View

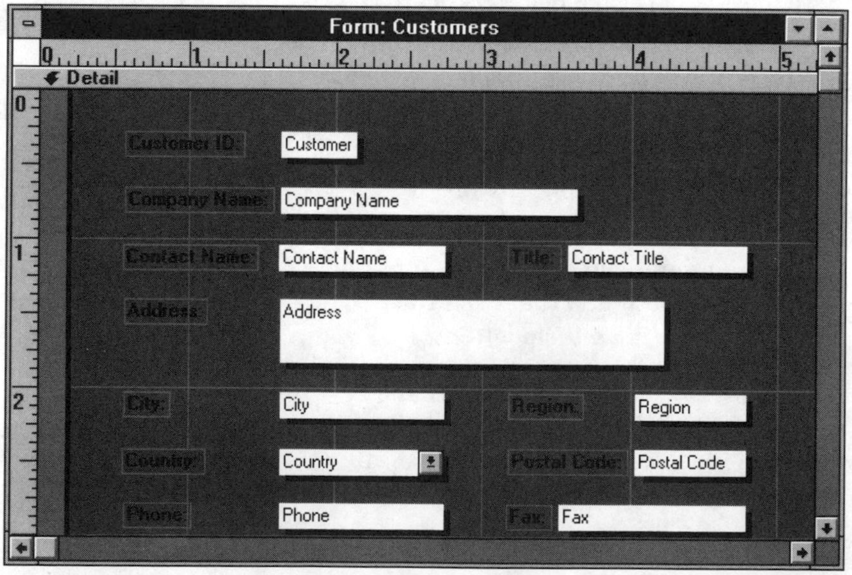

3. Click on the Form button to view forms, or the Report button to view reports.

4. Highlight the name of the form or report you want to modify in the Database window and click on Design.

You'll now see a form or report in Design View. Whether you chose a form or a report, the Design View window will look more or less the same.

Making a Switch

· · · · · · · · · · · ·

When you are viewing a form or report on screen, you can switch to seeing it in Design View by clicking on the Design View button on the toolbar. This is not the Design button (which has the word Design on it), this is the <u>Design View</u> button (which has a picture of design tools on it). Check out the inside front and back covers of this book to see the tools on Access' toolbars.

When you view a form or report in Design View, you'll see it in a window with lots of gizmos all around. Figure M.5 shows a form in Design View. Notice the Field List box and the Properties box. If for some odd reason you don't see these two dialog boxes when you view your form or report in Design View, you can make them appear by selecting (from the menu bar) View ➤ Field List and then View ➤ Properties.

See **Forms and Form Wizards; Reports and Report Wizards; Text: Toolbar Shortcuts for Changing**

MODIFYING FORMS: ADDING A DROP-DOWN BOX

Let's say you've got a field on your form in which you're just going to keep entering one of the same five pieces of data over and over. Maybe it's a table of U.S. Presidents and you've only got so many possibilities for what to put in the political party field. You can set up your form to include a *drop-down box*—a box that, when you click on it, will drop down, revealing a list of political parties from which you can choose simply by clicking. This can be a lot handier than figuring out which is the most common party and making that the default value for the field, and it sure beats typing in the same party names over and over. Figure M.6 shows such a drop-down box, placed on a form for the convenience of the user.

Using the Combo Box Wizard you can easily place these types of controls on your forms. All you need to do is place the control on the form and a series of dialog boxes will ask you about what you wish to display in the drop-down list. (For more information about the Combo Box Wizard, *See* Control Wizard.)

To place a drop-down box on an existing form:

1. View the form in Design View.

A B C D E F G H I J KL M N O P Q R S T U V W XYZ

When you click on a drop-down box, it drops down to reveal a list of choices. You can click on any of the choices, and that piece of data will then appear in the field.

2. You will need to use the toolbox. (*See* Toolbox) If the toolbox is not visible, select View ➤ Toolbox to get the toolbox.

3. Select the drop-down-box tool (also known as the combo box tool).

This will tell Access that you're going to add a drop-down box to the form.

4. Click on the form. The Combo Box Wizard dialog box will appear.

5. Since we are playing a Combo Box that will always display the same information, select the check box labeled "I will type in the values that I want." Click on Next to continue and Access will display the next Combo Box Wizard dialog box.

6. Now, enter 1 into the Number of Columns text box to tell Access that the combo box will only have a single row. Press the Tab key to move to the grid.

7. Enter the political parties into the grid in the dialog box. Between each value that will show in the combo box we

need to press the tab key. Enter Democrat and press the Tab key. Now enter Republican and press Tab. Enter Federalist and press the Tab key. Finally, enter Whig. Click on the Next button when you are done entering the values that will appear in the combo box.

8. The next dialog box in the Combo Box Wizard asks you where you want to store the results of the combo box. To store the results in a field from the table or query on which the form is based, select the field from the drop-down list labeled "Store that value in this field." Click the Next button to continue.

9. In the final dialog box, you should enter a name for the control you just created. You can either accept the suggested name—it will appear as the word *Filed* followed by a number—or type any descriptive name you prefer into the text box. Once you have named the control, click on Finish and you'll be returned to your form, which will now include a drop-down list of political parties.

It's quite possible—and often useful—to use a table or a query as the source of values for the drop-down list. If you do this, your drop-down list will change as your database changes.

You can even have a list of values in the drop-down box, and set things up so an associated value shows up in the field instead of the value that's listed in the box. For example, let's say you're setting up a drop-down box for an Employee ID field. You could set it up so a list of people's names appears in the drop-down box, but when you click on a person's name, their ID number shows up in the field.

While this particular setup is a bit of trouble to get working, it can provide a powerful method for automating your forms.

See **Controls; Control Wizards; Modifying Forms and Reports; Toolbox**

MODIFYING FORMS/REPORTS: ADDING A LOGO

To impress their company's image on stockholders and customers alike, many companies plaster their logo all over everything they have printed—from envelopes and letterhead to the reports they put out.

Often, big companies have developers modify business software to meet the company's needs, and as part of that, they even have the company logo appear on screen in the applications that were developed or modified for their use—in a data-entry form, for example.

A **logo** is an image that represents visually the company's style of doing business or their product line. Company logos are meant to represent something about the company's image. IBM, for example, wants to be known as the business person's computer company, so their logo—in which the three familiar letters (IBM) appear in the form of blocky text, with horizontal bars running through the letters in a graphically pleasing way—suggests stability and technology. Apple wants to be seen as a fun, accessible product, so their logo is colorful—a picture of a multi-colored apple, with a bite taken out of it. A logo provides a quick and easy way for the consumer to identify a company's product, and it reinforces the image the company wants to convey to the public.

You can do that, too. It's a simple matter of creating a form or report with the appropriate Wizard and then embedding your logo into the form or report, using the usual techniques for modifying forms. Figure M.7 shows a report we created in Access, with a logo included for extra flash and dazzle.

To do this, however, the logo must (of course) be in an electronic format Access

Figure M.7
••••••••••••••••••••••••••

This report gets its finishing touch from the logo.

Sybex Softball Lineup

10-Aug-94

Batting Order	Batting Index	Last Name	Position	1B	2B	3B
1	1	Simmons-	RF	2	2	0
10	10	Quan	C	3	0	0
2	2	Gular	3B	6	0	0
3	3	Krassner	CF	5	0	2
4	4	Spofford	P	3	2	0
5	5	Wright	LF	7	0	0
6	6	Potter	EH	2	0	0
7	7	Cassel	SS	4	0	0
8	8	Bruno	2B	3	0	0
9	9	Gilbert	1B	4	0	0
EH	11	Hart-Davis	EH	7	1	0
EH	12	Simmons	RC	1	0	0
Substitute	13	Chan	1B	0	0	1
Substitute	13	Myren	SS	3	1	1
Substitute	14	Clark	RF	0	0	0
Substitute	14	Albertson	EH	5	0	0
Substitute	15	Kyle	EH	2	0	0

can use. Unfortunately, Access knows nothing about graphics, so you'll have to use a Windows application that can display your logo. The Paintbrush program that comes with Windows will do just fine. It's also easy to work with, and uses the same sort of point-and-click techniques you already know.

Getting Your Logo into an Electronic Format

This isn't as difficult as you may think. If you work in a company with a graphics department, they probably already have the company logo in the format you need. If not, you can use a scanner, which will lift an electronic picture of your logo from stationery or any other paper source. And if you don't have a scanner, you can just hike on over to the nearest copy shop—they almost all offer scanning, along with a whole range of other desktop publishing services. At some point in the scanning process, you'll be asked in what file format you want your image (the logo) to appear. To get the best results, you want your logo in a *bitmap* format—a file that ends in the extension .BMP. This is the most common file format for graphic images, and it's the one with which Paintbrush is comfortable.

Placing the Logo

To place the logo on a report or form you first need to view the report or form in Design View. You'll also have to decide where on the report or form you want it to appear. You may have to move some of the controls on your report or form around, to make room for the logo.

To place your logo on a form or report:

1. While viewing the form or report in Design View, select Edit ➤ Insert Object. Access will display the Insert Object dialog box (Figure M.8). Right now, you are placing a *file* into the form or report, so you can ignore the list of object types.

2. The image you're placing—the logo—is in an electronic file, so click on the Create from File button.

3. Now you must select the file that contains the logo. You can either type

in the filename—along with the full path—in the File text box, or you can click on the Browse button and pick the file from the Browse dialog box.

4. Once you have specified everything in the dialog box, click OK.

Access will place the graphic on the report. Don't worry if it's covering up some other controls at the moment. Once we've got the logo placed and sized correctly, we'll tidy up the other objects as needed.

5. First, you'll want to make it the right size. If the Properties box is not already displayed, select View ➤ Properties or click on the Properties button

on the toolbar.

Figure M.8
••••••••••••••••••••••••••

In the Insert Object dialog box, we've selected the "create from file" option, C:\REPORT as the drive and directory containing our logo file, and LOGO.BMP as the file.

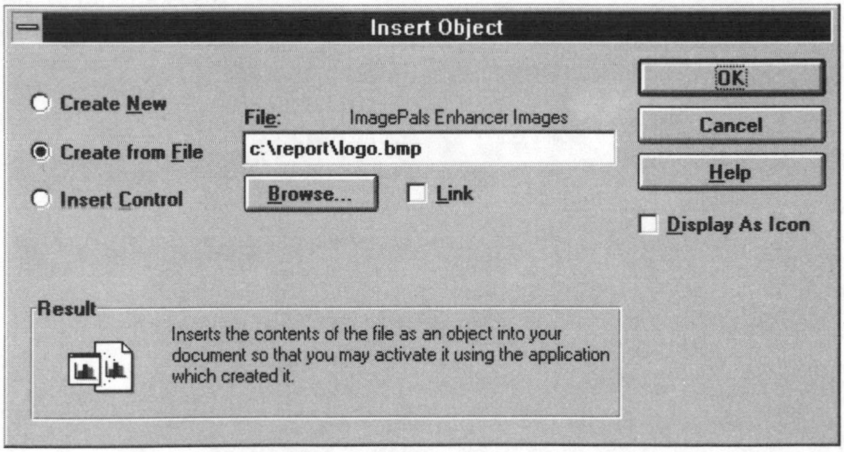

Insert Object

○ Create **N**ew

● Create from **F**ile

○ Insert Control

File: ImagePals Enhancer Images

c:\report\logo.bmp

Browse...   ☐ Link

OK

Cancel

Help

☐ **D**isplay As Icon

Result

Inserts the contents of the file as an object into your document so that you may activate it using the application which created it.

6. Set the Size Mode property for the graphic to Zoom. This will tell Access that you want to resize the graphic without changing the relationship between its height and width.

7. Click and hold the sizing handle in the lower-right corner of the graphic. An outline will appear. Drag the outline to make it the size you want for your logo. You can make it smaller or larger, as you like.

If you placed an exceptionally big graphic on the report you'll have to use the horizontal and/or vertical scroll bars to find the sizing handle on the graphic.

8. The graphic should still be selected. You'll know it is if handles are showing around it. If not, click on it once to make the handles appear. Then move the mouse pointer over the graphic (without pressing the mouse button down). The mouse pointer should change into a little hand.

9. To place the graphic where you want it, grab the graphic by clicking the hand-shaped mouse pointer on it. Then drag the graphic around, and drop it into place.

10. Click on the Form View button to see your logo appearing on your form, or on the Print Preview button to preview your logo on a report. If you print your report, the logo will appear where you placed it.

See   Controls; Control Wizards; Modifying Forms and Reports; OLE; Toolbox

MODULE

A *module* is an access object that holds Access BASIC code. Access BASIC is the programming language in Access. We don't cover programming in this book.

NETWORK ADMINISTRATOR

The person who manages a network is
known as the *network administrator*. (A
network is a lot of computers cabled together so programs, data, and even equipment can be shared by many users.)

NUMBER DATA TYPE

You can just put a number into a text field,
and sometimes you should—in the case of
ZIP codes, for example—on which you're
never going to perform any mathematics
calculations.

   You should put a number into a *number*
field, on the other hand, if you are going to
do any kind of math with it.

> **66** If the number relates to money,
> you may want to consider putting it
> into a special <u>currency</u> field.

A good example of when to use a number
in a number field instead of a text field is
when you want to place a discount percentage in a customer database. Maybe you
give a 45% discount to retail buyers, a
50% discount to distributors, and a 55%
discount to those who pay in advance. You
would have to have set up a number field
called Discount in your Customers table so
that you could later record in that field the
discount percentage for each customer.

   Of course, there are many uses for number fields, and a basic knowledge of those
properties associated with number fields
will help you decide whether a number
field is the right place to put a particular
number.

Number Data Type Properties

These properties are available for any field
set up as a number field:

- ✪ Field Size
- ✪ Format

- Decimal Places
- Input Mask
- Caption
- Default Value
- Validation Rule
- Validation Text
- Indexed
- Required

The **Field Size** property for a number field is a bit more complicated than it is for a text field. In a number field, the Field Size affects not just how long the field is, but also the range of numbers that can be stored in the field. Explaining all of this could take an entire volume—so let's just say that for most purposes, the default Field Size property—Double—will do. It allows for the storage of an unthinkably wide range of numbers.

When you are doing joins between this field and a counter field you'll want to use Long Integer for the Field Size property (see Joins and Relationships).

The properties available for Field Size in a number field are:

Byte A number that can range from 0 to 255 without a fractional part

Integer An number that can range from −32,768 to 32,768 without a fractional part

Long Integer An number that can range from −2,147,483,648 to 2,147,483,647

Single A real number between -3.402823×10^{38} and 3.402823×10^{38} that may include a fractional part

Double A real number between $-1.79769313486232 \times 10^{308}$ and $1.79769313486232 \times 10^{308}$ that may include a fractional part

If you're determined to mess with this, remember to pick the smallest field size possible.

The more flexible a field is—meaning the larger it is, and the more able it is to hold long pieces of information—the more space it takes up in your database. Just as you don't want your closets full of large boxes each containing one small item, you don't want your database tables to be full of large fields containing mainly small bits of data. It's wasteful, and you'll eventually run out of storage space.

The **Format** property determines the default way numbers will look when displayed in datasheets and forms. You can select any of these for the Format of a number field:

General Number Displays the number just as you enter it sans the commas (entering either *1,000* or *1000* will display *1000*)

Currency Inserts separators—usually a comma for thousands, and displays negative amounts either in red or surrounded by parentheses

Fixed Shows a fixed number of decimal places based on the Decimal Places property

Standard Adds a separator for thousands

Percent Multiplies the number you enter by 100 and then adds a percent sign (%) at the end

Scientific Displays numbers in standard scientific notation

The **Decimal Places** property controls the number of digits after the decimal place displayed by Access. Setting this property to Auto causes Access to use the number of places specified in the Format property.

The **Input Mask** property controls the way Access displays the field in an empty table before you have entered any data.

The *Caption* property holds descriptive text that Access displays in the Status Line while the field is active.

The **Default Value** property controls what is displayed in new fields. If you want the default value of the field to be zero, you would enter 0 into this property.

The **Validation Rule** property holds an expression that must be true for Access to store the data. You can use this property to ensure that data in your table meets certain criteria.

The **Validation Text** property contains a message that is displayed whenever data that does not meet the Validation Rule is entered.

The **Indexed** property determines whether Access keeps an indexed of the table based on the field. You should index fields that you use in Joins.

The **Required** property, if set to *true*, *will prevent the user from storing a new record in the table unless a value is entered into this field.*

See **Data Type; Data Types in Access; Text Data Type**

A
B
C
D
E
F
G
H
I
J
KL
M
N
O
P
Q
R
S
T
U
V
W
XYZ

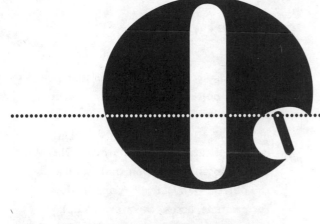

OBJECT

Objects are the things that make up your Access database. Tables, queries, forms, and reports are all objects. So are controls and fields. In fact, pretty much everything in Access is an object.

See Part I

OFF-SITE BACKUPS

Backup copies of your data or programs that are kept someplace other than your place of business are called *off-site backups*. Having up-to-date backups in a secure place is your best insurance against loss or damage to your data.

OLE

OLE stands for Object Linking and Embedding. The cool thing about OLE, a technology introduced in Windows 3.1, is that it allows an application (Access, for example) to store objects that were created in another application (a spreadsheet from Excel, for example). This means that each application can do what it does best, and the user gets the big-time benefit of extra power in both applications.

OLE also lets you store data in rich, new formats that communicate effectively—like pictures, sound, and video—as they become available. Okay, so maybe today you don't have a need to store video, but some time in the near future you might get snazzy new hardware and software, and there you'll be, *finding* a purpose for video in your database.

Not too long from now, you'll be including little movies that demonstrate your product's capabilities in your database. And you'll be set, because Access, and all your other Windows applications that can act as OLE *clients*, are set to use video. (*See* How OLE Works) In Figure O.1 you can see a still image of an animation embedded into an Access form.

Today, without any additional software or hardware, you can use OLE to store pictures in your database. The sample Northwind Traders database that comes with Access includes an Employees table in which each employee is represented by a record (including the employee's photograph) that appears on screen as an Access form. Figure O.2, shown here, illustrates a record from the Northwind Traders Employees table.

See **OLE Object Data Type**

How OLE Works

With OLE, Access can store and manipulate any object that belongs to another application, if that application "knows" how to be an OLE server. An OLE <u>server</u> is an application that can provide OLE objects to an application that can use the objects—an OLE <u>client</u> application. For example, Access can store and play back sound or video because they are both objects that belong to another Windows application.

Figure O.1

When you double-click on the OLE object field in this form, the train appears to rush past in a little video.

Figure O.2

The photograph of the employee in this form is actually an object stored in a field of the OLE data type.

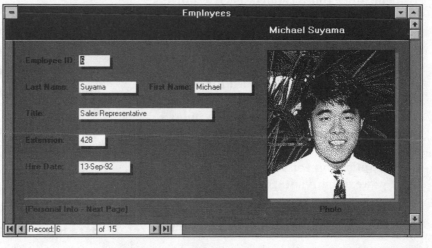

OLE Objects

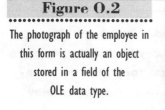 **To store an OLE object, you need another Windows application that can act as an OLE server and knows how to manipulate the object. You can store sound as a Windows Sound Recorder object, but you need to have a _sound driver_ (basically a piece of software that tells your PC how to play the sound) installed in Windows. To store and play video, you need an OLE server application that knows about video, like Video for Windows or QuickTime for Windows.**

Since Paintbrush, the painting program that comes with Windows, can act as an OLE server, the Northwind Traders employee picture is stored as an OLE object. Access lets Paintbrush handle the displaying and editing of the object.

Whenever you double-click on an OLE object in Access, Access transfers control to the application that "owns" the object. This means that you can edit an employee's picture by double-clicking on it in Access. (That will automatically start up Paintbrush.) When you do this, don't be alarmed if the file has a weird name. The filename does not represent an actual file on the disk, but an object that is stored inside another applications file.

With Access and other Windows applications that can act as OLE clients, you can create compound documents—documents that no single application could create. Let's say you have created a lot of nicely formatted reports in Word for Windows.

You can store those reports as OLE objects in records in an Access table. This will make it easier to keep track of the reports. So when you open a report by double-clicking on the Access OLE field that contains it, Access will actually open Word for Windows and let you edit or print your report. When you're finished, Word for Windows will close, and the edited report will once more be stored as an OLE object in Access. Each application will have been used to its most powerful advantage.

Linking and Embedding OLE Objects

The *object* that gets linked or embedded into an Access table using OLE can be an entire file—a document, spreadsheet, picture, or sound, for example—or it can be just part of a file. Whether you are linking or embedding, you should know the difference between the two ideas. Basically, in both linking and embedding, Windows maintains a connection between Access and the application in which the linked or embedded object was created. The difference is that:

✪ When you *link* an object into an Access table, the object still exists in the application in which it was created, and if the object is changed—either in Access or the other application—the changes will appear in the object in your Access table.

✪ When you *embed* an object into an Access table, the copy of the object in Access is separate from the application in which it was created. If the original object is changed in the other application, the change will not show up in the object in Access.

See **"Exporting" Data with DDE**

OLE is a memory hog. If you have only 4MB of RAM you can forget OLE as a practical tool. Even on a machine with 8MB of memory, you may be pushing your luck. If you don't have enough memory to run OLE effectively, you'll find your machine slowing down to an unusable crawl as Access and the other application exhaust themselves trying to send data back and forth using OLE. The solution to this, of course, is to add more RAM to your PC.

OLE OBJECT DATA TYPE

In Access, OLE is a data type. This means that when you are creating a table, you can assign a field to be of the data type *OLE*. Into that field, as a value like the data in any other field, you will place an OLE object.

An OLE field in Access has only two properties you can set:

Caption   contains a label for the field when it is used on a form.

Required   controls whether you *must* embed an object into the field when you add a new record to your table.

See   **Data Type; Text Data Type**

OLE Objects in a Database

Once you have created a table that includes a field of the OLE data type, you need a way to place objects that come from other applications into the field.

·············· Tip ·····················

In working with OLE, you'll find that different techniques are more or less successful, depending on what Windows application you are using as your OLE server. Play around with the methods described here to see which one works best with the specific combination of applications you're using.

Embedding an Object

To embed an object from another application into a field of the OLE data type in your Access table, you must have both Access and the other application running.

We're going to assume that you've already created a table that includes a field of the data type OLE.

Follow these steps to add an OLE object to a field of the OLE data type:

1. In Access, select the name of the table into which you want to place the OLE object. Click on Open. Access will display the table in Datasheet View, as shown in Figure O.3.

2. To switch to the other application (the server application), hold down Ctrl and press Esc. Then double-click on the name of the other application in the Task List, which appears.

3. In the server application, select whatever it is you want to embed into Access. (Exactly how you do this depends on the other application.)

4. Select Edit ➤ Copy to copy whatever you've selected to the Windows Clipboard.

5. Now switch back to Access by holding down Ctrl and pressing Esc, then double-clicking on Access in the Task List.

6. You should be in Datasheet View. Click on the cell into which you want to place the OLE object, to make that the active cell.

7. Select Edit ➤ Paste from the menu bar to copy the object from the Clipboard into the cell.

You will not see the object itself in the cell. Instead, you will see the name of the OLE server application (Figure O.4). If you double-click on the cell, you'll activate the server application, and the object will be displayed. To actually see the object in Access, you'll have to view the table in Form View. Figure O.5 shows an Object in a table viewed in Form View.

A B C D E F G H I J KL M N O P Q R S T U V W XYZ

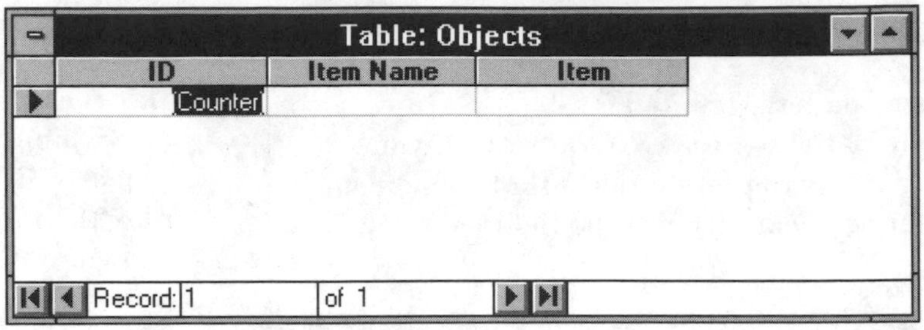

Figure O.3
....
In this table, the Item field is an
empty OLE field.

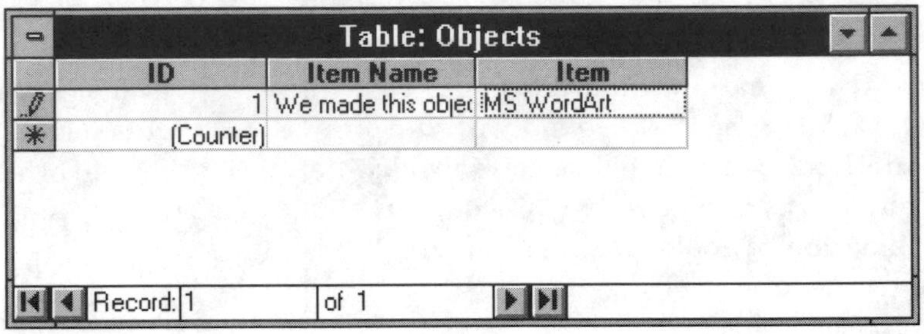

ID	Item Name	Item
(Counter)		

Table: Objects
Record: 1 of 1

Figure O.4
....
The same table shown in Figure O.3,
but with the server application
name appearing in the OLE field,
to indicate that the field contains
an object that came from that
application.

ID	Item Name	Item
1	We made this objec	MS WordArt
(Counter)		

Table: Objects
Record: 1 of 1

Embedding a File

You can embed the entire contents of a file (a document file, a spreadsheet, whatever) into an OLE field. To do so, you need to have Access open; you do not need to have another application open.

Follow these steps:

1. In Access, select the name of the table into which you want to place the OLE object. Click on Open. Access will display the table in Datasheet View.

2. Click on the cell into which you want to place the object. This will make that cell the active cell.

3. Select Edit ➤ Insert Object from the menu bar. Access will display the Insert Object dialog box (Figure O.6).

4. You are going to insert an object that is currently stored in a disk file, so click on "Create from file," then click the Browse button. Access will display the Browse dialog box (Figure O.7).

5. In the Browse dialog box, select the name of the file that contains the object you want to embed. Click on OK.

6. The name of the file you picked in the Browse dialog box will appear in the Insert Object dialog box's File text box. Click OK to go ahead and place the object into Access.

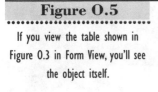

Figure O.5

If you view the table shown in Figure O.3 in Form View, you'll see the object itself.

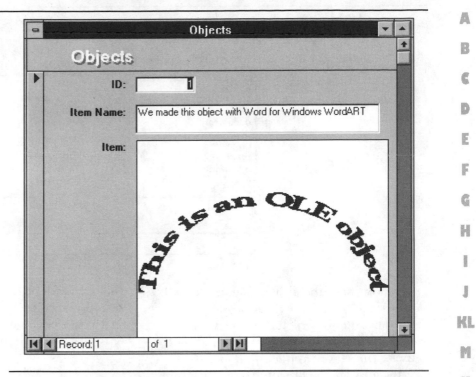

Figure O.6

The Insert Object dialog box

You won't see the object itself in the cell. Instead, you're going to see the name of the application in which the object was created. If you double-click on the cell, you'll activate the server application, and then you'll get to see the object. To see the object in Access, you'll have to view the table in Form View. There, you'll see a pictorial representation of the object, which will be different depending on what application was used to create the object itself. If it is a Paintbrush object (a picture), you'll see the picture itself.

Using Object Packager

Windows includes a small application, Object Packager, whose sole purpose is to package data files from applications into icons, which you can embed into other applications. If you have trouble embedding an entire file using the method described in the last section, try the Object Packager technique we're about to describe instead.

To use the Object Packager to embed an entire file into an Access table:

1. In Access, select the name of the table into which you want to place the OLE object. Click on Open. Access will display the table in Datasheet View.

2. Click on the cell into which you want to place the object. This will make that cell active.

3. Select Edit ➤ Insert Object from the menu bar. Access will display the Insert Object dialog box.

4. Select Package from the list of Object Types and click on OK. Access will start up the Windows Object Packager (Figure O.8) application.

5. In the Object Packager window, select File ➤ Import from the menu bar. The Object Packager application will display the Import dialog box.

Figure O.8

The Object Packager window

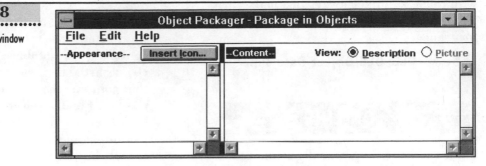

6. Select the name of the file you want to embed into the Access OLE field and then click on OK.

7. Now select File ➤ Exit from the Object Packager menu bar. Object Packager will display a dialog box asking if you want to update the Access Object. (This is just a quirky way of asking you whether you want to save the object in Access.) Click on Yes, because that's what we're doing here.

You will be returned to Access, in Datasheet View, and you'll see the word "Package" in the cell to indicate that a file has been embedded into the OLE field.

As usual, you can double-click on the cell to open the object. It will open in the application to which it belongs.

OLE: EDITING EMBEDDED OBJECTS

Remember that the active field is the highlighted field is the current field. Think about this—when the active field is one

that contains an OLE object, a new choice is added to the drop-down Edit menu. What the new choice is called will depend on what type of OLE object is in the field. Whatever it's called, this menu choice will allow you to edit (change) the OLE object.

For example, if you have embedded a Package object into the field, the new Edit menu option will be Package Object. If you select Package Object, you can choose from these options:

Activate Contents Causes the application that can manipulate the embedded data to start up, so you can edit the data

Edit Package Starts up the Object Packager application, so you can change aspects of the package itself

Change to Picture Converts the data to a picture (once this has been done you can no longer edit the data, because it is then stored only as an image)

Note again that these options will vary, depending on the type of object that is embedded into the OLE field. The only way to get to know these options is to play around with them, so tinker away. Just make sure you have a backup copy of your data as insurance.

See **OLE; OLE Object Data Type**

ON-LINE

To be ready or electronically connected is to be *on-line*. A printer, for example, is on-line when it's ready to print; a Help system is on-line when it is available to you electronically (on screen).

OPENING AN EXISTING DATABASE

You have to open a database before you can work with it; that's pretty obvious. There are two circumstances in which you might open a database:

○ You're just getting rolling and you haven't yet opened a database to work with

○ You've been working with a database already, and you want to open (switch to) a different one

To open an existing database (assuming you don't already have one open):

1. Select Open Database from the File menu on the menu bar. The Open Database dialog box will appear.

2. If you see the database file you want listed in the File Name box, just double-click on it or click the OK button.

or

If you don't see the database file you want listed, select the disk drive that contains your database file from the Drives list. Then select the directory that contains the file from the Directories list. Finally, select the database file's filename from the File Name list by double-clicking on it or by clicking the OK button.

3. The Database window for the database you selected in step 2 will appear.

You now have the database open.

See **Database Window**

OPERATOR

An *operator* is a piece of a mathematical sentence, like $+$, $-$, $\times$, $\div$, or $=$. A mathematical operator performs some function on the two pieces of data (usually numbers) that surround it.

See **Expressions: Components**

OPTIONS DIALOG BOX: CHANGING OPTIONS

You can change some of the defaults in the Options dialog box, using the Options command in Access' View menu. Changing some of these defaults may be to your advantage. Many of them are better left unchanged. We'll tell you what the options are, and what their default settings are, too, in case after your tinkering you want to go back.

66 **The View menu appears along the menu bar only when you have a database open.**

In the Category list in the Options dialog box, you can select the category of options you want to modify (Figure O.9). The categories are:

General Changes the general desktop settings

Keyboard Changes the way certain keys on the keyboard work

Printing Changes margin settings for *new* forms and reports

Form and Report Design Changes defaults in the form and report design screens

Datasheet Changes the look of the default datasheet

Query Design Changes some defaults used in query design

Macro Design Changes defaults used in macro design

Module Design Changes defaults used in creating Access BASIC procedures

66 **Some of these option categories— Macro Design, Module Design, and Multiuser/ODBC—have to do with advanced areas of Access that we didn't cover in this book. You can find out more about those options by checking out <u>Understanding Microsoft Access 2</u> (Sybex, 1994).**

Figure O.9

The Options dialog box

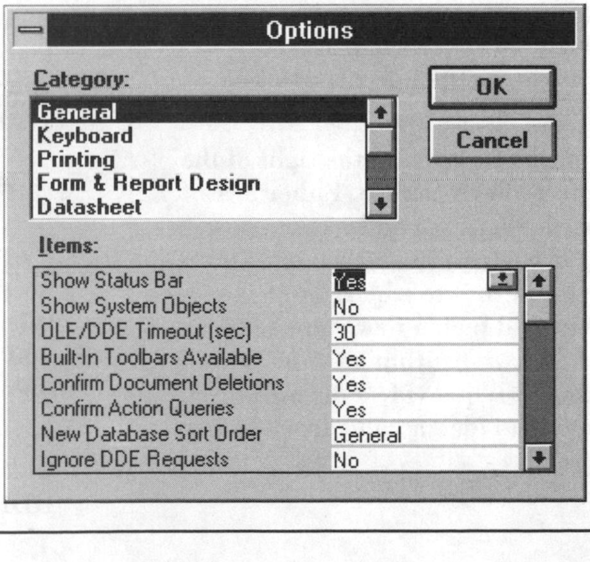

Multiuser/ODBC Changes some settings used on a network

Some details of setting Options dialog box options differ, but if you know one general procedure, you can pretty much change any of them.

The general way you go about setting an option is:

1. With any database open (so the View menu will appear on the menu bar), select View ➤ Options to display the Options dialog box.

2. In the Categories section of the Options dialog box, highlight the category for the option you want to change. If you don't see the category you want to change immediately, you can scroll around in the list using the vertical scroll bar along the list's right side.

3. Once you have the category you want highlighted in the Category list, Access will display all the options you can set for that category in an Items list. Find the option you want to set. If you can't see it right away, scroll around the Items list using the horizontal scroll bar along the right side of the list.

4. Click on the text box to the right of the item you want to change. Either erase the current setting and type in a new value, or click on the little box with the down-arrow in it to (the right of the text box) and pick a new value from the drop-down list that appears. (Not all options will provide a drop-down list for you to pick a value from—some

options will have it no other way but that you type in the value.)

The categories and options that can be changed (but not necessarily *should* be changed) are described in the following sections.

General Desktop Options

Using the General options category, you can change the way the desktop (your on-screen work area) looks and works in Access. You can set the following options under the General options category:

Show Status Bar Determines whether you'll see the status bar along the bottom of the Access window. You will gain a teensy-weensy bit of extra screen space by setting this option to No, but the status bar is generally very helpful, and you can only use it if you can see it, so leave this option set to Yes.

Show System Objects Access keeps track of itself and many aspects of your database in special tables—called *system objects*. If you were to set Show System Objects to Yes, you would see extra tables appear in the list of tables in your database. *You should not modify these tables.* Access uses them to keep track of your database. Just leave this option set to No, so you won't see and be tempted to change the system object tables.

OLE/DDE Timeout (sec) Access waits 0–300 seconds for an OLE or DDE communication to start between applications before giving up. The default is set to 30 seconds.

Built-In Toolbars Available The Built-In Toolbars Available option determines whether Access will display the toolbar along the top of every window. The toolbar is very useful, so trust us, you want to keep this set to Yes.

Confirm Document Deletion Controls whether Access will warn you—and give you a chance to back out—before you delete a database object (like a table or query). Keep this set to Yes.

Confirm Action Queries If set to Yes, Access will warn you before it runs an action query. The default is Yes. Leave it set to Yes to avoid accidentally deleting some of your data with an Action Query.

New Database Sort Order You can set the alphabetical sorting for new databases to General—which, oddly enough, means English and a number of other languages that follow English's alphabetizing system (including many European languages and "Modern Spanish")—or to one of a number of *other* languages, such as Icelandic.

Ignore DDE Requests Setting this option to Yes will prevent Access from responding to DDE request from other applications. You should leave this set to No.

Default Find/Replace Behavior Changing this option will change the way Access first looks for data when you select Edit ➤ Find or Edit ➤ Replace. Your options are Fast Search, which searches only the current field and matches against the entire field;

Start of Field Search, which searches the current field and compares the search string with the beginning of the field; or General Search, which causes Access to search all fields and match any part of the field. (Note that changes to this option do not take effect until the next time you start up Access.)

Default Database Directory Specifies in which directory Access will place new databases that you create, and in which directory Access will look for databases. If you leave it set to the default value, dot (.), Access will place your new databases into the current directory.

Confirm Record Change If set to No, Access will stop asking you to confirm any changes you make to records.

Can Customize Toolbars Setting this option to No prohibits you from customizing the toolbars that Access displays along the top of the window. You should leave this set to Yes.

Enable DDE Refresh Controls whether Access will attempt to refresh DDE data. Keep it set to Yes.

First Weekday Allows you to tell Access what day your week begins on. This is used in some group reports. For example, if you group data by the week, you might want the week to begin on Monday, on Sunday, or on some other day.

First Week Specifies the first week of the year. The choices are: Starts Jan 1, First 4-day week, or First full week. This is used in a number of Access BASIC functions. It's a programming thing; leave it alone.

Show ToolTips   Lets you turn on or off the labels that appear when you move the mouse over icons and tools on the toolbar and in toolboxes. We think those labels are very handy, so we recommend you keep this set to Yes.

Color Buttons on Toolbars   Controls whether Access displays color or black-and-white images on the toolbar. Keep this set to yes so you can have your tools appear in living color.

Large Toolbar Button   Allows you to choose whether Access displays large or small buttons on the toolbar. If you have this set to No, you'll see the normal (small) buttons.

Keyboard Options

With the Keyboard category options, you can change the way Access behaves when you press certain keys. You might want to do this to make the keyboard behave as it does when you're using another database with which you're more familiar, but *hey*, how about learning those handy Access ways?

Arrow Key Behavior   In Datasheet and Form View, this option determines whether pressing the → and ← keys will cause Access to move to the next field or will move the insertion point over one character at a time. Your choices are:

Next Field

Next Character

Move After Enter   Controls what happens when you press the ↵ key. You can select:

No, to have Access *not* move the insertion point

Next Field, to have Access move the insertion point to the next field

Next Record, to have Access move the insertion point to the next record

Cursor Stops at First/Last Field   Setting this option to Yes stops the insertion point from moving from the first or last field in a record to the next/previous record. For example, with this option set to Yes, when you are editing the last field of one record, pressing the right arrow will move you to the first field of the next record.

Key Assignment Macro   You can place into this option the name of a special macro that holds other macros that Access will execute when you press certain keys. (Macros are beyond the scope of this book. To find out more about them, check out Sybex's *Understanding Microsoft Access 2* by Alan Simpson.)

Printing Options

From the Printing category of options, you can change the settings for the top, bottom, left, and right margins of new forms and reports. Any changes you make to the margin settings will not affect existing forms or reports. The default margin on all four sides is 1″. You can change this to be expressed in inches, centimeters, or *twips* ($\frac{1}{1440}$ of an inch—wild, eh?) by typing that info into the appropriate text box.

Form and Report Design Options

This category of options allows you to change the initial settings for creating new forms and reports.

Form Template The *Normal* template is a form template that Access uses whenever you create a new form from scratch without the aid of the Form Wizard. You can enter the name or any form that's stored in your database file; Access will use that form as a template for any net forms you create without the aid of the Form Wizard.

Report Template Just like the Form Template option, except that it's for reports. You can type the name of any report that's stored in your database. Access will use this report as a template for any new reports that you create.

Objects Snap to Grid When this option is turned on (Yes), objects placed on the Design View grid will snap into place along the grid lines on screen. When you install Access, it sets this option to Yes. Having objects snap to the grid is very handy, so leave this option alone.

Show Grid If this option is turned on (Yes), you'll see the grid displayed when you first enter into Design View for forms or reports. By default, Access shows the grid.

Selection Behavior This option determines whether controls that are partially enclosed in the selection box will be selected as you click-and-drag over them. The default setting for this option is to select partially selected objects.

Show Ruler If this option is set to Yes, the ruler will appear at the top and left side of the Design View screen for forms and reports. By default, Access displays the ruler, which is handy, so leave this set to Yes.

Move Enclosed Controls If this is set to Yes, controls that are enclosed in another control will move only together. For example, option buttons will be moved automatically when the group control that contains them is moved. *The default setting of this is No*, but if you are using a lot of enclosed controls on your forms, setting this to Yes will make editing your forms easier.

Control Wizards Set this option to Yes or No to turn the Control Wizards on (Yes) or off (No) in Form- and Report Design View. When you install Access, the Control Wizards will be enabled. Unless you like doing everything yourself, you'll probably want to leave this option set to Yes. If you do turn off the Control Wizards here, though, you can enable them again while you are designing a form or report simply by clicking on the Control Wizards tool in the toolbox.

A
B
C
D
E
F
G
H
I
J
KL
M
N
O
P
Q
R
S
T
U
V
W
XYZ

Datasheet Options

The Datasheet category of options allows you to control the way the datasheet looks when you first open it in Datasheet View for tables and queries.

Default Gridlines Behavior Controls whether Access will display gridlines to separate cells in the datasheet. By default this is set to On.

Default Column Width Lets you set the width of columns on the datasheet. The default column width is 1".

Default Font Name Lets you select which font will be used to display data on the datasheet. Access provides a complete list of fonts. Click on the Default Font Name text box and a down-arrow will appear. Click on the down-arrow and select a font name from the drop-down list that appears. Access uses the font MS Sans Serif by default for text on the datasheet.

Default Font Size Lets you select the size of the font you want Access to use to display data on the datasheet. To pick a size, click in this text box and then on the down-arrow that appears. Then select a font size from the drop-down list that appears. When Access is first installed it displays data on a datasheet in 8-point text.

Default Font Weight Lets you control the *font weight* (how heavy, or dark, the type looks) that is initially used to display data on the datasheet. Access gives you a whole range of options from

which to choose, but many fonts don't support all the choices Access gives you. (Many fonts come in only two weights—normal and bold.) If you choose a weight that's not available in the font you've selected, Access will give you whatever's closest to what you picked. The default is Normal.

Default Font Italic Can be turned on by selecting Yes here, or off by selecting No. The default is No.

Default Font Underline Tells Access to initially underline all data on the datasheet (by selecting Yes), or not underline data (by selecting No). Again, the default is No.

Query Design Options

With this category of options, you can change the way the Query Design View grid appears when you open it to create new queries.

Output All Fields If this option is set to Yes, all the fields in the table on which you're basing the query will show up in the dynaset. The default setting here is No, and we recommend you keep it that way.

Run Permission This option is relevant only if you are using Access on a network and have set up Access' security features. In any case, just leave it set to User's to save yourself a lot of trouble.

Show Table Names Setting this option to Yes causes Access to display an extra row in the QBE grid—that row will show you from which table each field came. If you start using Access to create a lot of joins, setting this option to Yes might make your job with the QBE grid easier. The default for this option is No.

66 **We said up front that we were covering the most commonly used options. If you just can't stand to leave well enough alone, turn to the Access documentation for more information on changing the options we haven't covered.**

See **Customizing Access**

OUTPUT TO

Output To in Access is like a hybrid between exporting and printing. It allows you to export your data into a spreadsheet or word processor document, where you can use it as if it had been created in that program. This is something you can also do by exporting, but with Output To your data will appear in the other program looking a lot better.

To output data with Output To, follow these steps:

1. In the Database window, select the object you wish to output.

2. Select File ➤ Output To. Access displays the Output To dialog box (Figure O.10).

3. In the Output To dialog box, select the type of file you want to create. Your choices are:

❂ Microsoft Excel

❂ Rich Text Format

❂ MS-DOS Text

4. Once you have picked the format you wish to output the object to, click the OK button. Access will display the Output To dialog box shown in Figure O.11 (this is a different dialog box than the first one—oddly enough with the same name).

····· **Tip** ·····

You can either export all of your data or just the records you had selected when you picked File ➤ Output To by selecting one of the two option buttons in the dialog box. Select *All* to export all the records, or *Selection* to export the records you had selected.

5. Enter the filename you wish to output your data into and click the OK button.

6. Access will display a dialog box while it is working. When Access is done outputting your data, you will be returned to the Database window.

You now have your data in a file usable in other program such as Microsoft Excel or Microsoft Word.

Figure O.10

The first Output To dialog box

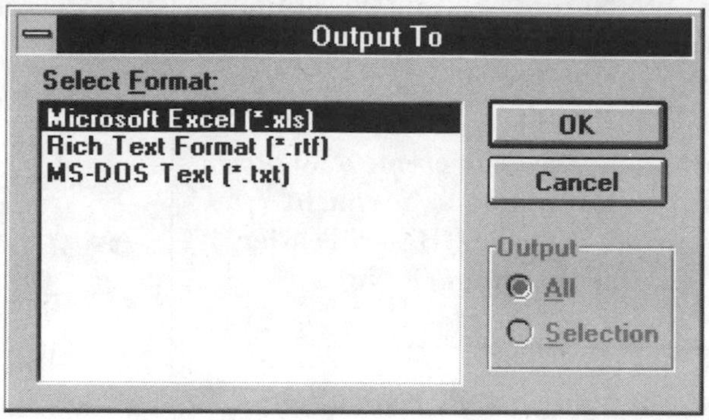

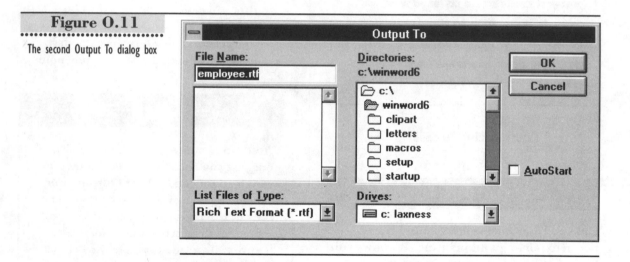

Figure O.11

The second Output To dialog box

See **Exporting; Mail Merge to Microsoft Word**

OVERTYPE MODE

Overtype is a mode of typing in which whatever you type covers up what was there in the first place. Overtype is also known (more sensibly and commonly) as *Typeover* mode,

and is sometimes known as *Overwrite* or *Overstrike*. They're all the same.

Rich Text Format is a format supported by many word processor programs, including Microsoft Word. MS-DOS Text produces almost the same results as exporting to a text file.

PASTE

See **Copy, Cut, and Paste**

PATH

The complete way to find a file starting at the root of a drive is the *path*. The list of directories your computer searches to find executable files is also the *path*. A path goes something like:

`C:\ACCESS\SAMPAPPS\NWIND.MDB`

See **Directories**

PERIPHERAL

Any piece of equipment that is extra to your computer is known as a *peripheral*. A modem or a mouse is peripheral; a keyboard is technically peripheral but not usually referred to as such because you can't do much without a keyboard. The CPU box definitely is not peripheral.

PORTRAIT

When you're holding a piece of paper so that it's an up-and-down rectangle, that's known as *portrait orientation*.

See **Printer Setup; Printing**

POSTSCRIPT

Postscript is a computer language developed by Adobe to describe printed pages electronically. Many high-end laser printers understand Postscript and are said to be "Postscript printers."

See **Printing**

PREVIEW

See Print Preview

PRIMARY KEY

A special field in a table that contains a value to identify the record is the *primary key* field. Each table can have only a single primary key field.

Every table *should* include a primary key field. The primary key field in a table's records contains a unique identifier—a number for each record that no other record can have. For example, a primary key like a Customer ID contains a number that identifies each record in the Customer table. No two Customer ID numbers can be alike—Whatzit Widgets can't have the same Customer ID as Turbo Diaper Pros. In the same way the government doesn't allow two people to have the same Social Security number, Access doesn't allow duplicates in primary keys.

The primary key in a table gives Access a quick and easy way to link tables. However, that's not the main purpose of primary keys—Access uses primary keys to speed things internally in a number of ways that are very technical. In our primary key discussion, we're going to stick to talking about how to make the linking of tables easier.

See **Joins and Relationships; Tables: Creating in Design View**

It's smart to use a field that is of the Counter data type for the primary key. Access automatically generates a new number for the counter field of each record if there is a field defined as a counter field. If you already have a counter field in your table, Access will use the counter field instead of creating a new counter field called ID when it creates a key field. You can also make a field of your database into the key field by selecting the field you want to turn into a primary key and clicking on the primary key icon on the toolbar.

PRINTER SETUP

For the most part, the options available to you on your printer depend on the type of printer you have, and who made it. Windows itself provides options for managing your printer and its setup. (For information on that, take a look at *Murphy's Laws of Windows* or *Mastering Windows 3.1*, both published by Sybex.)

In this section, we'll describe some of the options you can set that are more commonly used in Access. Everything we talk about here you set from the Access Print

Setup dialog box. You can get to this dialog box in one of three ways:

✪ Click on the Setup button in the Print dialog box

✪ Click on the Setup button in Print Preview mode

✪ Select Print Setup from the File pull-down menu

Printing Sideways

So you take your $8\frac{1}{2}'' \times 11''$ sheet of paper, and you hold it so it's taller than it is wide, and people call that the *portrait* view (it's vertically rectangular, like your head). Then you take the paper and turn it sideways, and that view is called *landscape* (it's wide, like Wyoming).

If you want something printed landscape, select the Landscape option in the Print Setup dialog box. (Not all printers support this option. Check your printer's documentation to see if it does.) Figure P.1 shows you the definitive difference between portrait and landscape orientation.

Picking Where the Paper Comes From

If you have a printer that uses a paper tray—for example, a laser printer—you may be able to choose the paper source (where the printer will get sheets of paper). Some common choices are:

✪ Upper Tray

✪ Lower Tray

✪ Envelope Tray

✪ Manual Feed

Most laser printers today have at least an Upper Tray and Manual Feed option. Not all printers have all the other options, but some of the extra snappy and more expensive printers have even more.

You select the paper source in the Source drop-down list in the Paper section of the Print Setup dialog box.

Using Manual Feed or the Envelope Tray

Manual Feed is handy when you need to print a few pages on letterhead, envelopes, or label paper. Manual Feed is pretty much what it says—you hand feed the paper into the printer. This saves you the time and hassle of pulling out the paper tray, removing the usual paper, inserting the special paper, putting the tray back in, printing, pulling out the paper tray again, reinserting the usual paper, and placing the tray back into the printer.

When you use Manual Feed, you may have to stand by the printer, though, to pay attention to its instructions and pop the paper in at the right time.

Some printers come with a special envelope tray, which allows you to place envelopes in a space just the right size for them. Other than that, printing envelopes is usually a matter of feeding them through one by one with the Manual Feed option.

A
B
C
D
E
F
G
H
I
J
KL
M
N
O
P
Q
R
S
T
U
V
W
XYZ

Figure P.1
....

Portrait vs. landscape orientation

Portrait

Landscape

Paper Size

Most of the time, you'll print to the standard paper size—$8\frac{1}{2}$" × 11". Other sizes may be available to you—sizes that are available for the printer you're using will appear in the Print Setup dialog box's Paper: Size drop-down list. You should usually leave this set to Letter $8\frac{1}{2}$" × 11", unless you want to print on paper that is some special size and that your printer supports.

If that's the case, simply select your special paper size from the drop-down list.

Changing Printers

Some lucky folks (and many businesses) have more than one printer. This is the sort of thing that gets set up first in Windows, and then is available to you in Access.

If you change the paper size, Access will stick with the new size you've chosen until you change it back.

Just because you've changed the paper size in Access doesn't necessarily mean your <u>printer</u> is set up for the new paper size. You may have to make a change in your printer's setup, too. Check your printer's documentation to find out what you have to do.

If you have more than one printer available to you, you can switch between them in Access' Print Setup dialog box. Selecting the Default Printer option will send your print jobs to whatever printer you have set up as the default printer in Windows (Access lists the name of the default printer in the Print Setup dialog box). To pick a different printer for your print job, select the one you want from the Specific Printer drop-down list. As soon as you select a new printer, the options available in the Print Setup dialog box will change to reflect the capabilities of the printer you've selected. Other than living with those changes, you can then go about printing just as you did with the other printer you were using.

When you save your report, Access saves information about the printer you used, too. If you change printers and open the report later, Access will point out the printer change in a dialog box, and ask if you want the report reformatted for the current printer.

PRINTING

For a decade or more, computer futurists have been chanting promises of the paperless office—the office that will do all its

work electronically, sparing trees and conducting business faster than we can think.

This is not likely to happen *next week*. Many people still believe the only reliable copy of a document is a paper one (probably stored off-site in a fire-safe cabinet). So for the time being, we must still rely on printed copies.

See   **Printer Setup; Printing Datasheets; Printing Forms; Printing Mailing Labels; Printing Reports; Printing Transparencies, Print Preview**

PRINTING DATASHEETS

You have two basic options in printing the datasheet. You can print either the entire datasheet or just part of it (a *range*).

See   **Datasheet; Datasheet View**

A
B
C
D
E
F
G
H
I
J
KL
M
N
O
P
Q
R
S
T
U
V
W
XYZ

Printing the Entire Datasheet

To print the entire datasheet, you must first (of course) be in the Database window. You can select the name of the datasheet or the name of a query (the results of that query will appear as a datasheet, as well). Or you can view the datasheet or query in Datasheet View.

In either case, once you've got the datasheet selected or in view, you can:

1. Select File ➤ Print. Access displays the Print dialog box.

2. Click on OK.

The entire datasheet—all of the fields of all of the records in that datasheet—will print out in a very ordinary-looking but organized way.

Printing Part of the Datasheet

You're not always going to want to print the whole datasheet. Sometimes you'll want to print a few pages—maybe 1 through 50, or just 12 through 17, for example. Sometimes you'll want to print just a few records.

Printing a Range of Pages

You can also tell Access you want it to print a certain *range* of pages by selecting Pages and entering the starting and ending pages in the From and To boxes in the Print dialog box, as shown in Figure P.2.

Once you've told Access which pages to print, go ahead and press the OK button to print those pages.

Figure P.2

Only pages 12–17 will be printed.

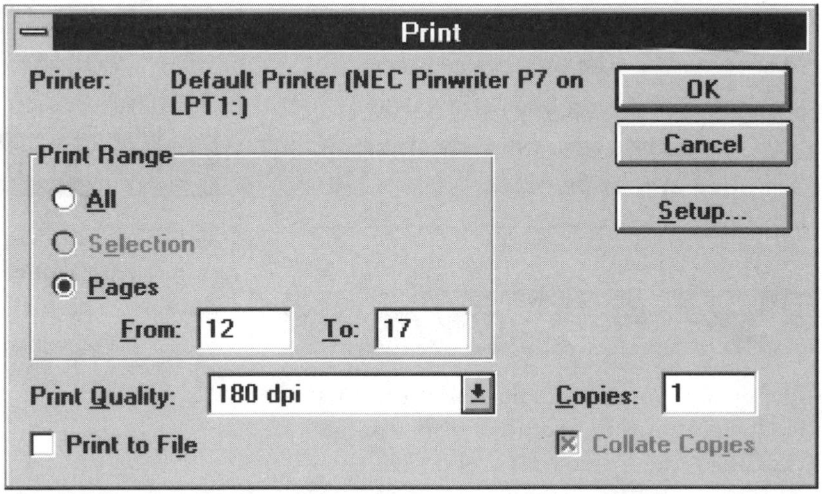

Print
Printer: Default Printer (NEC Pinwriter P7 on LPT1:)
Print Range
○ All
○ Selection
● Pages
From: 12   To: 17
Print Quality: 180 dpi
☐ Print to File
OK
Cancel
Setup...
Copies: 1
☒ Collate Copies

Selecting Certain Records to Be Printed

To print a selection of your records from Datasheet View:

1. Select the records you want to print while viewing your table or dynaset in Datasheet View. You can select a single record by clicking on the record indicator to the left of that record. Or you can select multiple records by holding down the Shift key and clicking first on the first record you want and then on the last record you want. (Note that you can print only a *continuous* range of records in the datasheet.)

2. Select File ➤ Print.

3. In the Print dialog box that appears, select the Selection option. This tells Access to print only those records you selected in step 1.

4. Click OK and Access will print your records.

Changing the Font

The datasheet is displayed entirely in a single, utilitarian font. If you want to jazz it up, you can change the font and its look by following these steps:

1. While viewing the datasheet in Datasheet View, select Format ➤ Font.

2. In the Font dialog box, you can select the new font from the font list that appears.

3. The Font Style list lets you specify the style of the font—bold or italic, for example. Your choices will depend on the font you have selected.

4. If you want to change the size of the font, select a new size from the Size box. You may need to widen columns in the datasheet, though, to allow your data to fit, if you increase the size of the font. (*See* Datasheet: Modifying Columns and Rows for more on widening columns.)

5. The results of your choices will show up in a little box that displays sample text in the styles you've chosen. Once you're happy with your choices, click on OK.

The datasheet should now appear on screen in the new font, and when you print it, the datasheet will also appear in print in its new font.

If you make changes to the font used in a table's datasheet, when you close the datasheet, Access will ask if you want to save the changes. If you do save the changes, the table will forever after appear sporting its new font when you view it in Datasheet View.

See **Options Dialog Box: Changing Options; Printing**

PRINTING FORMS

Let's say you have a nice form, you're looking at your data in the form of that form, and you get the wild idea you might want to *print* what you see so beautifully displayed on-screen.

We've been describing forms as something you view on screen, and that's what they were intended for, but hey, there's a little flexibility in software. You *can* actually print either a single record or an entire table or dynaset as a form.

See   **Forms and Form Wizards**

Printing a Single Record as a Form

To print a single record laid out as a form:

1. Start with the record you want to print, displayed on screen in a form.
2. Select Edit ➤ Select Record.
3. Select File ➤ Print.
4. In the Print dialog box, choose Selection.
5. Click the OK button to print the record.

That particular record, laid out neatly in the form of a form, will pop out of your printer like magic. (As long as your printer's working.)

Printing a Table or Dynaset as a Form

You can print either an entire table or dynaset, or a portion of one, using a form. To do this, open the form and then follow these steps.

1. Select File ➤ Print.
2. In the Print dialog box, enter the starting and ending numbers for the pages you want to print into the From and To boxes. Note that these are page numbers, not record numbers. Each page, when it's printed, may include many records. Make sure that the Pages option is selected. (To print all of your data just select All.)
3. Click OK to print.

Again, your printer will spit out whatever you asked for—a whole query or dynaset, or just the part you asked for—in the fine form of a form.

See   **Printing**

PRINTING MAILING LABELS

Mailing labels are just another type of report in Access, so you print them the same way you print any other report. There are a few details to keep in mind, though, when you're printing mailing labels.

✪   When you're placing labels in the paper tray of your HP Laserjet II or *most* other modern laser printers, the labels go face up.

○ If your laser printer has a paper exit at the rear, you should use it. In the course of going through your printer, paper usually has to turn over through a kind of barrel-and-roller system that sometimes peels the labels off their paper backing.

○ When you're printing on expensive paper—label sheets or stationery—you probably won't want to waste sheets by printing them just to see how your report or labels will look.

Viewing the thing in Print Preview will give you a good idea of roughly where gizmos will appear on the printed page, but sometimes it's hard to relate the Print Preview image with real paper. To get a better idea how things are lined up relative to labels on a label sheet or the letterhead on your stationery, print a sample of your document or labels on plain white paper. Place this copy over a clean sheet of labels or stationery, hold it up to the light so you can see through both sheets, and check out how things line up. If everything looks okay, go ahead and print.

See **Printing; Printing Reports; Reports and Report Wizards**

PRINTING REPORTS

You've created your report, you've saved your report, and now you want to print it out. That's what reports are for, right? There are some tricky ins and outs of printing, but there's also a quick and easy way. As long as your printer is already set up correctly this technique will work.

To quickly print out any kind of report:

1. Select the report in the Database window.

2. Click either on the Preview button or the

in the toolbar.

Access will create a window that shows you what the report will look like on paper. You can move around this window using the horizontal and vertical scroll bars, as usual. You can also change pages by using the VCR-type controls that appear next to the page number at the bottom of the window.

3. Click on the Print... button:

66 **You can also get to the Print dialog box from Print Preview by clicking on the Print button.**

4. Access will display the Print dialog box. You shouldn't have to do much of anything here, but if you want, you can change the range of pages Access will print. (Other options may depend on what type of printer you have.) Click on OK to print out your report.

PRINTING TRANSPARENCIES

You can print transparencies of reports for presentations simply by replacing the regular paper in the paper tray with transparent "paper." You don't have to change anything else in Access, and almost certainly not in your printer.

You should first proof a copy by printing it on plain paper in the usual way, though—you really, really want to catch your errors before you print your document on the more expensive transparencies.

See   **Printing Reports**

PRINT PREVIEW

You don't have to actually *print* your datasheet, form, or report just to see what it's going to look like—you can preview the printed page on screen instead, by using Access' Print Preview feature. The Print Preview feature opens up a window that shows you just what your print job will look like when it's actually printed. You can even zoom in close to see details or zoom out to get an overview of the entire document.

To view your datasheet or report in Print Preview mode, select the table, query, form, or report you want to see in the Database window, then select File ➤ Print Preview. Or, if you are already viewing

your data in Datasheet or Form view, select File ➤ Print Preview or click on the

button on the toolbar.

 Whenever you double-click on a report name in the Database window or select a report in the Database window and click the Preview button, you get to see your report in Print Preview mode.

Once you are viewing something in Print Preview mode, you can manipulate the image in a number of ways by using these buttons, which appear along the top of the window:

 Click this button and you will see the standard Print dialog box.

 Clicking on the Setup button makes Access display the Print Setup dialog box.

 Click on the Zoom button to switch back and forth between a view of the entire page in a window and a close-up view of part of the page, in which you can use horizontal and vertical scroll bars to move around the image.

Click on Close to exit Preview mode without printing the document, and return to wherever you were when you selected Print Preview.

Print Preview is a great way to look before you print. Of course, some errors may escape you, and then—once you have committed your document to paper—show up like a boo-boo on a baby's butt. You can always go back and fix anything that's not quite right, using the techniques we've described throughout this book. For example, if you see an error in your data (like a misspelled product name), you can edit in the datasheet or in a form. (*See* Editing Data in Datasheet View; Editing Data with a Form) If you see that something was incorrectly aligned or misspelled when you created your report, you can correct that in Report Design View. (*See* Modifying Forms and Reports)

See **Printing**

PROGRAMMING

We do not cover Access programming in this book. That's because the beauty of Access is its ease of use, and *you're not supposed to have to know* how to program it. But if you want to delve deeply into Access, you can investigate Access' programming features on your own. With Access you can create objects called Modules that contain Access BASIC programs. All that and more is explained in the language reference provided with the program by Microsoft.

PROPERTIES

Those qualities or characteristics of objects in Access that you can change are known as *properties*.

A
B
C
D
E
F
G
H
I
J
KL
M
N
O
P
Q
R
S
T
U
V
W
XYZ

Q

QBE

QBE stands for **Query By Example**, which allows you to describe a query by filling out sections of a grid.

See **Queries: Creating**

QBE GRID

The *QBE grid* is the column-and-row grid on which you lay out your queries using simple point-and-click or point-and-drag mouse techniques.

See **Queries: Creating**

QUERIES

A *query* is just a question—sometimes a group of questions bundled together—designed to come up with a specific set of answers. An Access query may be as simple as "List all the customers who haven't

paid," or it may include a combination of questions, like, "List everyone who hasn't paid in the last three months, *and* owes in excess of $1,000.00, *and* has an office in Tucumcari."

The tricky part here is that Access doesn't understand English—at least not as we speak it. So you have to learn how to phrase your queries so Access can understand them. This isn't terribly difficult—but you do have to learn to do it Access' way, because, unfortunately, Access can't learn yours.

When you ask Access to answer a query, it will sift through the records in whatever table you specify, process the question, and produce an answer. The answer will appear in the form of yet another set of records, called a *dynaset*. (*See* Figure 1.7 in Part 1).

66 **You can base a query on a table or on the results of a query (a dynaset).**

A B C D E F G H I J KL M N O P Q R S T U V W XYZ

The Secret Truth about Dynasets

. . . .

The dynaset <u>looks</u> like a new table, and you can use it as if it were one, but it's not a table. It's really a kind of illusion to the computer—a set of complicated instructions that point to fields that actually exist in the table(s) on which you based your query.

Creating a query is like instructing your computer to "put a picture of the Last Name field from the Employees table here," and "a picture of the Bonus field from the Benefits table here." In other words, the Last Name field still actually <u>exists</u> in the Employees table, and the Bonus field still exists in the Benefits table. Those fields will <u>appear</u> in the dynaset that results from your query, but they appear as representations of the fields that actually exist in the underlying tables—in this case, the Employees table and the Benefits table.

Be careful when you change data in a dynaset. The dynaset is based on a table, but it is not its own separate table; <u>if you make a change to data in a dynaset, you will also be changing that piece of data in the underlying table.</u>

See Queries: Basic Types; Queries: Creating; Query Wizards

QUERIES: BASIC TYPES

There are three basic categories of queries in Access:

- ○ Select queries
- ○ Crosstab queries
- ○ Action queries

Because they're the most commonly used, we're going to dwell on *select* queries, which are queries that select and present information from the tables or dynasets on which they're based. Some examples of select queries are (in plain English), "List the names of all employees who elect to carry dental insurance," or "Find all the dancers' shoe sizes." For obvious reasons, you'll often use select queries as the basis of forms and reports.

In this book, when we refer to a query without saying what type of query it is, you can bet that we're talking about the ever-popular <u>select</u> query.

A *crosstab query* sums up information from tables in rows and columns—it *cross tabu*lates information. An example of this might be a summary of company names and the average prices of their stock over some period of time.

An *action* query modifies data in a table—either the one it is based upon, or another one. For example, you might want to move records that are no longer relevant to what you're currently doing to an *archive* table—a table that holds old data you don't want to keep active (but which you don't want to delete permanently.) You can automate the process of moving these records from one table to another using action queries.

See   **Queries; Queries: Creating**

---

66   **You can bring together related information from many tables using a single query with a join. Then you can either display that information, or base forms or reports on it. You cannot, however, edit data that results from some types of joins. (See Joins and Relationships)**

---

66   **A query is an object, just like everything else in Access. That means that the query has to be stored, just like any other object, in the database file. Why store a query? Well, because you may have to ask the same question more than once, and if you stored the query the first time, you won't have to repeat the whole process again.**

Queries Used as Tables

Whenever you execute a select query, Access builds what it calls a *dynaset*, which is a collection of records that are the answer to the query. You can use a dynaset anyplace you would use a table. This means that you can use the results of a select query as the basis of a form or a report.

You can also view and edit the results of a select query in Datasheet View. Do this with some caution, though—when you edit the data in the select query, you'll be changing the tables on which you've based the query.

See   **Queries; Queries: Creating**

QUERIES: BASING FORMS ON

You can use a dynaset (the results of a query, which will look like a table) just as you would a table, so you can base forms on queries—but there is an easier way to filter your information into a form. You can use a Forms Filter/Sort property to specify the filtering conditions (which data to work on) and sort order (in what order the data should be sorted) for the form.

Also—because the way you specify criteria is the same in queries and in the Filter/Sort property of forms, and because the grids look similar—everything you learn about queries you can directly apply to the Filter/Sort property of forms.

See   **Forms and Form Wizards**

A
B
C
D
E
F
G
H
I
J
KL
M
N
O
P
Q
R
S
T
U
V
W
XYZ

QUERIES: CREATING

66 You can use the Query Wizards as a shortcut to create queries, but you'll almost invariably find that you need to alter those queries. You'll also often need to create custom queries. This section is about creating queries from scratch. (See Query Wizards)

Because a query is just another object in your database, you must have the database file open in order to create and store a query. (The query will be based on the table(s) or dynaset(s) contained in that database file, *and* the query will itself become a part of that database file.)

To create a new query:

1. With the Database window of your choice open, click on the Query button. You will see either a list of existing queries or, if no one has created a query in this database file before, an empty list.

2. Click on the New button. The New Query dialog box will appear.

3. In the New Query dialog box, click the New Query button.

4. A dialog box will appear, asking you to choose the table upon which you want to base the query. You can select any table or dynaset from the list. To do this, either double-click on the name of the

table or dynaset you want, or select the name by highlighting it and clicking on Add. You can switch the listing to tables, queries, or even both, by clicking on the buttons near the bottom on the dialog box.

66 You can base your query on more than one table or dynaset. (See Joins and Relationships)

5. When you are finished selecting the table(s) and/or dynaset(s) on which you'll base your new query, click on the Close button. The Query Design View window will appear. This is where you will design your query.

Tip

If you are currently viewing a table or dynaset in either Datasheet or Design View, you can quickly create a new query based on that table or dynaset by selecting File ➤ New ➤ Query.

Now you are looking at the Query Design View window. There are two parts to this window. Along the top are one or more smaller windows, each of which shows a table or dynaset upon which you're basing your query.

These windows are called *Field Lists*, because they contain a list of all the fields in the table or dynaset with which they're associated. Take a look at the Field List in the top part of the Query Design View window shown in Figure Q.1. Keep in mind, though, that we're covering only queries with a single source here, so you will see only one Field List for now.

The grid along the bottom of the Query Design View window is what the folks at Microsoft call the graphical *QBE grid* (QBE is short for **Query By Example**). Of course, whatever the folks at Microsoft call it is also what we call it. This is where you tell Access the question you want it to answer. You will describe your query in the QBE grid by first placing fields, and then entering criteria, sort options, and other things into the grid.

To create a query, you click and drag field names from the Field List box in the top of the window to the QBE grid in the bottom of the window. Then you specify *criteria*—certain conditions the field has to meet for its record to be included in the dynaset of the query—along with other options. The steps for placing field names in the QBE grid and for specifying criteria and options are outlined below.

Adding a Field to a Query

Every field you want to appear in the dynaset that results from the query must be

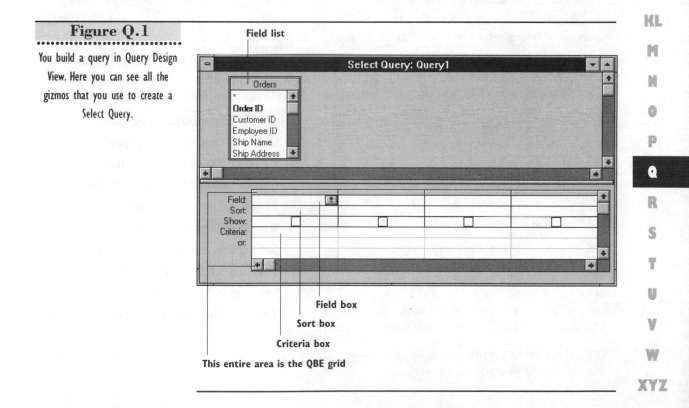

Figure Q.1

You build a query in Query Design View. Here you can see all the gizmos that you use to create a Select Query.

Field list

Select Query: Query1

Orders

Order ID
Customer ID
Employee ID
Ship Name
Ship Address

Field:
Sort:
Show:
Criteria:
or:

Field box

Sort box

Criteria box

This entire area is the QBE grid

SQL and What It Means
. . . .

When you create queries, you are actually programming a computer by drawing pictures. (See the box in the Queries section titled The Secret Truth about Dynasets.) The heart of Access is a SQL (pronounced sequel) "engine" that takes commands in a standard database language (called SQL) and executes them. The graphical QBE grid gives you a visual way to tell Access what you want it to do. Access then takes the "picture" you draw and translates it into lines of computer code. These lines of code are what the Access SQL "engine" actually can understand. You can see the lines of code that Access is creating from the pictures you draw, by clicking on the SQL View icon (the one with "SQL" on it) the Query Design toolbar.

included in the QBE grid. To place a field in the QBE grid, you can use either of two methods:

- Click and drag
- Use the pull-down menu

The result will be the same in either case, so you can choose the method that's more comfortable or convenient for you.

To use the *click-and-drag* method:

1. In the Field List box, click on the name of the field you want to place.

2. Hold down the mouse button and drag the field to an empty slot in the top row—the Field row—of the QBE grid.

3. With the pointer over the cell you've targeted in the Field row, lift the mouse button, and the field name will appear in the cell.

To use the *pull-down menu* method:

1. Click in the Field row of the cell you wish to change to make that cell the current one. A small down-arrow button will appear in the cell. Click on the down-arrow button, and a drop-down list will appear, listing all the available field names.

2. Select the field you want by clicking on its field name. The field name will then appear in the current cell of the Field row.

Once you've placed field names in the Field row of the QBE grid, you can move down the columns of the grid, specifying criteria and options for each field.

See Criteria; Datasheet View; Queries; Queries: Basic Types; Queries: Executing; Queries: Fields Combined With; Queries: Prompts to Enter Data; Queries: Renaming Fields; Queries: Running Existing; Queries: Saving for Later Use; Queries: Showing and Hididng Fields; Queries: Sorting Data on a Field; Queries: Viewing Their Results; Query Wizards

QUERIES: EXECUTING

Every time you use a query to get data—when you look at the query in Datasheet View or as a form or report—you are doing what's called *executing* the query. This is when Access takes the SQL code that the query generated and uses it to create a collection of records.

---

66 The SQL code is a set of instructions to Access that tell it what kind of a picture to create from the data in the underlying table(s) or dynaset(s). (See the box in the previous section titled SQL and What It Means.)

See Queries; Queries: Running Existing

QUERIES: FIELDS COMBINED WITH

You can have Access calculate new fields (combine two fields into one new field) that will appear in the results of your query.

As an example, you might want to create a calculated Full Name field that combines the First Name and Last Name fields. To do this, you would enter the following expression in the QBE grid:

```
Full Name: [Last Name] & ", " &
[First Name]
```

The result then would be a field called Full Name, which would contain the contents of the Last Name field, a comma, and the contents of the First Name field, like this:

Wickerface, Mildred

Some of the more useful operators that you can use in an expression include:

Operator	Meaning
+	Add one number to another
−	Subtract one number from another
*	Multiply one number by another
/	Divide one number by another
^	Raise one number to the power of another
mod	Modulus (or remainder)
&	Combine two strings into one

---

66 You can also use any Access BASIC function in an expression. For a complete list of hundreds of functions you can use in expressions, search Access' on-line Help for the topic "Functions: Reference."

A
B
C
D
E
F
G
H
I
J
KL
M
N
O
P
Q
R
S
T
U
V
W
XYZ

See **Expression Builder; Expressions; Queries: Creating**

QUERIES: MODIFYING EXISTING

Remember, you can always change an existing query by switching to Query Design View and then simply making any adjustment within the boundaries of Access and morality.

See **Queries; Queries: Creating**

> ·············· **Tip** ··············
>
> **If you want to set up a query that's only somewhat different than an existing one, open the existing query, make changes to it, and choose File ➤ Save As to give it a new name.**

QUERIES: PROMPTS TO ENTER DATA

What do you do if you want to use different values in a criteria every time you run a query? Access lets you place variables (parameters) in the criteria and calls this a *parameter* query. Every time you run the query, Access will ask you to supply values for the variables. Let's say you want to create a dynaset that includes all the records of a table that has a Date Entered field that falls between two dates that you enter when

you run the query. You can enter the following in the Criteria box for the Date Entered field in the QBE grid:

```
Between [Beginning Date] and
[Ending Date]
```

When you execute the query that includes the above criteria, Access will display two dialog boxes—one right after the other. The first will ask you for the beginning date. Once you have typed in that date and pressed ↵, the second dialog box will appear, asking for the ending date. Type it in, press ↵ again, and Access will run your query.

See **Queries; Queries: Creating**

Be sure the names you put in brackets are not also field names in the table or dynaset on which you're basing your query. If they are, Access will attempt to get and use the value from those fields and will not prompt you to enter a value.

QUERIES: RENAMING FIELDS

Let's say you want the field name in your query to be called something different from the name for the same field in the table on which you're basing your query. Maybe you're listing contributors and their potential gifts to a fund-raising event, for example. In the underlying table, a Contributions table, the field might have the name "Amount." But in your dynaset you might want a more specific name for the same field—something like "Previously Gave," for example, to tell you what this contributor gave in the past, and to allow you to anticipate what they might give at an upcoming event.

You can give a field in your query a new name—one that is used only in the query—by prefixing the field name in the QBE grid's field box with the new field name, followed by a colon—like this:

```
Previously Gave: Amount
```

As another example, Figure Q.2 shows a QBE grid that takes a field called "Order Date" from the underlying table and renames it "Transaction Date" in the query.

See **Queries; Queries: Creating**

QUERIES: RUNNING EXISTING

So you've got your handy queries all saved up, and you want to just run one of them. Now what?

You can execute an existing query by following these easy steps:

1. Click on the Query button to get a list of the queries that are available in the Database window. The Query button looks like this:

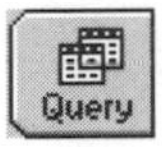

2. Select a query from the list and click on Open. If you want to look at the structure of the query, click on the Design button.

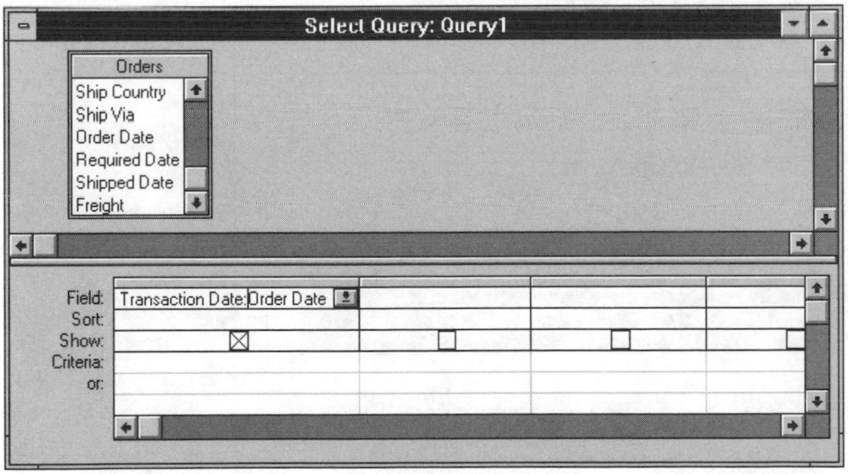

Figure Q.2

You can rename the field for the purposes of your query <u>without</u> changing the name of the field in the underlying table.

Select Query: Query1

Orders
Ship Country
Ship Via
Order Date
Required Date
Shipped Date
Freight

Field:	Transaction Date:Order Date				
Sort:					
Show:	☒		☐	☐	☐
Criteria:					
or:					

If you are opening a select query, you will see a datasheet. If you picked an action query in step 1, Access will warn that you are about to start an action query. You can execute the query or bail out.

Select queries and action queries have two different icons that appear next to their names in the Database window.

Icon	What It Is
🗔	Select Query
🗔!	Action Query

---

(66) **If you click on an existing Action Query, it will try to perform its duties and a warning message will appear to verify that that is what should happen. This warning message does not occur when you click on any other type of existing query.**

See **Datasheet View; Queries; Queries: Creating**

QUERIES: SAVING FOR LATER USE

In database management, as in life, you often find yourself asking the same questions over and over, sometimes with a little variation. When you meet people, you may ask them, "Where are you from?" Or you vary the question a little, asking instead, "Are you from here?" Either way, it's basically the same question. To save yourself time and energy re-creating queries that you commonly use, you should save those puppies. You can save a query by any of the following methods:

- ✪ In Query Design view, Select File ➤ Save, or File ➤ Save As.

- ✪ In Datasheet View, select File ➤ Save Query, or File ➤ Save Query As.

- ✪ If your query is new or if you have changed it since the last time you ran it, when you close the query window, Access will ask you if you want to save the thing. Better yet, if you haven't saved your query before, Access will prompt you for a name for the query.

············· Tip ·····················

When you name a query, a file, or anything else in life, you should name it something that will remind you what the thing is. In the case of queries, try to come up with a name that tells you what the query actually does. Since a query is stored as an Access object, you can use up to 64 characters, including spaces, in its name. You can't use periods, exclamation marks, @, or brackets. Other than that, the limits have to do more with what's reasonable and helpful than with what's possible. Naming a query W or % isn't very helpful. Naming it WomenManagers or RenewingSubscribers% would be better.

QUERIES: SHOWING AND HIDING FIELDS

Sometimes you will want to include a field in a query just to sort on it or to use it in a criteria. For example, if you were combining the First Name field with the Last Name field in your query—so as to present only a full name in the results of the query—you would not then want to sort on the full name, because the sort would alphabetize your data based on the first letter of the first name. To solve this problem (having set things up to combine the First Name and Last Name fields), you can include a duplicate Last Name field, make that a hidden field, and perform your sort on just the hidden Last Name field.

When you have a field that you need to include in the QBE grid but don't want to appear in the resulting dynaset, turn off (deselect) the Show check box. This causes the field not to show up the resulting dynaset, although the field is still in the QBE grid.

See **Queries; Queries: Creating**

QUERIES: SORTING DATA ON A FIELD

Let's say you want the results of your query to be presented to you in some specific order—alphabetical, for example—to make it easier for you to read the results.

You can sort the dynaset that will result from your query, and you can base that sort on any of the fields you include in your query. To do this:

1. From the top row of the QBE grid, find the name of the field on which you want to base the sort. Follow that column down 'til you get to the cell that's in the Sort row.

2. Place your mouse pointer on that cell and click. A button with a little down-arrow will appear in the cell.

3. Click on that button to pull down the Sort list.

4. Select a Sort order from the following options:

   Ascending Sorts from the beginning of the alphabet to the end, or from the smallest number to the largest. (Ignores the case—uppercase or lowercase—of letters.)

   Descending Sorts from the end of the alphabet to the beginning, or from the largest numbers to the smallest. (Again, ignores the case of letters.)

   (not sorted) Does not sort. (Select this to turn off the sort for an individual field.)

5. Finally, to execute the query, click on the Execute button.

See **Filters and Sorts; Queries; Queries: Creating; Quick Sort**

A
B
C
D
E
F
G
H
I
J
KL
M
N
O
P
Q
R
S
T
U
V
W
XYZ

QUERIES: STATISTICAL ANALYSIS WITH

If you're the type to want your data to do a lot of dancing through hoops, you can also use queries to produce statistical information based on your tables.

See **Queries; Totals Queries**

QUERIES: VIEWING THEIR RESULTS

Sooner or later you're going to want to have a look at the results of your query. Maybe you'll want to check things out during the process of designing your query, or maybe you're finished with the design and you want to see the data that's resulting from all your heavy questioning.

To see the data that's resulting from your query displayed in Datasheet View, click on the Datasheet icon in the toolbar:

To switch back to the Query Design View window, just click on the Query Design View icon (the one that's two to the left of the Datasheet icon):

You can switch back and forth as often as you like, making changes when you're in Query Design View, then looking at the results, making more changes…and on, and on.

66 **In addition to viewing the results of your query in Datasheet View, you can save your query and then use it as the basis of a form or report.**

QUERY

See **Queries; Queries: Basic Types**

QUERY WIZARDS

Access 2 is chock full of new Wizards. The Query Wizards are meant to help you create a number of popular queries in the blink of an eye. Using the Query Wizards, you can create any of these queries:

- ✪ Crosstab query
- ✪ Find Duplicates query
- ✪ Find Unmatched query
- ✪ Archive query

To use any Query Wizard, you must open the database file you want to query.

Then, with the Database window open, you can either:

○ Click the Queries button to display the list of existing queries, then click the New button.

○ Select File ➤ New ➤ Query from the menu bar.

Access will display the New Query dialog box (Figure Q.3).

Click on the Query Wizard button and the Query Wizards dialog box will appear. To choose the Query Wizard you want to use, highlight its type in the list of type names and click on the OK button. Access will display a series of dialog boxes; which specific ones appear will depend on which type of query you chose. In the next sections that follow, we'll go over each of the queries you can create with the Query Wizards.

See **Queries; Queries: Basic Types; Queries: Creating**

Crosstab Query Wizard

The Crosstab Query Wizard allows you to create a crosstab query—which displays your data in row-and-column format, taking column heads from actual data in your tables—in a snap.

To use the Crosstab Query Wizard, from the Query Wizards window:

1. Highlight Crosstab Query in the list of types and click on the OK button. The Crosstab Query Wizard dialog box appears (Figure Q.4).

2. In the list box near the top of the Crosstab Query Wizard dialog box, you'll select the source of data for the query. You can base your crosstab query on any table or dynaset in the current database file. You can list Tables, Queries, or Both in the list box by selecting the buttons just below the list box. For example, when you select the Queries button, all the queries in the current

A B C D E F G H I J KL M N O P Q R S T U V W XYZ

Figure Q.3
••••••••••••••••••••••••••••••
The New Query dialog box

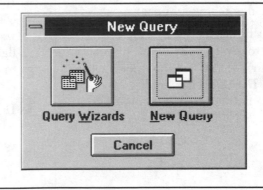

Figure Q.4
....

The Crosstab Query Wizard
dialog box

Crosstab Query Wizard

This Wizard creates a
crosstab query that displays
data in a compact,
spreadsheet-like format.

Select the table or query that
contains the data you want for
your crosstab query, and then
click the Next button.

Categories
Customers
Employees
Order Details
Orders
Products

View:
◉ Tables   ○ Queries   ○ Both

Sample:

	Header1	Header2	Header3
	TOTAL		

Hint   Cancel   < Back   Next >   Finish

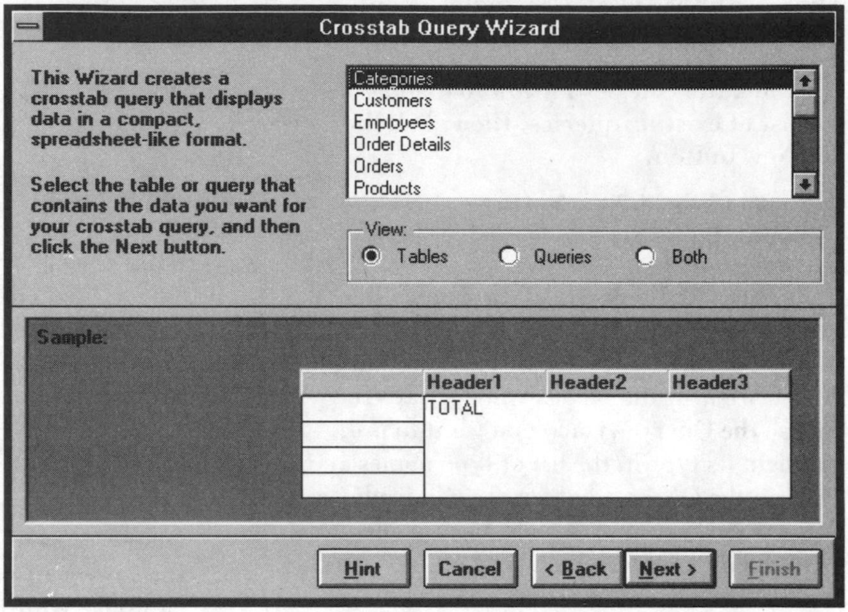

database file will appear in the list box.
Selecting Tables will display all the tables in the current database file. Once
you have selected the source of data
for the crosstab query, click on the
Next button. Another Crosstab Query
Wizard dialog box will appear.

3. Here, you'll tell Access on which fields
you want to group your data. You can
group your data on as many fields as
you wish. Highlight the field(s) you
want and click on the move-one-field
button

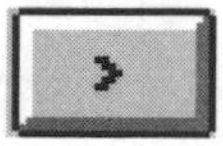

to move the fields into the list box on
the right. When you're finished, click
on the Next button. Yet another Crosstab Query Wizard dialog box will
appear.

4. In this dialog box, you need to tell Access which field holds the data you
want to turn into row headings. Highlight the field and click the Next button
to continue. Another dialog box appears, asking for more information.

5. In this dialog box, you'll tell Access
where (from which field) to get the information you want to display. Select
the field by clicking on its name in the
Available Fields list box.

6. Then, in the Function list box, pick any aggregate functions you want Access to use when the query is executed. (For more on aggregate functions, *see* Totals Queries.) When you're done with this, click on Next to continue. The final Crosstab Query Wizard dialog box will appear.

7. Here, you can either accept the name Access proposes for your query, or type a more descriptive name in the text box near the top of the window.

8. Be sure to select "Open the query to view the data." Click on the Finish button and you're all done.

Access will create the crosstab query you and the Wizard just whipped up, and execute it. In just a moment, you'll see a datasheet showing the results of your crosstab query.

66 You can have only 1,000 column heads in a crosstab query. If Access displays an error message when you run your query telling you that you have too many column heads, cancel out of the Wizard by clicking OK. Then go back and start again. This time, swap the fields you are grouping on with those you're using as column heads.

See **Crosstab Queries: Creating**

Find Duplicates Query Wizard

With the help of the Find Duplicates Query Wizard, you can quickly find duplicate records in your tables. In a mailing list, this is *really* handy. You can find duplicate records and then purge them from your mailing list, which obviously will save beaucoup postage costs if your mailing list has been around the block a few times.

To use the Find Duplicates Query Wizard, from the Query Wizards window:

1. Highlight Find Duplicates Query in the list of types and click on the OK button. The Find Duplicates Query Wizard dialog box appears.

2. In this dialog box, you'll select the source table or dynaset—the one that contains the data for which you want to find any duplicates. The source can be any table or query in your current database file. Highlight the name of the source table or dynaset in the displayed list, then click on Next. The next Find Duplicates Query Wizard dialog box will appear.

3. Select the fields in the source table or dynaset for which you want to find duplicates. Highlight each field you want to include and click on the add-one-field button:

When you're done, click on Next. Access displays yet another Find Duplicates Query Wizard dialog box.

4. Here, you can tell Access which *additional* fields you want to display. These fields will be displayed in the datasheet, but will not be used as part of the criteria for finding duplicate records. Highlight the name of each field you want to include and click on the add-one-field button. When you're done, click on Next to continue. The final Find Duplicates Query Wizard dialog box will appear.

5. Now you'll tell Access what you want to name your query. You can accept the name the Wizard suggests or you can type a more descriptive name into the text box. Click on Finish when you're done.

Access will create your query and execute it, taking just a few seconds to do so. Then the results of your query will appear in a datasheet.

Find Unmatched Query Wizard

The Find Unmatched Query Wizard helps you find those records in one table that have no related records in a second table. This is the sort of thing you might want to do when you want to find out which customers haven't placed orders, for example. You could check the Customers table against the Orders table using a Find Unmatched query, and the result would be a list of Customers with no records in the Orders table.

To use the Find Unmatched Query Wizard from the Query Wizards window:

1. Highlight Find Unmatched Query in the list of types and click on the OK button. The Find Unmatched Query Wizard dialog box (Figure Q.5) appears.

2. Here, you'll select the source table or dynaset (the Customers table is the source table in our example). The source can be any table or query that is in your current database file. Highlight the name of the source from the list displayed in the dialog box, and click on Next. The next Find Unmatched Query Wizard dialog box will appear.

3. In this dialog box, you'll select the table or dynaset you want to check records against. (This would be the Orders table in our example.) Highlight the name of the table or dynaset to select it, then click on Next to continue. Another dialog box will appear (Figure Q.6), asking for more information.

4. Here, you'll tell Access which field in the two tables contains related information. *(This is the same field you'd use to create a* join *between the two tables.)* In our Customers/Orders example, this would be the Customer ID field—the field that appears in both tables. Two boxes appear in the dialog box; the one on the left shows the fields in the table (or dynaset) you chose first, and the one on the right shows the fields in the table (or dynaset) you chose to check against. In both boxes, the name of the shared field (Customer ID in our example) will be highlighted. This is usually the appropriate choice; if it isn't, you

Figure Q.5

You'll start telling Access about the query you want to create in the Find Unmatched Query Wizard dialog box.

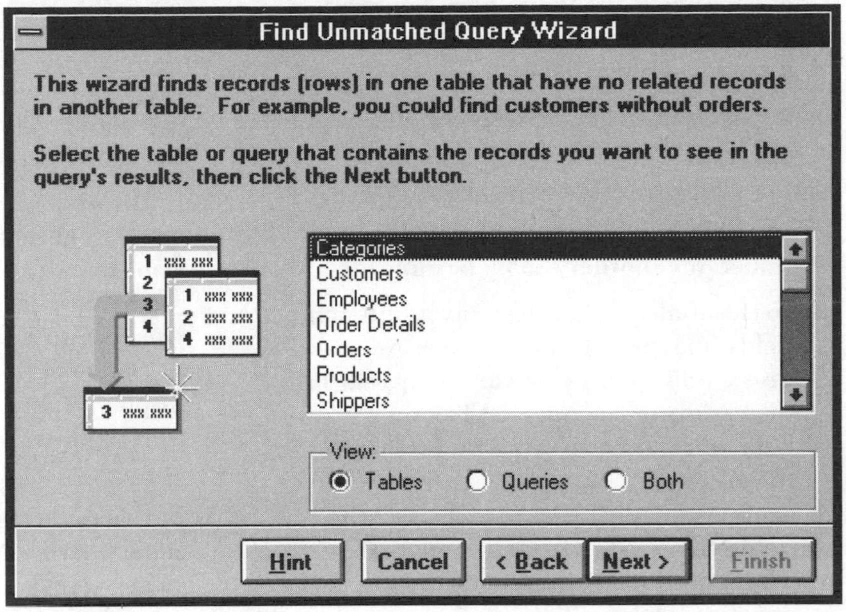

Find Unmatched Query Wizard

This wizard finds records (rows) in one table that have no related records in another table. For example, you could find customers without orders.

Select the table or query that contains the records you want to see in the query's results, then click the Next button.

Categories
Customers
Employees
Order Details
Orders
Products
Shippers

View:
● Tables   ○ Queries   ○ Both

Hint | Cancel | < Back | Next > | Finish

Figure Q.6

The name of the shared field will be highlighted.

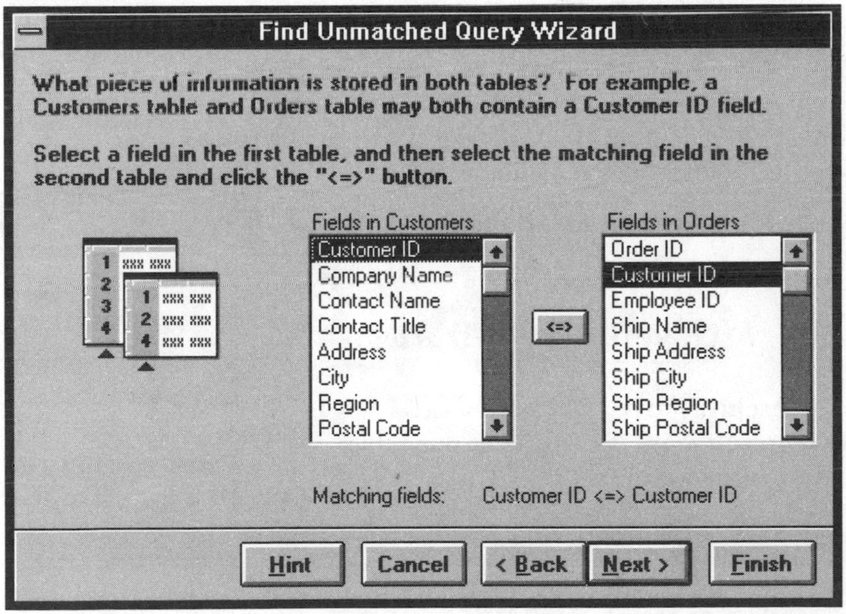

Find Unmatched Query Wizard

What piece of information is stored in both tables? For example, a Customers table and Orders table may both contain a Customer ID field.

Select a field in the first table, and then select the matching field in the second table and click the "<=>" button.

Fields in Customers
Customer ID
Company Name
Contact Name
Contact Title
Address
City
Region
Postal Code

<=>

Fields in Orders
Order ID
Customer ID
Employee ID
Ship Name
Ship Address
Ship City
Ship Region
Ship Postal Code

Matching fields: Customer ID <=> Customer ID

Hint | Cancel | < Back | Next > | Finish

A B C D E F G H I J KL M N O P Q R S T U V W XYZ

can highlight the field names you prefer to use and click on the button with a double-headed arrow:

In either case, click on Next to continue. Yet another dialog box appears.

5. In this dialog box, select any additional fields (maybe Customer Name, Address, and so on) you want to appear in the results of the query. Click on a field you want to include and then on the add-one-field button, and do that again in turn 'til you've picked all the fields you want. Then click on Next. The final Find Unmatched Query Wizard dialog box will appear.

6. Here, you'll name your query. You can either accept the name the Wizard has come up with for the query or you can type a more descriptive name into the text box. Click on Finish when you're done.

Access will create, then execute, the query. When all this is done, you'll see the results of your query in a datasheet.

See **Joins and Relationships**

Archive Query Wizard

The Archive Query Wizard works its magic to help you move records from one table into a second table.

To use the Archive Query Wizard, from the Query Wizards window:

1. Highlight Archive Query in the list of types and click on the OK button. The Archive Wizard dialog box appears.

2. In the dialog box, you'll select the table or dynaset that contains the data you want to move into another table. The source can be any table or query in your current database file. Highlight the name of the data source from the displayed list and click on Next. The next Archive Wizard dialog box will appear.

3. In this dialog box, you'll describe the criteria Access will use to decide to archive records. Select the field from the drop-down box labeled "This value," and the relational operator from the drop-down box labeled "Is." Type a value in the *text* box labeled "This value." Click on Next to continue.

4. In the next dialog box, Access actually shows you the records it will archive based on the criteria you specified. If

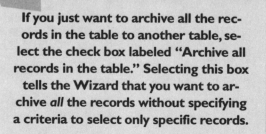

·············Tip·····················

If you just want to archive all the records in the table to another table, select the check box labeled "Archive all records in the table." Selecting this box tells the Wizard that you want to archive *all* the records without specifying a criteria to select only specific records.

this list is correct, click on Next. If it's not, go back by clicking on the Back button and change the criteria. When you're finished, click on Next. Another dialog box will appear.

5. Here, you'll tell Access if it should copy the records from the original table to the new one without deleting them in the original table (*copy records*), or copy the records *and delete them* from the original table (*move records*). Select one of the options and click on Next. The final Archive Wizard dialog box will appear.

6. You can either accept the Wizard's suggested query name as it appears in the dialog box or type a more descriptive name in the text box instead. Click Finish when you're done.

Access will create and execute the query. Depending on which option you chose, the records will be copied or moved. You can view the results of your query by viewing each of the tables or dynasets involved in the procedure.

See **Queries; Queries: Basic Types; Queries: Creating; Queries: Saving for Later Use**

QUICK SORT

Quick Sort is a handy feature that allows you to sort data with a single click of the mouse.

To use Quick Sort, you must start with a table displayed on screen in Datasheet View *or* with a table or query displayed in

a form. In the toolbar at the top of your screen, you'll see two Quick Sort icons:

Operator	Meaning
	Sorts in ascending order—from A to Z
	Sorts in descending order—from Z to A

Using Quick Sort is a snap:

1. Click in the field on which you want to sort, to make it the active field.

2. Click on either of the two Quick Sort icons in the toolbar.

In an instant, your data will be sorted in the order you specified.

Every table's datasheet or form has a Sort/Filter property (which we discuss in Filters and Sorts). Quick Sort is just a shortcut built into the program—it works by modifying the Sort/Filter property.

If, after you've sorted the data, you change your mind, just click on the Show All Records icon

on the toolbar. The data will appear in its original, unsorted version.

See **Filters and Sorts; Queries: Sorting Data With**

QUITTING ACCESS

See **Exiting Access**

R

r

RANDOM ACCESS MEMORY

RAM is the short way to say **Random Access Memory**. Random access memory, also just called *memory*, is where your computer stores information that it is processing. You need at least 6 MB of memory to run Access. Believe us when we say you'd rather have 8 or 16 MB, and the more the better.

Unfortunately, this memory thing is a bit complicated. Sometimes when you're opening windows or doing something else seemingly simple in Access or any other Windows application, a message might pop up saying you're out of memory.

The total amount of memory (both physical RAM and *virtual memory*, or disk space that Windows tricks your computer into treating as memory) usually is not what stops you. Windows has two 64K *heaps*, or special data structures in which it stores information. No matter how much more memory you put in your computer, these two 64K heaps are always 64K big in Windows versions 3.*x*.

If you try to open a new window or start up a new application and you get a message that sounds like "Out of Resources" or "Out of Memory," it means that one of these 64K heaps is full. Windows 3.1 reduces the amount of information it tries to keep in these heaps as compared to Windows 3.0, and that helps. This may be fixed in Windows 4.0.

RDBMS

A relational database management system, or *RDBMS* (like Access), is a database system in which the data is stored in tables which can be related to each other through those fields that they have in common.

See **Part I**

A
B
C
D
E
F
G
H
I
J
KL
M
N
O
P
Q
R
S
T
U
V
W
XYZ

RECORD

In an Access table, the collection of data about one particular thing is known as a *record*.

See **Part I**

REFERENTIAL INTEGRITY

Referential integrity is the feature in Access that makes the relationships between different tables stable.

See **Joins and Relationships; Joins: Referential Integrity In**

RELATIONAL DATABASE

See **Part I**

RELATIONAL OPERATOR

See **Comparison Operator; Expressions: Components**

REPORT

A printed, meaningful analysis of data is a *report*.

See **Reports and Report Wizards**

REPORTS: CREATING WITH REPORT WIZARDS

Report Wizards are the almost supernatural feature in Access that creates forms or reports based on your answers to a few questions.

Here is what you do to start creating a report using the Report Wizard:

1. Display the reports in the Database window.

2. Click on the New button.

3. In the New Report dialog box (Figure R.1) shown below, enter the name of the table or dynaset you are basing your report on, or click on the little box with the down arrow in it and pick the name from the list that appears.

4. Click the Report Wizards button to start the Report Wizard. You'll see a dialog box (Figure R.2) in which you pick the type of report you want the Wizard to whip up for you. There are six alternatives:

Single-Column Produces a report in which the fields appear one below another, in a *single column* (that's how it got its name).

Groups/Totals Produces a report showing data displayed in rows and columns, allowing you to group data by a common field, and to total certain fields.

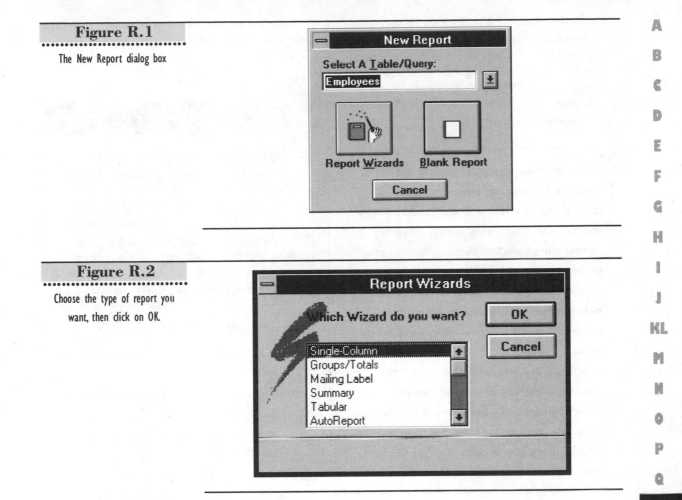

A
B
C
D
E
F
G
H
I
J
KL
M
N
O
P
Q
R
S
T
U
V
W
XYZ

Figure R.1

The New Report dialog box

Figure R.2

Choose the type of report you want, then click on OK.

AutoReport Produces a report that looks like a Single-Column report—you aren't asked any questions while the Wizard is creating this one, though, so it looks pretty generic. The Auto-Report report displays *all* the fields in the table or dynaset on which the report is based.

Summary Produces a report showing data summarized in groups. Both totals and grand totals are included for selected fields.

Tabular Produces a report showing data displayed as fields in columns across the page, like a table.

Mailing Label Produces a report showing data laid out in mailing list format. (In fact, you'll get to choose from a list of all the Avery label stock numbers, so you can print any standard layout for your mailing labels. This is a *real* boon to humankind.)

In many database programs, you must describe the mailing labels you plan to use by saying what size the labels are (in inches) and how many labels there are across the page. The Report Wizard assumes you're going to use Avery labels, and asks the stock number for the labels you're using. If you're using some other brand of labels—Winky Mailordermaven's Brand X labels, or whatever—you'll usually find that the label sizes are the same as one or another of Avery's label sizes. Sometimes they'll even tell you on the Brand X package which Avery stock number they correspond to, in size and layout.

Single-Column Reports

A Single-Column report places each field of data on its own line. One field appears below another, in a single column running down the report. One record appears as a column of fields, and then another record appears the same way, then another, and another....

This just keeps going as long as you want.

Single-Column reports are ideal for data that does not lend itself to a column-and-row grid.

Tip

Unlike forms, reports do not have a Sort/Filter property. You can tell the Wizard to sort the fields in your report in a certain order, but you cannot filter out records to be included in the report. If you want to get around this, base your reports on dynasets rather than tables. This allows you to modify the underlying query to make it select those records you want to include in your report.

To create a Single-Column report using the Report Wizard:

1. Select Single-Column in the first Report Wizards dialog box.

2. The Report Wizard displays a dialog box (Figure R.3) in which you pick fields to include in the report.

At first you'll find that all the fields in the table or dynaset you picked to base the report on are listed in the Available Fields list box on the left side. Your mission, should you choose to accept it, is to get those fields you want to include in your report from the Available Fields list box to the Field Order on Report list box on the right side of the window.

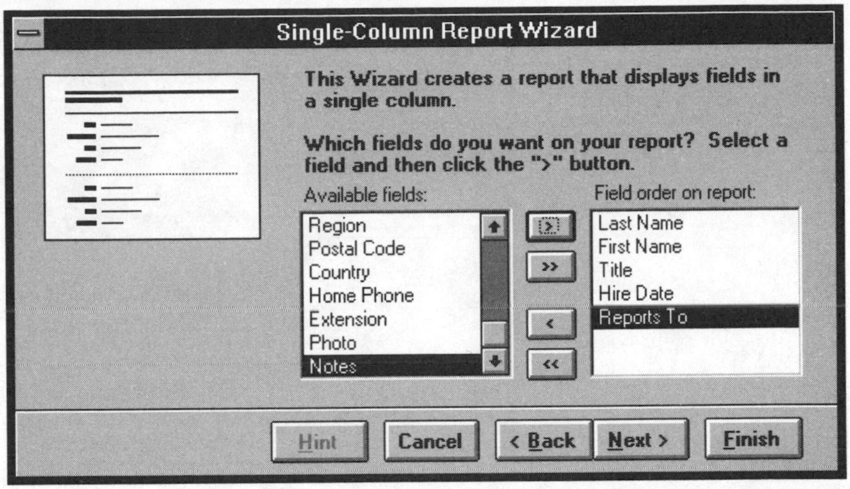

Figure R.3

In this dialog box, you'll select the fields you want included in your report.

Single-Column Report Wizard

This Wizard creates a report that displays fields in a single column.

Which fields do you want on your report? Select a field and then click the ">" button.

Available fields:

Region
Postal Code
Country
Home Phone
Extension
Photo
Notes

Field order on report:

Last Name
First Name
Title
Hire Date
Reports To

Hint | Cancel | < Back | Next > | Finish

To move one field from the box on the left to the box on the right, highlight the field on the left and click on this button:

To move *all* of the fields in the box on the left to the box on the right, click on:

If you make a mistake and want to move some fields back to the left from the box on the right, you can highlight those fields and click on:

And if you completely change your mind and want to hustle *all* of the fields in the box on the right back to the left, click on:

Once you have moved fields all around to your heart's content, and you have all the fields you want to include on your report listed in the box on the right, click the Next button. The Wizard will instantly display another dialog box (Figure R.4) where it asks you to tell it which of the fields in the report you want to use for the *sort*. (The sort order tells Access in what order you want the records to appear on your report.)

A B C D E F G H I J KL M N O P Q R S T U V W XYZ

Figure R.4

Figure R.4
....
In this dialog box, select the field
you want to sort by.

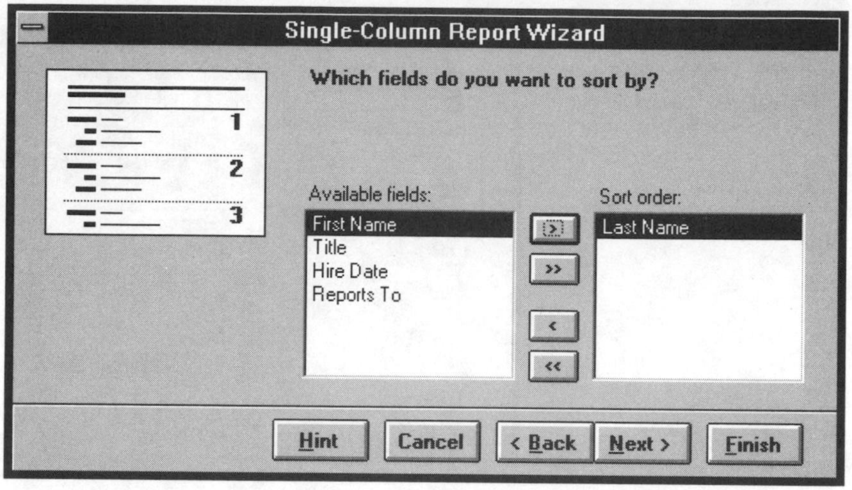

Single-Column Report Wizard

Which fields do you want to sort by?

1
2
3

Available fields:

First Name
Title
Hire Date
Reports To

Sort order:

Last Name

Hint   Cancel   < Back   Next >   Finish

You pick the sort order of the report by moving the fields you want to sort on from the Available Fields list box on the left side to the Field Order on Report list box on the right using the same set of buttons with funny pointers on them that you used to move fields around. You can put a bunch of fields in the box—all of them, if you want. Access is going to sort your report in the order in which you listed the fields.

So let's say you're working with a gigantic mailing list, chock full of Swopes, Szmuks, and Heffendragers. If you put in the Last Name Field first, all the Heffendragers will come first, then all the Swopes, then all the Szmuks. If you listed only the Last Name field, that'll be the end of things. But if you put the First Name field in second, all the Heffendragers will still be before the Swopes, *and* they'll be sorted again, this time by their first names. Then if you put in the ZIP code as your third field in the sort order, all the Gilda Heffendragers (how many can there be?) will be sorted by ZIP code.

Once you have specified the order in which you want your report sorted, click on the Next button to move on.

The one last thing the Report Wizard needs to know is the style you want for your report. You'll be presented with a dialog box asking for the "Kind of look" you want your report to have. Your choices for looks are:

Executive has double lines above and below column headings.

Presentation has single, bold lines above and below column headings.

Ledger has a column-and-row grid around data.

As you click on different looks, the Wizard will display a sample along the left hand side of the dialog box.

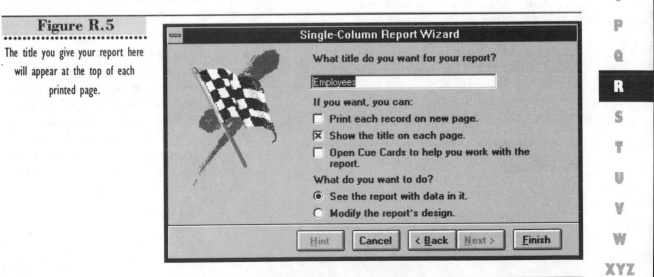

You can tell Access whether you want the report to print in portrait or landscape orientation by clicking on either the Portrait or Landscape option box. (See Printing) You can also control the amount of space between each line of the report the Wizard creates by selecting a value from the Line Spacing drop-down list. The default value of ¹/₁₂" works well.

Once you have picked the look you want, click on the Next button to move along.

In the Report Wizard's last dialog box (Figure R.5) you'll get to title your report. The Wizard in its wisdom will suggest that you give your report the same name as the underlying table or dynaset. You can follow the Wizard's advice, or you can type in any name you want. If you're going to have a number of reports based on the same table or dynaset, you probably want to give your reports different names—not Customers1, Customers2, and Customers3, but something more memorable and informative.

The name you give to your report will appear as a title at the top of each printed page.

Once you have named the report you can view it either in Print Preview mode, or in Design View. Click on the button labeled "See the report with data in it" to see the report in Print Preview mode, or click on the button labeled "Modify the report's design" to bring the report up in Design View. Then click on Finish.

When you close the Report Preview or Design window, Access will prompt you to save the report.

See   **Reports: Saving**

Figure R.5
....

The title you give your report here will appear at the top of each printed page.

Groups/Totals Reports

Groups/Totals reports are great for summarizing information. They allow you to group related records of your database together and display the totals of selected fields within the group. For example, you might want to use this to produce a report that groups sales by salesperson and sums up each salesperson's sales for the month.

To use the Report Wizard to create a Groups/Totals report:

1. Follow the directions in Reports: Creating with Report Wizards to start creating your report.

2. Select Groups/Totals from the list of available report types, and click on OK.

3. Access will display a dialog box asking you for the fields to place on the report. All the fields that are available to include on the report are listed in the Available Fields list box on the left side of the dialog box. The fields that will be included on the report are in the Fields Order on Report list box on the right side. Move fields from the Available Fields list box (on the left) to the Fields Order on Report list box (on the right) by highlighting the field you want to move and clicking on this button:

If you want to move all of the fields from left to right, click on:

You can remove single fields from the Fields Order on Report list box by highlighting them and clicking this button:

If you want to remove *all* the fields and start over, click on this button:

4. Once you are satisfied that all the fields you want to include on the report are in the Fields Order on Report list box on the right side of the window, click on the Next button. (That's the one that says *Next* on it.)

5. The Report Wizard now wants to know which of the fields you are including in your report make up a group. (Remember—a field that makes up a group contains the same data for related items— a company name, or a date, or two things you would commonly group your data on.) Pick the fields you want to group on and move them over to the box labeled "Group records by," using the same buttons you have used before. You can have as many as three groups in a single report.

6. Once you have selected the fields you want to group on, click the Next button.

7. Now you have to tell the Wizard how you want it to group data for each of the fields you have selected to group on. You can group data either on the entire field or on the first however many (*n*) characters of the field. If each related record contains the same data in the field which you are grouping, you should select Normal. If you want to group on some prefix in a field—say the first two characters of an ID field—you should select the appropriate choice. Each of the fields you picked to group on appears in the list on the right side; you should pick each in turn and tell the Wizard how to group the data within them.

8. Once you have told the Wizard how to group your data, click on the Next button to move onward.

9. In the next dialog box (Figure R.6), you tell the Wizard on which of the fields in your report you want to sort. Your data will be sorted by these fields, within each group.

This determines the order of items within the groups you have already defined. Select the sort fields by moving them from the Available Fields window to the window labeled "Sort within groups by," by highlighting fields and clicking on the now familiar buttons with arrows on them.

10. Once you have told the Wizard how to sort the fields, click on the Next button.

11. The next dialog box allows you to pick the look of your report. Click on report styles, and the Wizard will display a sample along the left side of the dialog box. You can choose from:

Executive has double lines above and below column headings.

Presentation has single, bold lines above and below column headings.

···Tip···

Sometimes you'll want a row-and-column report—one that displays all your information in nice rows and columns. The Report Wizard doesn't list a row-and-column report as one of your options, so you may think it can't create a report of this type. By using the Groups/Totals report in a tricky way, you can create a report that looks like column and rows. To do this, leave the box labeled "Group records by" empty. The report that results will show data arranged in rows and columns—not grouped together. It's a bit like having another Wizard at your disposal.

A
B
C
D
E
F
G
H
I
J
KL
M
N
O
P
Q
R
S
T
U
V
W
XYZ

Figure R.6

Select the sort order here.

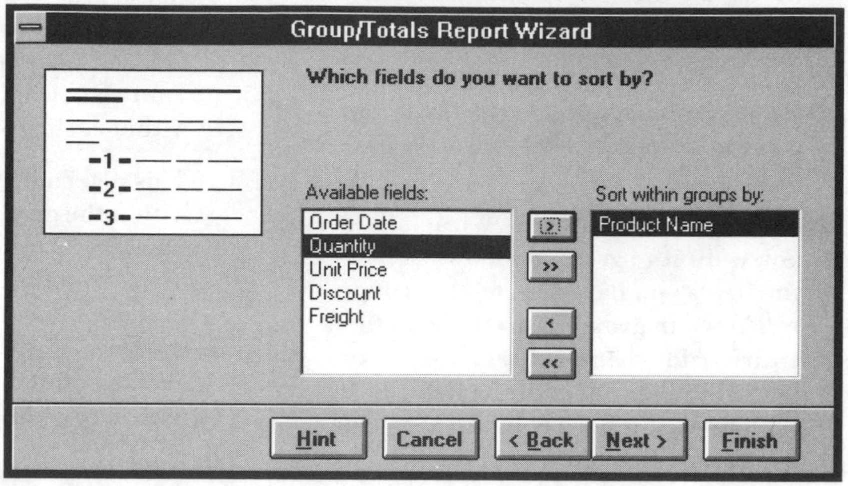

Group/Totals Report Wizard

Which fields do you want to sort by?

Available fields:
- Order Date
- Quantity
- Unit Price
- Discount
- Freight

Sort within groups by:
- Product Name

Hint | Cancel | < Back | Next > | Finish

Ledger has a column-and-row grid around data.

> 🛣️ **You can control the amount of space between each line of the report the Wizard creates by selecting a value from the Line Spacing drop-down list. The default value of ¹/₁₂" works well.**

Once you have selected the look you want, click on Next to move on.

12. In the last dialog box you get to name your report. The name appears as a title at the top of each page that you print out. The Wizard suggests using the same name as the table or query upon which you've based the report,

but you can type anything you want into the Report title field.

> 🛣️ **If you want the Wizard to force all of the fields you've selected to fit across a single page, select the box labeled "See all the fields on one page." The Wizard will then shrink the fields to make them all fit.**

13. Once you have entered a title for it, you can view the report either in Design View or in Print Preview mode. Click on the button labeled "Modify the report's design" to view the report in Design View. Or click on the button labeled "See the report with data in it" to take a look at it in Print Preview mode. Print Preview mode lets you see how it will look when you print the thing. When you are done, click on Finish.

When you close the report's Preview or Design window, Access will ask you if you want to save your report.

See **Reports and Report Wizards; Reports: Saving**

Creating Mailing Labels

If you have ever wrestled with another database program or a word processor to get it to print out sheets of labels, you'll really appreciate how much easier it is now, with the help of the Access Report Wizard.

To call a mailing label feature a *report* may seem a bit odd at first. But think about this a minute—you print other reports in Access by pulling data from your table or dynaset and organizing it on the page in an appropriate way. So why shouldn't you do the same with mailing labels?

The Report Wizard makes creating and printing mailing labels on a laser printer a real breeze. All you need to know is the Avery stock number of the labels you are printing on and which fields you want to place on the label. You don't even have to remember that you need to know these things—the Wizard will ask you, and offer you choices. You answer with multiple-choice-style answers, pop your labels into the printer's paper tray, and before you can say "Bibbity-Bobbity-Boo," out they pop, ready to stick on envelopes, and mail.

To create labels using the Report Wizard:

1. Follow the directions in the section called Reports: Creating with Report Wizards to get started.

2. Select Mailing Label as your report type, and click on OK.

3. The Report Wizard will present you with a dialog box (Figure R.7).

Now, this dialog box looks a bit more complicated than some, but not to worry. The Wizard wants to know which fields you want to place on the label and where they should appear. Use the buttons shown in Table R.1 to place text on the labels.

4. Once you have placed all the fields and other characters that you want to appear on the label, click on the Next button to move along.

5. The Wizard will display the dialog box in which you tell the Wizard on what field it should sort. You'll usually want to sort on

A B C D E F G H I J KL M N O P Q R S T U V W XYZ

Figure R.7
·····················
In this dialog box, you'll set up
your mailing labels in a snap.

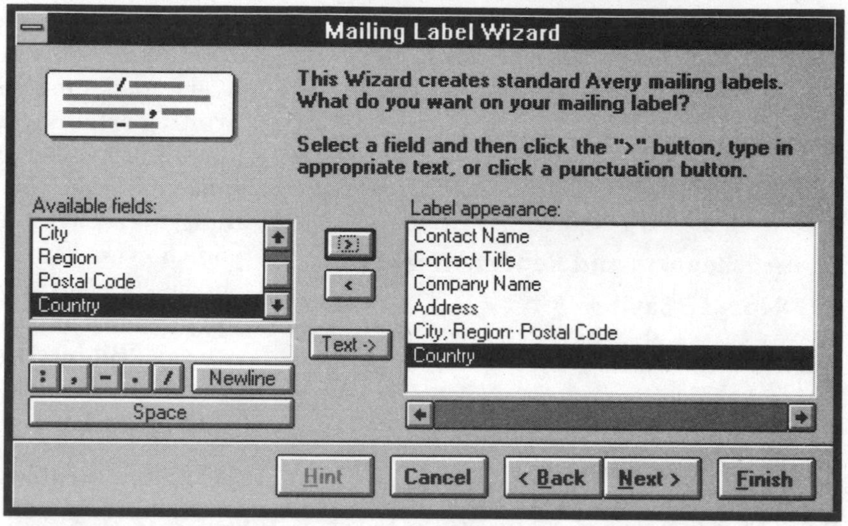

either ZIP code or Last Name. Pick the fields you want to sort on by highlighting them and clicking on the now familiar arrow buttons to move them around. Once you have selected the fields on which you want to sort, click on the Next button to continue.

6. In the dialog box shown in Figure R.8 Access gives you a list of Avery label stock numbers, along with a list telling you the number of labels across the sheet and the size of the labels for each stock number. All you need to know is the stock number for the Avery labels you are using. You can get that number from the Avery label packaging. To select the Avery label you're using, click on its stock number in the list.

7. Once you have selected the labels, click on the Next button.

66 **If, for some reason, you want to use metric measurements instead of English, select the Metric button, and the list of Avery label sizes will be converted.**

8. Now a dialog box appears which allows you to pick the font used on the mailing labels. You can either leave the default settings as they are or you can pick a new font name, font size, or font weight. You can select a style (italic or underline). You can even pick a text color (although, you need a color printer to print out color labels). Once you have specified the font to use, click on the Next button.

Table R.1

Use These Buttons to Place Text on Mailing Labels

Button	What It Does
[>]	Adds the highlighted field to the label.
<	Removes the highlighted field from the label.
Text ->	Places the text you have typed into the text box on the label. (To use this button, first point and click in the text box to its right and enter the text you want to include on the label. Then click on the button to add the text to the label.)
:	Adds a colon (:) to the label.
,	Adds a comma (,) to the label.
-	Adds a hyphen (-) to the label.
.	Adds a period (.) to the label.
/	Adds a slash (/) to the label.
Newline	Starts a new line on the label.
Space	Adds a space to the label. (Spaces appear as dots in the Label Appearance box so you can tell where they are located.)
→	Allows you to scroll around from left to right in the window that contains what you are placing on your label—pretty handy when you want to place more stuff on a line than the Wizard can display in the box labeled "Label appearance."
←	Allows you to scroll around from right to left in the window that contains what you are placing on your label. Again, this is handy when you want to place more stuff on a line than the Wizard can display in the box labeled "Label appearance."

A B C D E F G H I J KL M N O P Q **R** S T U V W XYZ

Figure R.8

Now, this is the dialog box that's worth a million.

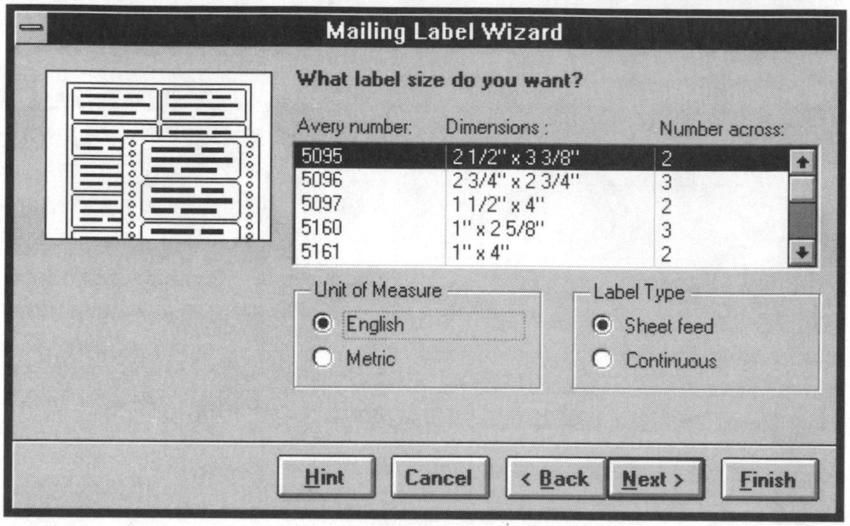

9. Another dialog box will appear, telling you that you can preview the labels you have created by selecting the button labeled "See the mailing labels as they will look printed" or view them in Design View by selecting the button labeled "Modify the mailing label design." Click on Finish when you're ready to move in.

Mailing labels are reports, so you save and print them in the same way you would any other report.

After you view your labels, you are prompted to save the report, and to provide a name for them.

See **Form Letters: Creating by Using Reports; Mail Merge to Microsoft Word; Modifying Forms and Reports; Printing Reports; Reports and Report Wizards; Reports: Saving**

Tip

Mailing labels, unlike other reports the Wizard creates, can't be changed much. Once you've created them, take a look at your mailing labels in Design View to see what the Wizard has done for you, but if you need to change them it's really much easier to start over and create new labels from scratch.

REPORTS: PRINTING

See **Printing Reports**

REPORTS AND REPORT WIZARDS

The Report Wizard in Access works its magic on printed reports—the kind you use to explain or summarize information. Printed reports are the sort of thing you might want to give to your board of directors (to explain this year's budget), to the IRS (to justify your deductions), or to your boss (to justify your employment).

The Report Wizard does for reports what the Form Wizard does for forms—it turns the tedious, time-consuming work of creating a report into the simple matter of answering a few questions. You answer them, and the Report Wizard churns out businesslike sheets of printed data, all neatly arranged in easy-to-read styles and formats.

You can also use the Report Wizard to print mailing labels. If you're printing the ever popular and ever present standard-sized Avery labels, you don't even have to count how many are on a page or pull out a ruler to measure them. You just tell the Wizard the stock number for the Avery labels you're using (the number's on the package), and the Wizard lays out your mailing labels for you. The Wizard seems to know all.

Picking the Report Source

A report, like a form, is based on a table or dynaset. To create your report, you must start with an open Database window (remember, the database file contains the tables and dynasets on which you'll base your report). You can see a list of all the existing reports any time. Just click on the Report button.

Access will list all the existing reports for this particular database file in the Database window.

See **Reports: Creating with Report Wizards**

REPORTS: SAVING

So you're finished creating your report, whatever type and style it might be. It's a dandy report, and you want to keep it to use, modify, or print later.

It's a great idea to save some reports to use as a model for later reports that might be similar. That way, you won't have to create your report from scratch every time you want to set one up that's basically the same.

When you start to close either the Preview window or the Design window for a report you have created with the Wizard, Access will present a dialog box asking if you want to save the report. The dialog box will look like Figure R.9.

To save your report, click on the Yes button and a dialog box will appear asking you to name the report. Type a name into the Report Name box and click on OK. If you don't want to save your report, just click the Cancel button.

See **Save/Save As**

Tip

Access will suggest a name for your report. The suggested name will appear in the Report Name box, and will be woefully inadequate, in that it will provide no specific information or description for the report. As you know, it's really important to name things in a way that helps you remember what the thing is and why you kept it around. So don't just accept Access' naming suggestion. Think independently—you're a lot smarter than Access, and you know more about your business.

Figure R.9

This dialog box asks whether you want to save the report.

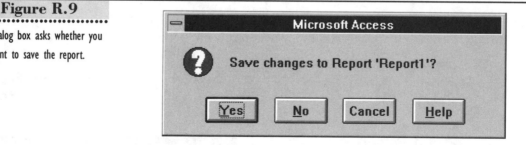

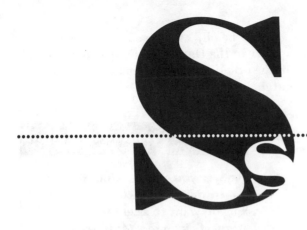

SAVE/SAVE AS

Save and Save As are standard Windows commands that generally appear in the File pull-down menu of any Windows program. They usually let you save whatever you're working on into its own file—either using an existing filename (Save) or using a new filename (Save As).

All the objects that make up your database are stored in a single Access database file. (You know this because you read Part 1, right?) Because of this, the Save command works a little differently in Access than in other Windows programs. In Access, when you save an object, it is saved *into the database file*. It is not saved into a separate file of its own, like a word processed document or a spreadsheet would be. The command's behavior even changes a little *within* Access, depending on what type of object you're dealing with, but generally it'll be like this.

After you've created or modified an object (a table, query, form, report, or any other object) in Access, you'll often want to save it so you can use it again in the future. You can save an object with the Save command in the File pull-down menu. The object will then be saved with the same name it had before you changed it.

When you open, use, and modify an existing object, you may find that you want to save it with a *new* name, so you'll later have both the original object and the new, modified one. In that case, you'll use the Save As command, which will give you the opportunity to provide a new name.

> **66** You don't have to do anything explicit to save the data in your tables. Access saves data for you as you enter it and close the tables. We are talking about saving <u>objects</u> here, not data. Remember that all the objects that make up your Access database are stored in a single .MDB file.

That's the way it generally works, but as we mentioned, it's sometimes a little different. As an example, when you have a query in Datasheet View, the menu items will read Save Query and Save Query As rather than Save and Save As.

Saving an Object with Its Existing Name

Select File ➤ Save to save an object if it already has a name. The cursor will turn briefly into an hourglass shape, and when it turns back into its usual shape, you'll know the object has been saved.

If you use Save and Access finds that the object does not have a name yet (oops!), the Save As dialog box will appear, and you can proceed as described in the next section.

Saving an Object with a New Name

Select File ➤ Save As to save an object with a new name. The Save As dialog box will appear. Access will suggest a name for the object, but the name will be very generic. You can accept that name if you like, by clicking on OK; or you can type in a new, more meaningful and descriptive name, and then click OK.

You can use up to 64 characters when you name the object, because it's an *object* and not a file. (For info on naming *Files*, *All* Database File: Naming)

Once the object is saved, its name will appear in the Database window along with all the other objects that make up your database.

·············Tip·············

Whenever you close a window that holds a modified object, Access will ask if you want to save the object. If you click on the Yes button, Access will act as if you selected File ➤ Save from the menu bar.

See **Part 1; Forms: Saving; Reports: Saving**

SELECT QUERY

A *select query* is a query that finds data, selecting only what meets your specifications.

See **Queries**

SORTING

Sorting is putting records in order based on some orderly system that you impose.

See **Filters and Sorts; Queries: Sorting Data on a Field; Quick Sort**

SORT ORDER: CHANGING

You can change the sort order specified in a datasheet, a form's Filter/Sort property, or a query. If, for example, you have a query that displays a list of the dates people were hired and you wanted to know who was hired most recently, click in the Sort cell for the date in the QBE grid, and then select Descending from the drop-down menu. You could also choose Not Sorted.

See **Filters and Sorts; Queries; Queries: Sorting Data on a Field; Quick Sort**

SPREADSHEET

See **Datasheet; Exporting to Lotus 1-2-3 or to Excel; Importing from a Spreadsheet**

SQL

SQL is short for Structured Query Language—a standard computer language for databases, first developed by IBM but now used throughout the industry.

See **Importing from a Text File (using SQL Database Servers)**

STARTING ACCESS

To start Access, double-click on the Access icon in the Program Manager's Microsoft Office group (see Figure S.1).

Tip

With the Windows File Manager, you can start Access and load a database file at the same time by double-clicking on the database file. (Database files have the extension .MDB.)

When you start Access, you may see the Welcome screen (shown in Figure S.2). Double-click on its control button in the upper-left corner of the screen to move along.

A
B
C
D
E
F
G
H
I
J
KL
M
N
O
P
Q
R
S
T
U
V
W
XYZ

Figure S.1

Double-click on the Access icon in
the Microsoft Office group.

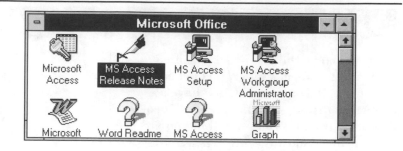

Figure S.2

The Access Welcome screen

Control button

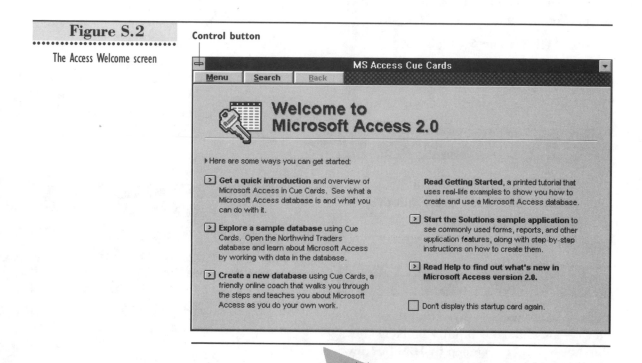

GET RID
OF THE WELCOME SCREEN

·············Tip··············

To make the Welcome screen go away
forever, first click in the check box
that says <u>Don't display this startup
screen again</u>. Then double-click on the
control button.

See **Database File: Creating; Database: Opening an Existing; Exiting Access**

STATISTICAL ANALYSIS

See **Queries: Statistical Analysis With; Totals Queries**

STRING

A *string* is any sequence of characters, strung together. In Access strings are kept in text fields or memo fields.

See **Data Type; Text Data Type; Memo Data Type**

SUB FORM

A *Sub form* is the form inside a Main form.

See **Forms and Form Wizards**

A
B
C
D
E
F
G
H
I
J
KL
M
N
O
P
Q
R
S
T
U
V
W
XYZ

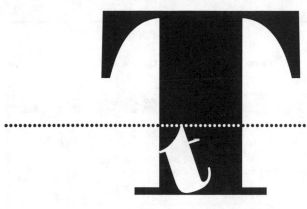

TABLE

A *table* is an organized list that contains data. Tables contain records which contain fields, which is where you enter your data. Tables can be linked with one another in relational databases like Access.

See **Part I; Table Wizard; Tables: Creating in Design View**

TABLE WIZARD

The Table Wizard's magic lets you quickly create a table customized to any of a number of data-keeping tasks. To use the Table Wizard, display the list of tables in the Database window of the database you wish to add the table to and follow these instructions:

I. Click on New. Access will display the New Table dialog box.

2. In the New Table dialog box, click on the Table Wizards button. The Table

Wizard dialog box will appear as shown in Figure T.1.

3. Select either the Business or Personal option button, depending on what type of table you wish to create.

4. Pick a sample table from the Sample Tables list by clicking on its name.

5. Add fields to your table by selecting fields for data you wish to store in the Sample Fields list box and click in on the add one field button. You can add all the sample fields to your table by clicking on the add-all-fields button.

6. Once you have placed all the fields you wish to have in your table in the list labeled "Fields in my new table," click on the Next button. Access will display another Table Wizard dialog box.

7. In this dialog box, you can enter a name for the table you are creating. Type the name into the text box near the top of the dialog box.

Figure T.1

The Table Wizard dialog box makes creating tables magically easy.

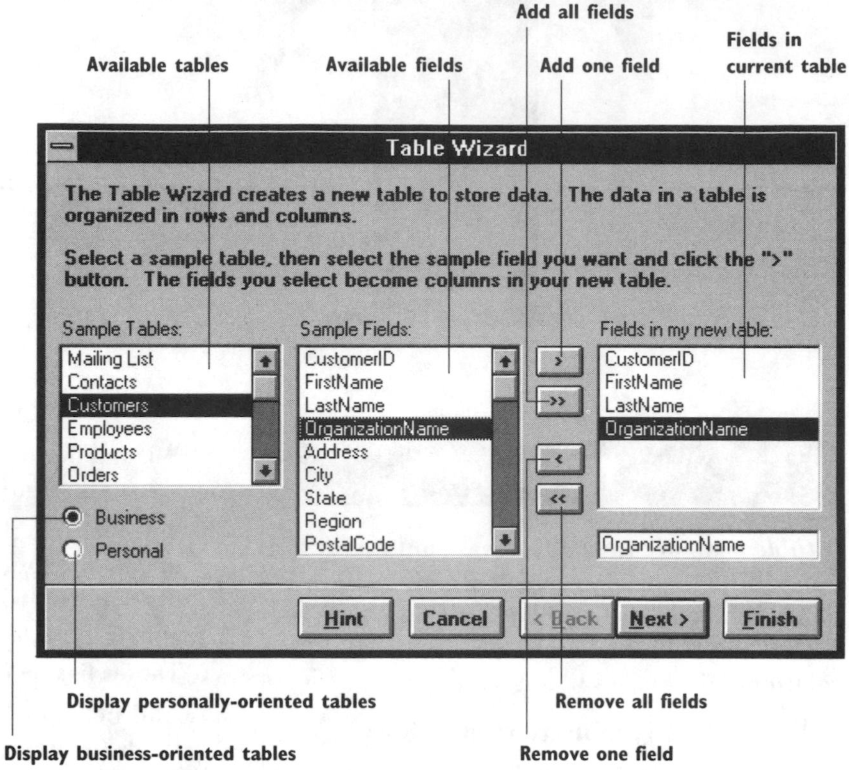

Available tables

Available fields

Add all fields

Add one field

Fields in current table

Table Wizard

The Table Wizard creates a new table to store data. The data in a table is organized in rows and columns.

Select a sample table, then select the sample field you want and click the ">" button. The fields you select become columns in your new table.

Sample Tables:
- Mailing List
- Contacts
- Customers
- Employees
- Products
- Orders

◉ Business
○ Personal

Sample Fields:
- CustomerID
- FirstName
- LastName
- OrganizationName
- Address
- City
- State
- Region
- PostalCode

Fields in my new table:
- CustomerID
- FirstName
- LastName
- OrganizationName

OrganizationName

Hint | Cancel | < Back | Next > | Finish

Display personally-oriented tables

Remove all fields

Display business-oriented tables

Remove one field

Tip

If you decide you do not want to include one of the fields you have moved from the *Sample Fields* list to the *Fields in my new table* list, you can use the remove-one-field or remove-all-fields buttons to remove fields. These buttons look just like their add-one-field and add-all-fields counterparts, except that the arrows point left instead of right.

8. Once you have entered a name for the table, you can tell Access if you want it to add a primary key field, or if you wish, you can specified the primary key field. If you want Access to add the primary key field, select the option box labeled "Let Microsoft Access set a primary key for me." Once you are done, click on the Next button.

9. If you elected to have Access create the primary key, Access will check all the other tables in the current database and figure out how your new table is related to them. Click on Next to continue.

10. A dialog box will appear, showing you how the new table is related to all the other tables in your database. In the list labeled "My new table is… " you'll see how the Wizard thinks the new table is related to the other tables in the database. You can change any of these relationships by selecting the relationship in the list and clicking the Change button. Once you are satisfied with the way the new table will relate to the other tables in the database, click on the Next button.

11. In the final Table Wizard dialog box, you can elect to:

❂ Modify the table using Table Design View

❂ Enter data into the table using Datasheet View

❂ Enter data into the table using a form Access creates with the AutoForm Wizard

Select one of these options by clicking on the options button and click the Finish button.

See **Tables: Creating in Design View**

TABLES: CREATING IN DESIGN VIEW

To create a new table, first open the database file that will contain the table. Select File ➤ Open to do this. (To find out how to *create* a database file, *see* Database: Creating.)

1. Click on the Table button along the left side of the Database window. The icon should look pressed down.

2. Then click on the New button along the top of the Database window.

3. When the New Table dialog box appears, click on the New Table button.

This will open up a new table in Access' Design View—the place where you create or modify tables. You can see an example of this in Figure T.2. In Design View, you'll see a three-column grid.

See **Tables: Creating**

TABLES: CREATING FIELDS IN

Table Design View (shown in Figure T.2) is the view of your table that allows you to add or modify fields.

Figure T.2

The Table Design window

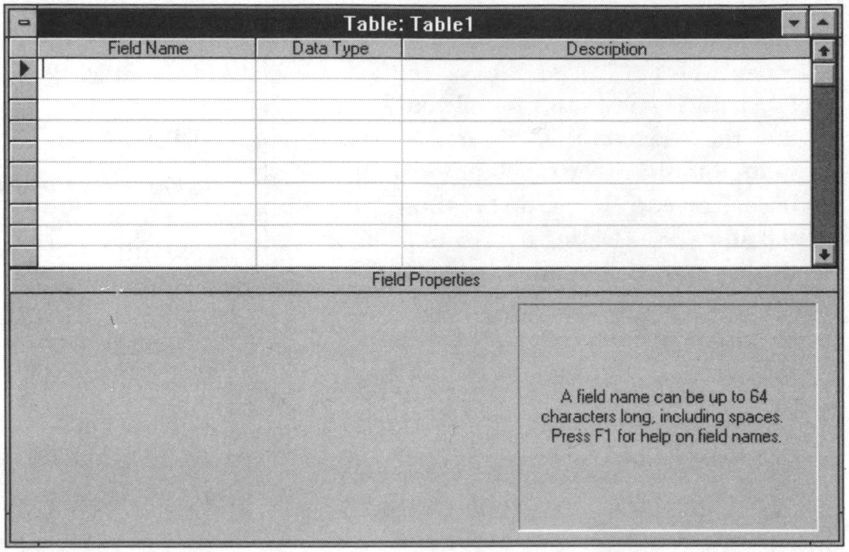

	Table: Table1		
Field Name	Data Type	Description	

Field Properties

A field name can be up to 64 characters long, including spaces. Press F1 for help on field names.

66 A single database can have almost as many tables as you want—there is a limit, but it's in the thousands, so you have plenty of room to maneuver. In reality, creating and using more than 150 tables is not a great idea, because of the speed limitations of the machines that are currently available.

You can enter into Table Design View in a number of ways:

❂ Create a new table by clicking on the New button while the Database window is listing tables

❂ Create a new table by selecting File ➤ New ➤ Table from the menu bar

❂ Select a table in the Database window and click on the Design button (the one with the word Design on it)

❂ Click on the Design View button

while looking at a table in Datasheet View

You can specify the data type of each field either when you create a new table or when you modify an existing table.

Adding a New Field

To add a new field to a database:

1. Enter a new field name in the Field Name column.

2. Click on the Data Type pull-down menu and pick a data type from the list that appears.

3. If it is a data type that requires a field size, you then enter this in the Properties box along the bottom of the Table Design View window.

4. Set any other Field Properties that you want to set.

See **Tables: Creating in Design View**

TARGET FILE

The *target file* is the file an operation is doing something to. For example, an Append action query can copy records from the current database file (the *source* file) to the target database file.

TEXT

In Access, *Text* is a data type that contains strings of characters, usually of letters or numbers (numbers that don't have to be used mathematically, that is). Text is also, of course, whatever's written in a text field.

See **Data Type; Memo Data Type; Text Data Type**

TEXT DATA TYPE

Access defaults to the Text data type. That means Access assumes, at first, that this is the data type you're going to want. So whenever you create a new field, Access drops text into the data type.

That's no accident. In a field of the data type text, you can store any relatively short piece of data that will be typed in in letters and numbers. This includes: names, street addresses, favorite ball teams—you name it. You can store up to 255 characters in a text field, and then you can do text-like things to these fields—like sorting and indexing.

Now, when it comes to the properties from which you can choose…well, some options you get with text fields, and some you don't.

Tip

Use a text field to store ZIP codes. You never sum up ZIP codes, so you don't need them to be a number field. ZIP codes are simple, they're always set up the same way, and usually all you do to play with them is some kind of *sort*, which is a common enough thing to do with text fields. (Another consideration is that if you store ZIP codes in a number field, Access will drop all the leading zeros from those ZIP codes that start with 0; 02345 would become 2345, which would confuse the postal system all the way to Oz.

Text Data Type Properties

You can pick from the following choices when you assign properties to a text field:

✪ Field Size

✪ Format

✪ Input Mask

✪ Caption

✪ Default Value

✪ Validation Rule

✪ Validation Text

✪ Required

✪ Allow Zero Length

✪ Indexed

Field Size determines the maximum number of characters you can store in the field when you enter your data. You can tell Access to allow anywhere from 1 to 255 characters in a given text field.

Format describes the way the contents of the text field will look in the on-screen display or in print. You have these choices for the field:

✪ You can make **uppercase or lowercase characters** happen by typing in > for uppercase or < for lowercase.

✪ You can make **left-justified characters** happen by typing in ! (an exclamation point).

You can also specify the way single characters are displayed, by using the @ symbol where you want a letter, number, or space, and the & symbol for characters— like dashes—that are *not* letters, numbers, or spaces.

> **If you format a field to be displayed on screen in uppercase (all capital letters) or lowercase (all small letters), you can enter your data in any combination of upper- or lowercase, and Access will display—and print—it the way you formatted it (as opposed to the way you typed it). <u>However</u>, the data will be stored the way you typed it, and that's what you'll see when you edit the data. So if you type ICkaBoDd into a field formatted with the > character to force uppercase display, you're going to see ICKABODD on screen and in your mailing labels, but ICkaBoDd when you edit the field.**

Some examples of how you might use this business are shown in Table T.1.

Input Mask controls how Access displays the field before data is entered into it. For example, in a text field that contains the longer type of ZIP codes (nine-digits), an input mask might make the field look like 00000-0000. In this case, the user could enter any *number* where the zeros are, and the hyphen would automatically appear. (*See* Input Mask Wizard)

Table T.1

You Can Specify the Format for a Text Field to Control How Characters Will Be Displayed

When You Format a Text Field	If You Type This	It Will Be Displayed As
>	Nixon	NIXON
(@@@) @@@-@@@@	5105551212	(510) 555-1212
@@@&@@@@	555-1212	555-1212
Job @@@@	1234	Job 1234

Using the **Caption** property, you can set up a caption for the field. The caption will be displayed next to the field when the data is displayed as a form or report. The caption you write might, for example, tell the person entering the data how to do the entry. If you don't type anything into the caption property box, the field name will appear as the caption next to the field.

Default Value lets you set up a default data entry for the field. For example, if you were setting up a field for "Department," and you knew that 80% of the time the department was going to be "Editorial" you could set that up as the Default Value. Then you won't have to type "Editorial," into the department field of every record when you do data entry. Instead, they will all say "Editorial" and you'll have to type in the department name only for those records that have to do with some other department.

You can set up a **Validation Rule** that will require the data being entered to meet some specified rule—for example, if you're setting up a Last Name field, and you want every last name to start with a capital letter.

Tip

If you are setting up a character field to hold numbers (ZIP codes, for example), you may want to set a Validation Rule to accept only numbers. This will prevent the person doing data entry from typing a lowercase l instead of the number 1, or an O instead of a 0.

A **Validation Text** property holds a message to be displayed by Access if the user tries to enter data that violates the Validation Rule. So if you've set up a Validation Rule that says the data entered must start with an uppercase letter, you can get Access to display some message like, "Please capitalize the first letter."

Required controls whether data must be entered into the field for every new record.

Allow Zero Length determines whether the field is allowed to be empty.

A B C D E F G H I J KL M N O P Q R S T U V W XYZ

Indexed tells Access to keep a list of the fields in order—alphabetical order, if it's a text field. Now what Access does with these indexed fields never shows up in any display. Instead, the results are a little abstract—they have to do with making things easier for Access. For example, indexing a field makes it easier for Access to use that field to link one table to another, and run the link faster. In the same way you would have to take a while to sort through a stack of unalphabetized names to find the one you're looking for and to match it up with the one you have, Access is going to take a long time flipping through unindexed fields to connect those that are supposed to be linked.

See **Text Field: Creating**

TEXT FIELD: CREATING

To create a text field in Table Design View:

1. Enter a field name in the Field Name column.

2. The Text data type is the default data type, so you do not have to change anything in the Data Type column.

3. You can enter a description in the Description column. Access will display the contents of the Description column along the bottom of the Access window when you are entering data in the field. Make sure your description will remind you what should go into the field.

4. Now you can go ahead and set the field properties in the Field Properties box along the bottom of the window.

······································· Tip ·······································

If you want to store text that might be one length in one record and a very different length— say, a dozen characters in one record but many thousands in another record—in another record, consider using a memo field, which will stretch and shrink to fit the text that's stored in it. If you used a text field, you'd have to make it big enough to accommodate the largest piece of data that is going to go in it. If you're storing biography notes for a bunch of writers, for example, you're going to find that **Writer A** went to a certain university and lived forever in his hometown, while **Writer B** did her undergraduate, master's, and Ph.D. work at three different schools, traveled extensively, and has won a Pulitzer. You wouldn't want to put this information for each writer in a text field called Biography, because every writer's Biography field would have to be big enough to contain the most accomplished writer's bio. It's simply more space-efficient to use memo fields. However, when you store information in a memo field, you are limited in the ways you can search the data—so you may find it useful to break some information down into a short piece (that you'll put in a text field) that you can use for searches, and a larger piece (that you'll keep as a variable length memo field.)

See Text Data Type; Tables: Creating in Design View

TEXT: TOOLBAR SHORTCUTS FOR CHANGING

In this section, remember that to change the appearance of text that appears in fields on your form or report, you must change the control that represents the field or label in Design View. You can go through a lot of hoops to change text using the Properties box, or you can click on a few handy buttons appearing on the toolbar at the top of your screen.

 Makes text bold

 Makes text into italics

 Makes text left-aligned

 Centers text within the control

Makes text right-aligned

To use the icons on the toolbar to change the look of text as it will be displayed on the form or report:

1. Select the control or controls you want to change.

2. Click on the icon on the toolbar that makes the change you want.

3. Repeat step 2 until you are happy with the look of the text you wanted to change.

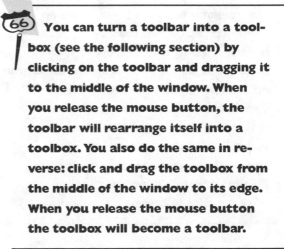

You can also change the font the control is displayed in, by moving the mouse pointer to the Font Name box in the toolbar, clicking on the little box with the down arrow in it, and finally picking a new font from the drop-down list that appears. To change the size the text will be displayed in, do the same where the size appears.

TOOLBAR

The row of icons (tiny pictures that mean something) that appears along the top of the Access window is a *toolbar*. The toolbar changes depending on what you are doing. The most commonly used toolbars are shown in the charts on the inside front and back covers of this book.

See Toolbox

You can turn a toolbar into a toolbox (see the following section) by clicking on the toolbar and dragging it to the middle of the window. When you release the mouse button, the toolbar will rearrange itself into a toolbox. You also do the same in reverse: click and drag the toolbox from the middle of the window to its edge. When you release the mouse button the toolbox will become a toolbar.

A B C D E F G H I J KL M N O P Q R S T U V W XYZ

TOOLBOX

Access, like many other Windows programs, includes a *toolbox* in its Design View for forms and reports. The toolbox is a group of icons that represent controls you might want to use in the design of your form or report.

Toolboxes vs. Toolbars

· · · · · · · · · · · · · ·

The big difference between a toolbox and toolbar is that the toolbox is a vertically rectangular batch of tools that appears in the work area of your screen, while the toolbar is a strip of tools that appears across the edge of your screen. The toolbox can be dragged around your screen and dropped into more convenient locations while you're working, but the toolbar can't. It just spans the edge of your screen.

One nifty new thing in Access is that you can transform toolboxes into toolbars and vice versa. Just click on the title bar of any toolbox and drag it to the edge of your screen, then drop it where a toolbar normally appears, and it will become one. Click between buttons in any toolbar and drag it out into the work area of your screen. It will rearrange itself into a toolbox, which you then can plop anywhere in the work area that's convenient, or drag off to the edge to become a toolbar again.

These are the control tools Access makes available to you in the toolbox:

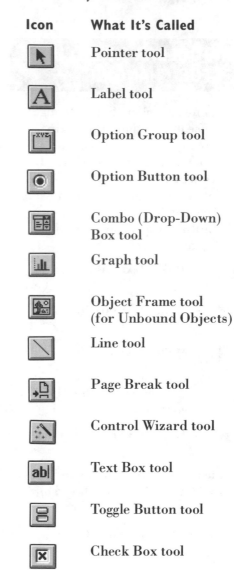

Icon	What It's Called
	Pointer tool
	Label tool
	Option Group tool
	Option Button tool
	Combo (Drop-Down) Box tool
	Graph tool
	Object Frame tool (for Unbound Objects)
	Line tool
	Page Break tool
	Control Wizard tool
	Text Box tool
	Toggle Button tool
	Check Box tool
	List Box tool

Icon	What It's Called
	Subform/Subreport tool
	Bound Object Frame tool
	Rectangle tool
	Command Button tool
	Tool Lock tool

To use a tool from the toolbox, click on its icon. For example, if you click on the Text tool icon, and then click on the form or report, you'll place a Text Box control where you clicked.

Also, you'll be using the tool you've selected only until you've placed the control the tool represents. Immediately after that, the usual mouse pointer will return. If you select a tool and then change your mind, you can click on the Pointer tool in the toolbox and the pointer will be its usual familiar self, without the ability to place a control. If you do want the tool you select to remain in effect for a while, first select the Tool Lock tool, and then select the tool with which you want to work.

If, while you are working, the toolbox seems to be in your way, you can move it. Just click on the toolbox, hold the mouse button down, and drag that toolbox to a more convenient spot.

> *See* **Modifying Forms and Reports; Toolbar**

TOTALS QUERIES

You can use queries to produce scads of statistical information based on your tables.

You can group your data by categories and then calculate *aggregate functions*, based on fields, for all the records in a group. An aggregate function is a function that you apply to a collection of numbers with a single number as a result. A simple example of an aggregate function is *Max*—a function that takes a group of numbers, and figures out the (single) *maximum* number among them.

To group your data by categories and calculate aggregate functions:

1. Create a new query based on the table or dynaset about which you want statistical information.

2. Click on the Totals icon on the toolbar; this causes a new Total row to appear in the QBE grid.

3. Start adding fields that you want to group by into the QBE grid, using either the click-and-drag method or the pull-down menu method. The Total box should read Group By for each field you are using to group your data. You group your data on common fields that describe related records in your database. In a Stock Prices table, for example, you would group your data on Company Name (for the name of the company issuing the stock).

A B C D E F G H I J KL M N O P Q R S T U V W XYZ

4. Once you have entered all the fields you are using to specify groups, start adding fields for which you want to specify aggregate functions.

5. In the Totals box, pick the aggregate function you want to perform on each field. Here's a list of the aggregate functions that are available in Access.

Select **Group By** for fields upon which you want to base record grouping

Sum Sums all values in the group and displays the result

Avg Displays the average of all data in the group

Min Displays the minimal value in the group

Max Displays the maximal value in the group

Count Counts the data elements in the group

StDev Calculates the standard deviation of the data in the group

Var Calculates the variance of the data in the group

First Returns the first piece of data in the group

Last Returns the last piece of data in the group

Expression Select Expression when you have entered an expression instead of a field name in the Field box

Where Choose Where when you want to use the field as part of a criteria to select records

You now have a query that will perform aggregate functions on your table. To see the results, just click on the Datasheet View button. Figure T.3 shows the Query Design View of a query that calculates the standard deviation on closing stock prices based on a table of stock prices. Figure T.4 displays the results of running the query.

See **Queries; Datasheet**

Figure T.3

This query groups data by company name and then calculates the standard deviation of the closing stock prices for each company.

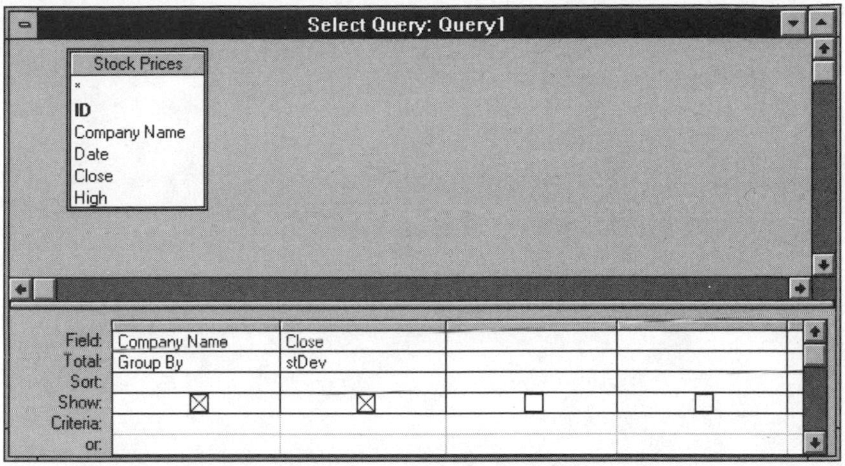

Figure T.4

Executing the query shows us that STAX is a more volatile stock than is APC over the period for which we have data.

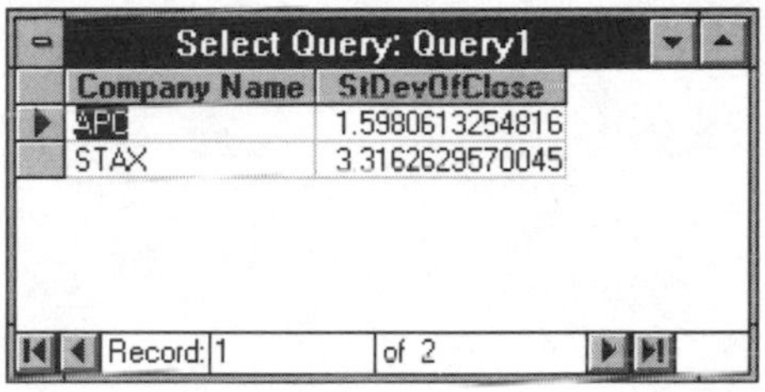

A
B
C
D
E
F
G
H
I
J
KL
M
N
O
P
Q
R
S
T
U
V
W
XYZ

A
B
C
D
E
F
G
H
I
J
KL
M
N
O
P
Q
R
S
T
U
V
W
XYZ

UNDO

See   **Editing Data in Datasheet View**

USER

The person (you or someone else) who uses the computer and the programs on it is called a *user*.

UPDATE ACTION QUERIES

An Update action query modifies the data in the table upon which the query is based. This type of query comes in handy, for example, when the phone company changes the area code for your city. You can set up a query to select all the records that contain that city name in the City field, and have the Phone Number fields of those records updated to show the new area code.

The first step in creating an Update action query is to create a Select query that

produces the dynaset of those records and fields you want to modify. Once you have a query that produces the proper dynaset, do the following to turn it into an Update action query:

1. In the Query Design window, Select Query ➤ Update.

2. In the QBE grid, enter whatever you want to change *to* in the Update To row. (You can enter either a value or an expression.)

3. Click on the Execute icon on the toolbar to run your Update action query.

4. Access displays a dialog box telling you how many records are about to be changed. If you click OK, Access will update the data. If you click Cancel, you can bail out now.

You can enter any expression (mathematical sentence) you want into the Update To row of the QBE grid. You can include the value from the field that is being updated—or from any other field in the table—by enclosing its name in square brackets.

Let's say all the employees in your small company have been slaving away for weeks to make an important deadline. You were going to reward them anyway, but you've just watched "A Christmas Carol" on late night TV, and you're inspired to increase their bonuses. To use an Update action query to increase everyone's bonus by 5%, you would build the Update action query shown in Figure U.1.

Executing the Update action query shown in Figure U.1 will increase the value of the bonus field by 5% for everyone listed in the Employees table.

See **Action Queries; Queries; Query Wizards**

Figure U.1
....

An Update action query that increases all the values in the Bonus field by 5% (1.05 times)

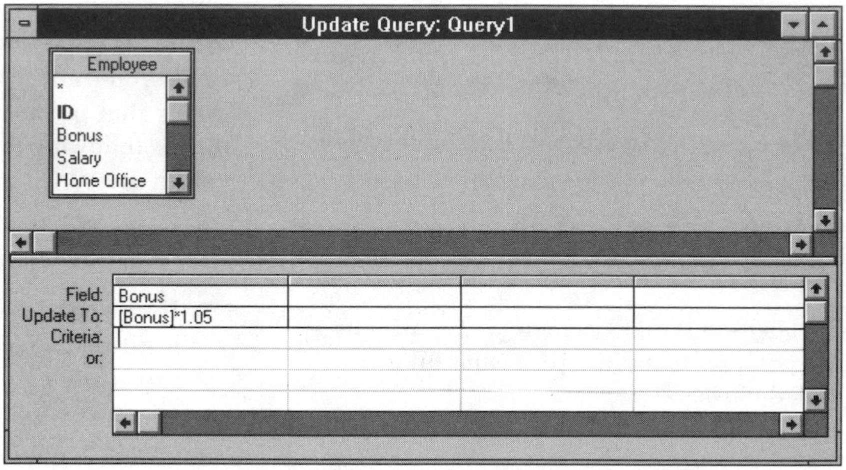

V

A B C D E F G H I J KL M N O P Q R S T U **V** W XYZ

VALUE

A *value* is piece of data in a field or elsewhere.

VIEWING DATA

You can view data on screen as a *form* or as a *datasheet*. A form (Figure V.1) is an

Data shown in the form of a form

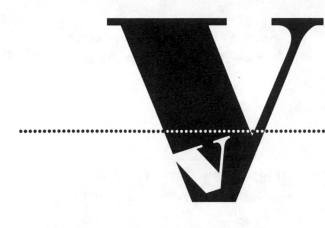

	Order ID	Ship City	Ship Country	Shipped Date	Freight
▶	10000	Torino	Italy	15-May-91	$4.45
	10001	Montréal	Canada	23-May-91	$79.45
	10002	Bräcke	Sweden	17-May-91	$36.18
	10003	København	Denmark	24-May-91	$18.59
	10004	Århus	Denmark	20-May-91	$20.12
	10005	Oulu	Finland	24-May-91	$4.13
	10006	Torino	Italy	24-May-91	$3.62
	10007	Leipzig	Germany	11-Jun-91	$36.19

Record: 1   of 1078

attractive presentation that makes entering data into one record at a time especially easy; a datasheet (Figure V.2) is a column-and-row layout that resembles a spreadsheet and that allows you to see a lot of records at once.

See **Part 1; Datasheet; Datasheet View; Forms and Form Wizards**

Figure V.2

The same data shown in Figure V.1, this time in a form of datasheet

Order ID	Ship City	Ship Country	Shipped Date	Freight
10000	Torino	Italy	15-May-91	$4.45
10001	Montréal	Canada	23-May-91	$79.45
10002	Bräcke	Sweden	17-May-91	$36.18
10003	København	Denmark	24-May-91	$18.59
10004	Århus	Denmark	20-May-91	$20.12
10005	Oulu	Finland	24-May-91	$4.13
10006	Torino	Italy	24-May-91	$3.62
10007	Leipzig	Germany	11-Jun-91	$36.19
10008	Lisboa	Portugal	29-May-91	$74.22
10009	London	UK	31-May-91	$49.21
10010	København	Denmark	30-May-91	$3.01
10011	Resende	Brazil	03-Jun-91	$31.54
10012	I. de Margarita	Venezuela	03-Jun-91	$102.59
10013	Genève	Switzerland	07-Jun-91	$50.87
10014	Caracas	Venezuela	12-Jun-91	$17.67
10015	Salzburg	Austria	20-Jun-91	$22.10
10016	Lille	France	11-Jul-91	$113.01
10017	Strasbourg	France	10-Jun-91	$111.81
10018	Albuquerque	USA	05-Jul-91	$65.46
10019	Bergamo	Italy	20-Jun-91	$2.42
10020	Reims	France	26-Jun-91	$27.51
10021	Graz	Austria	02-Jul-91	$75.17

Orders

Record: 1 of 1078

W

WILDCARDS

See   **Datasheet View: Finding and Replacing Text**

WINDOWS

Microsoft Access is a Microsoft Windows application. That means you have to know how to paddle around in Windows to get anything done in Access. If you already know what you're doing in Windows, you can skip this section.

Windows has what's called a GUI (pronounced *gooey*), which stands for Graphical User Interface. A GUI allows you to interact with your computer by manipulating images on the screen, instead of by typing commands. GUIs like Windows are supposed to make your computer easier to use. Windows is an add-on to Microsoft DOS (another Microsoftism), which controls the more fundamental aspects of your computer.

Scenes from Microsoft

We're talking a lot of "Microsofts" here. Microsoft, as you can probably guess, is an industry giant—Microsoft DOS (also known as MS-DOS) is the operating system software of choice for most PCs. It makes your PC do its basic functions. And <u>Windows</u> is the "umbrella" program that makes it possible for you to use different applications (database, spreadsheet, word processing, and others) without having to learn new commands for each one. (Or, as Mac fanatics say, Windows makes your machine "look like a Macintosh.")

Microsoft, having developed and marketed the more fundamental DOS and Windows, is therefore in a position to develop applications that work especially smoothly with DOS and Windows.

To run Access, you need not one but three programs installed on your machine:

- ✪ DOS
- ✪ Windows
- ✪ Access

Almost all PCs come with DOS already installed, so that is nothing to worry about. DOS takes care of the most fundamental aspects of your PC, and, in the same way you don't have to think about breathing, you should not have to think about DOS as long as you've got Windows. Some machines will also arrive on your desk with Windows pre-installed. Windows gives you intuitive control over the somewhat less fundamental aspects of your machine— things you have to do consciously, but not with a lot of thought, like moving your arms and hands. To take this a little further, Access is then like a tool in your hands that you use consciously to perform some kind of work.

See **Part I**

WINDOWS BASICS

Throughout this book, we assume that you know Windows. But just in case you don't, we're going to give you a quick overview of Windows basics right here. We'll just tell you to select a menu item or to close a window without going into great detail about where to move the mouse pointer or which keys you should press.

Opening Windows

When you start your machine, you'll see one of two things. If you are very lucky and have been good all year, Windows will just run, and you'll see the Program Manager (Figure W.1).

If your machine is not set up to run Windows automatically when it starts up, you will first see a DOS prompt that looks something like:

```
C:\>
```

In that case, to start Windows you type win and press ↵ (Enter). *Then* you should see the Program Manager window shown in Figure W.1. The Program Manager is the Windows application that you use to start other applications. In that way, it is like the DOS command line—that place after the DOS prompt where you typed in win to start Windows.

You may see quite a different-looking setup on your machine. That's because you can move and change the windows whenever you like, and some people set up Windows on their machines to keep the changes they've made when they close up shop for the day.

Figure W.1

The Program Manager showing the Microsoft Office window open

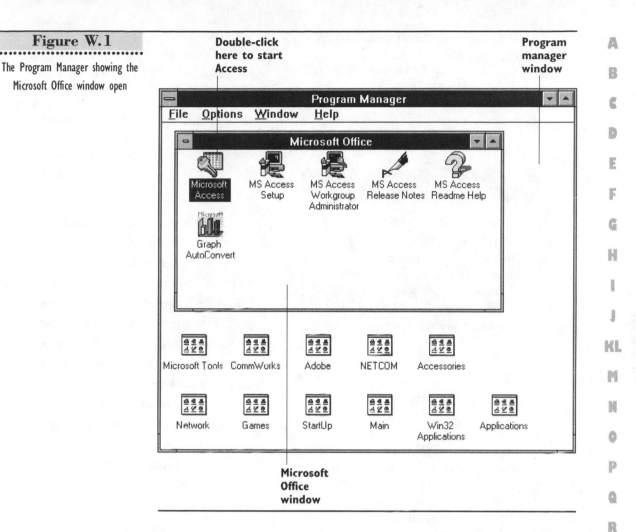

Double-click here to start Access

Program manager window

Microsoft Office window

Clicking and Double-Clicking

When you are using Windows, *clicking* means pointing the mouse pointer (the on-screen arrow) at something and then pressing and releasing the left mouse button. Windows allows (and in fact *requires*) you to do one of two types of clicking:

○ **Single-clicking** means just pointing the mouse pointer at something and clicking once. You usually single-click on something to select it, or make it active. When we say "click" we mean single-click, or click once.

○ **Double-clicking** means pointing the on-screen mouse pointer at something and clicking twice very fast. You double-click on something to perform an action on the thing on which you are double-clicking. For example, double-clicking on an icon in the Program Manager causes the program that is associated with the icon to run.

Tip

A number of mouse manufacturers make left-handed mice and the software to run them. If you are using a left-handed mouse, everything's turned around for you—you actually click and double-click on the right button, not the left button.

Icons and Menus and Bars

Look at almost any window and you'll find that it's topped by a *toolbar* (a strip of square buttons identified by tiny inscrutable pictures) just below a *menu bar* (that row of words you see). Each *icon* on the toolbar represents a function—printing, for instance—that you might want to do quickly.

An icon is a little picture that represents something the program does. Icons are meant to be "intuitive," which means you're supposed to know just from looking at it what the icon does. Of course, if they were truly intuitive, there'd be no need for this book.

It's like this: say last month you set up a database. Now, you've got your table on screen, and you just want to print it, not mess around with a lot of details. The Print button—the one with the picture of a printer on it—is a shortcut for the Print menu selection. Just click on the Print button, and—bingo!—out pops your database info.

As you move along from one task to the next, Access changes the icons that appear on the toolbar. This isn't meant to confuse people, but it does. You'll find all the tools you most often need in the charts on the inside covers of this book. And if you run the mouse pointer across a tool on your screen, pausing for a split second, a little yellow box will appear telling you the tool's name and a more descriptive message will appear at the very bottom of the screen.

Drop-Down Menus and Dialog Boxes

When you click on a title in the menu bar, a menu drops down—these are *drop-down menus*. Once you have dropped down a menu, you can select an item from the resulting list to make the program do something specific. The Access File menu, shown in Figure W.2, allows you to select from commonly used functions like Print..., Rename..., Exit, and so on.

If you click on menu items like Exit, which appears as a single word with no complications, it'll just do it's job—in the case of Exit, that means exiting the program. But if the menu item you select ends in three periods (for example, Rename...) a *dialog box* will appear. A dialog box is a special window that asks you to type in some kind of information (usually in answer to a question) before it does anything else—in other words, you *talk* to a dialog box. It talks to you. You and the dialog box have a *dialogue*. Got it?

Tip

In the case of some menu items, you'll see a *shortcut key* combination—something like Ctrl-X, for example—that allows you to take the same action without going to all the trouble of pointing at and selecting a drop-down menu item. (Pressing the shortcut key combination is the same as selecting the menu item with the mouse.)

A
B
C
D
E
F
G
H
I
J
KL
M
N
O
P
Q
R
S
T
U
V
W
XYZ

Figure W.2

Many Windows programs are designed to have similar menus and commands. You'll find drop-down menus that give you options much like these in other Windows applications.

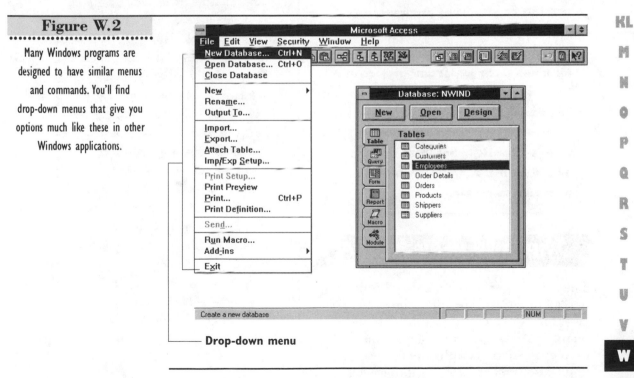

Drop-down menu

Closing Windows

As usual, you have several options. You can either double-click on the window's control box in the upper-left corner (it's the box with the minus sign in it), or you can click on File in the menu bar, and then click on Exit in the drop-down menu. In either case, if you have a document window open somewhere, you will usually (in most Windows-based programs) be asked whether you want to save your work. Try not to get in the habit of clicking your way thoughtlessly through this message—it will often be your last chance to save your work.

Don't count on any program to prompt you to save your work. Nothing—nothing—is worse than working for hours on an important project, and then, with your deadline fast approaching, closing the document window and—bam!—realizing you've forgotten to save your work. In database work, as in all of life's matters, the key to security is to save, save, <u>save</u>.

WINDOWS: MANIPULATING

The most powerful thing about Windows and all those Windows programs—like Access, for example, is that you get to have many windows open all at once. You can even open windows for many different applications all at once, right there next to

each other, for all the world to see and for you to tinker around in. Having lots of windows open at once is great. You can have one or more windows displaying Access tables, another window showing a Windows word processor document, and a third that contains a Windows spreadsheet program document (see Figure W.3).

Big and Little Windows

You have two types of windows to pay attention to. Basically it comes down to big windows and little windows, but some people call the big ones <u>parent</u> windows and the little ones <u>child</u> windows. First, you need to know that the parent window contains the child window, and that means the child window can't be bigger than the parent. All applications will have a main window—a parent window—usually named after the program. In Access, you'll see "Microsoft Access" at the top of this window. A second window—a child window—will be the document window. (Note that document windows exist only in applications that let you open more than one file at a time.) Remember that the document window is the child window of the main window. The program runs in the parent window, while individual files are shown in the child windows. Take a look at Figure W.4 to see all the common elements of an Access window.

Figure W.3

Windows allows you to have a bunch of windows open at once.

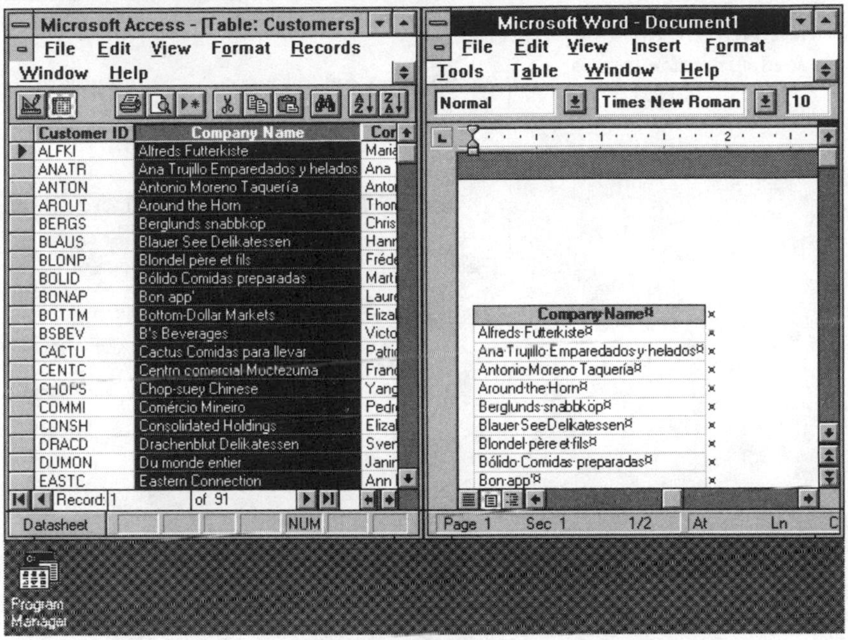

With a bunch of these windows open, you can click on one and then another to switch back and forth between them, or you can cut-and-paste material from one window to the other, without any fuss or muss.

The most common things you do to windows are listed below. We're going to tell you how to do these things with a mouse, because that's the best way to do it in Access, although you could use the keyboard if you insisted.

Maximize a window Sometimes you might want to make the parent window fill the entire screen or make a child window fill the entire parent window. If this sounds familiar, you can do *one* of the following:

✪ Double-click on the window's title bar

✪ Click on the Maximize button

✪ Click on the control box and select Maximize from the menu that appears

Minimize a window Other times you might want to reduce the window to a little icon (and get it out of the way). If so, do *one* of these:

✪ Click on the Minimize button

✪ Click on the control box and select Maximize from the menu that appears

Restore a window Every once in a while, you're going to want to return the window to the size it was before it was maximized. You

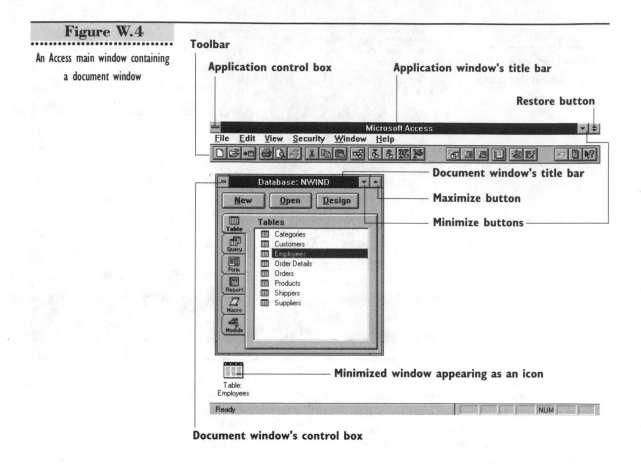

Figure W.4

An Access main window containing a document window

Toolbar

Application control box

Application window's title bar

Restore button

Document window's title bar

Maximize button

Minimize buttons

Minimized window appearing as an icon

Document window's control box

can do this in one of the following ways:

- ○ Double-click on the title bar
- ○ Click on the Restore button
- ○ Click on the control box and select Maximize from the menu that appears

Move a window And what if you need to reposition the window on the screen? It's

easy—just follow these steps:

1. Point at the window's title bar and click and hold down the mouse button.

2. Drag the window to the new location. (You'll actually be dragging an *outline* of the window—not the window itself.)

3. When the outline is where you want it, release the mouse button and the window will appear in its new location.

You can't move a maximized window around— it's already filling up the screen and there's simply nowhere for it to go.

Scroll a window Sometimes portions of a window don't fit on-screen because the window's too big. When *scroll bars* appear (as shown in Figure W.4) at the side or bottom of a window, you can click on the arrows at the ends of the scroll bar to move by short increments, or you can drag the little box in the scroll bar in the direction you want to go to cover more territory faster.

Tip

This isn't going to get you dates or cure cancer, but for real windows fun, you can get yourself a "billboard-sized" screen. Also, the difference between normal 640×480 VGA display and way-cool high-resolution 800×600 display is like night and day. Hi-res displays give you more room on the screen to fiddle around with your windows. Overall, the wider your monitor and the higher the resolution of your display card, the better. Watch out, though, because using real hi-res displays with slow machines can make your windows "crawly."

WIZARDS

Creating many of the most commonly used Access objects is a matter of real wizardry— Access includes more than 20 Wizards (built-in helpers that create pieces of your database for you). To use a Wizard, all you have to do is answer some on-screen questions; then tables, queries, reports, forms, and more will seem to appear on screen magically.

With the Access Wizards listed here, you can create complicated database objects really quickly and easily.

Table Wizard will conjure up a number of tables you might use every day—tables to organize your home video collection, CD collection, plants, friends, customers, invoices, or many other things.

Query Wizards will whip up in a jiffy some of the most popular types of queries. The **Crosstab Query Wizard** creates a query that crosstabulates the information in the table or dynaset on which the query's based. The **Find Duplicates Query Wizard** helps you locate duplicate records. The **Find Unmatched Query Wizard** finds all the records in a table or dynaset that have no linked records in another table or dynaset. The **Archive Query Wizard** helps you create a query that copies the records you specify from an existing table or dynaset into a new one.

Form Wizards make creating on-screen forms for viewing and entering data a snap. The **Single-Column Form Wizard** creates a form that just lists the contents of each record in a column, with labels to the left of the fields. The **Tabular Form Wizard** shows a bunch of records at once—this is a lot like the datasheet, but in the form of a form. The **Graph Form Wizard** creates a form that contains one of several kinds of handy graphs. The **Main/Subform Wizard** creates a form with a subform. (This is a convenient way to display data from two tables (or dynasets) in a single form.) The **AutoForm Wizard** creates a form like the one the Single-Column Form Wizard creates, but without asking any questions, so the form that appears is *really* generic, and doesn't select out specific data—everything in every record is displayed.

Report Wizards create printed reports in a flash. The **Single-Column Report Wizard** just lists the data in all the records of the table or dynaset in a single column. The **Groups/Totals Report Wizard** creates a report that groups related data together and calculates subtotals for each group. The **Mailing Label Report Wizard** generates mailing labels before you can say *abracadabra*. The **Summary Report Wizard** groups data and can include both a subtotal for each group and a grand total for all groups. The **Tabular Report Wizard** produces a report listing all the records in the table—again, this is like the datasheet, this

time in the form of a report. The **AutoReport Wizard** creates a form like the Single-Column Report Wizard does, but without asking any questions. The report it creates is pretty basic, and doesn't select out specific data—everything in every record shows up in print. The **MS Word Mail Merge Wizard** helps you create mail merge documents in Word for Windows.

Control Wizards are there for you when you want to customize forms. The **Option Group Wizard, Combo Box Wizard, List Box Wizard, Graph Wizard**, and **Command Button Wizard** each work with specific kinds of *controls* (the visual pieces that make up mainly forms, but also reports).

You usually start using a Wizard by clicking the Wizard button when you start creating a new object. Access will start presenting you with a series of dialog boxes asking about what you want to create. For example, when you use the Forms Wizard, Access asks for the type of form and what data you wish to display. Once Access has determined the information needed to create the object for you, it creates the object with no fuss, no muss, no fanfare. And guess what? If the object Access creates isn't *exactly* what you had in mind, you can always modify the thing.

See **Table Wizards; Query Wizards; Form Wizards; Report Wizards; Control Wizards**

XYZ

YEARS

See **Date/Time Data Type**

YES/NO DATA TYPE

The Yes/No data type can hold two values—
sometimes called Yes and No, sometimes
called True and False, and sometimes
called by other names that basically mean
the same thing. You'll want to use this data
type for fields when a simple question or
condition can be answered in only one of
two ways—something like, *Paid to date?*
or *Pass/Fail*, or even *Female/Male*.

Yes/No Data Type Properties

You can set these properties for Yes/No
data types:

- ✪ Format
- ✪ Caption

These days, you probably **don't**
want to use a Yes/No data type to indicate marital status—the answer
then could be Single/Married/Di-
vorced/Widowed/Separated/Living
with Someone, or Who Knows What.
The Yes/No data type lends itself to
questions that have utterly unambi-
guous answers—it's got to be either
Yes, or **No**.

- ✪ Default Value
- ✪ Validation Rule
- ✪ Validation Text
- ✪ Required
- ✪ Indexed

Format lets you determine how the Yes/No answer will appear when it is displayed—something that, of course makes a big difference in what questions you can ask. The predefined formats for a Yes/No field are:

Yes/No To display *Yes* or *No*

True/False To display *True* or *False*

On/Off To display *On* or *Off*

The big news here is that you can set up a custom format! To do this, type—within quotation marks—any word you want to display for true values, a semicolon (;), and then whatever word you want to display for false values. For example, the format

```
"Positive"; "Negative"
```

will cause what is really Yes—a *true* value—to be displayed as the word *Positive*, and what is really a No—a *false* value—to show up as the word *Negative*. Similarly,

```
"Female"; "Male"
```

will result in an answer of *Female* or *Male*.

66 **If you are typing literal text like this into a Format property for any data type, you should surround it with quotation marks. This stops Access from interpreting it as obscure special formatting codes that are beyond the scope of this book.**

Caption lets you type in a caption that will appear along the bottom of the Access window when data is being entered into the field. This can help to direct the person doing data entry. For example, the caption might read, "Answer true or false only."

Default Value lets you specify a value—or an expression—that will appear automatically in the field when a new record is created. Don't worry, though; you'll be able to change it later. This is useful when you anticipate that a certain value usually will appear in the field—perhaps, for example, you expect that the answer will almost always be Yes. You can make the default value Yes, and that value will appear automatically in this field in every record. In the cases where the answer is No, the data entry person can change the field's value to No.

Validation Rule lets you check the value entered into the field. Whenever data is entered into the field, it is compared using the Validation Rule. If the data violates the Validation Rule, the message specified in the Validation Text is displayed and the user must re-enter data into the field. Generally speaking, Validation Rules are not useful for Yes/No fields, because there are only two possibilities for a Yes/No field. If you know one of those is wrong, just set the other as the default value.

Validation Text holds a message to be displayed if the user enters data into the field that violates the Validation Rule property. This is totally unnecessary unless you've entered a Validation Rule.

Required lets you require that an entry be made into the field. If, for example, you have a field that asks "Male or Female," every record in the table will have to have one or the other of those values in the field.

Indexed lets you specify whether Access indexes the database on this field. It makes no sense whatsoever to index your database on a Yes/No field, so leave the Index property empty.

See **Data Type; Data Types in Access; Text Data Type**

ZEROS

See **Number Data Type**

ZIP CODES

Use a text field to store ZIP codes. You never sum up ZIP codes, so you don't need them to be a number field. ZIP codes are simple, they're always set up the same way, and usually all you do to play with them is some kind of *sort*, which is a common enough thing to do with text fields. (Another consideration is that if you store ZIP codes in a number field, Access will drop all the leading zeros from those ZIP codes that start with 0, so that 02345 would become 2345, which would befuddle the postal system and delay your mail.)

See **Data Type; Data Types in Access; Text Data Type**

ZOOM BOX

Access provides inadequately small spaces into which you're supposed to enter data. To cope with this, you can press Shift-F2, and—zowie!—a Zoom box will appear. You can then type your data into the larger space of the Zoom box. A Zoom box is shown in Figure Z.1.

Figure Z.1

If you find that Access is allowing only a dinky space into which you are trying to type a lot of memo field data, press Shift-F2, and a Zoom box like this will appear, allowing you more space.

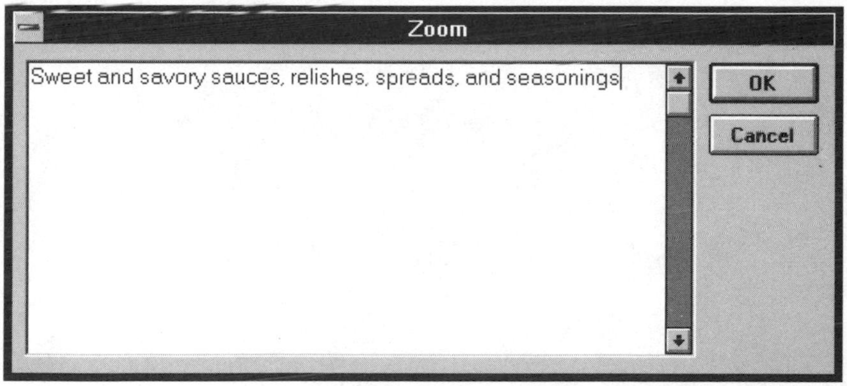

Note, however, that Access allows you to enter data into the larger space of the Zoom box, which implies that you have the ability to enter more data, but you cannot enter any more data than will fit the data width that was specified for this field. So the Zoom box means nothing if the field width is 3 characters wide. The Zoom box will let you type in the text of *War and Peace* and then scream at you when you try to enter it as data, allowing you to actually use only what fits into the width of the field. Because of this, memo fields are the best use of this feature.

See   **Datasheet; Datasheet View: Adding a Record**

ZOOM BUTTON

See   **Print Preview**

ZOOM PROPERTY

See   **Modifying Froms/Reports: Adding a Logo**

Index

Boldface page numbers indicate definitions and principal discussions of topics and subtopics. *Italic* page numbers indicate illustrations.

Symbols

& (ampersand), as concatenation operator, 123, 249
* (asterisk)
  as multiplication operator, 122, 249
  in searches, 87
\ (backslash)
  as division operator, 122
  for root directory, 100
[ ] (brackets)
  in expressions, 123
  for field names, 43, 64
  in searches, 87
  for variables in query criteria, 250
^ (caret), as exponential operator, 122, 249
: (colon), in field names, 126
, (comma), in delimited text files, 172
= (equal to)
  in expressions, 123, 124, 126
  in query criteria, 64
! (exclamation point), in searches, 87
> (greater than)
  in expressions, 123, 126
  in query criteria, 64
>= (greater than or equal to)
  in expressions, 123
  in query criteria, 64
- (hyphen), in searches, 87
< (less than)
  in expressions, 123
  in query criteria, 64
<= (less than or equal to)
  in expressions, 123
  in query criteria, 64

- (minus sign), as subtraction operator, 123, 249
<> (not equal to)
  in expressions, 123
  in query criteria, 64
() (parentheses), in expressions, 122, 123
+ (plus sign), as addition operator, 122, 249
# (pound sign)
  in expressions, 124
  in query criteria, 63
  in searches, 87
? (question mark), in searches, 87
/ (slash), as division operator, 122, 249

A

Access. *See* Microsoft Access
Access BASIC
  defined, **31**
  function calls in expressions, 122, 124, *125*, 249
  modules and, 208
  object properties, 58
accessing, objects across database files, 8
action queries. *See also* queries
  Append action queries, **34–35**
  backing up before using, 32, 97
  Confirm Action Queries option, **225**
  defined, **32, 244**
  Delete action queries, **97–98**
  expressions in, 124
  icon for, *252*
  Make Table action queries, **197–199**
  running, **252**
  Update action queries, **299–300**, *300*
  warning messages, 252
actions, **31**

active or current cell, **32, 70, 80**
Add New Library dialog box, 33
Add Table dialog box, 183, 186
Add-In Manager dialog box, **32–33**, *33*
adding
  annotations to Help, *164*
  controls to forms and reports, 56, 201, 203–205
  dates to form letters, 136–137, *136*
  drop-down boxes to forms, 201, **203–205**
  fields to forms and reports, 56
  fields to queries, 247–248
  logos to forms and reports, 201, **205–208**, *206*
  page breaks to form letters, 138–139
  records
    with Append action queries, 34–35
    in Datasheet View, 80–82
    shortcut key for, 77
add-ins
  Attachment Manager, **37–39**
  Database Documentor, **73–74**
  defined, **33**
  deleting, 33
  Import Database, **165**
  installing, 33
addition operator (+), 122, 249
aggregate functions, **295–296**, *297*
alignment
  Center Text button, 293
  Left Align button, 293
  Right Align tool, 137, 293
Allow Zero Length property, 200, 291
Alt key
  data entry with, 77
  for special characters, 82–83, *83*
ampersand (&), as concatenation operator, 123, 249
"and" criteria, **64–65**, *65*
annotating Help, **164**, *164*

Properties box, 203
switching to, **99**, 203
viewing queries in, **14**, *15*
designing databases, **19–25**, *26–27*.
See also creating
assigning primary keys, 21, 23–24
example, 7
mapping relationships, 24
normalization and, 25
planning database structure, 19–21
planning fields and records, 22–23
planning table structures, 21–22
desktop
General desktop options, **224–226**
maximizing space on, 90
dialog boxes, **99**, **307**
directories
for database files, **74–75**, *75*
for installing Access, 179
paths, **231**
root directory, **99–100**
setting default directory, **225**
subdirectories, **99**
disk space, **100**
disks. *See* floppy disks; hard disks
displaying. *See also* hiding; Show
Datasheet View, 79
Field List box, 56
gridlines, 227
labels for toolbar and toolbox, **226**
objects in Database window, 10
Properties box, **54**, 60, 207
ruler, 227
status bar, 224
system objects, 224
table names in QBE grid, 229
tables as datasheets, 11
toolbar, 225
toolbox, 49
ToolTips, 226
View menu, 223
division operators (/ and \), 122, 249
documenting, database objects, **73–74**. *See also* annotating
DOS
creating directories in, 74
defined, **8**, **100**
DOS Text format, 229, 230
TYPE command, 172
viewing text files in, **172**
Windows and, 303–304

Double property, 210
double-clicking, **305–306**
DPI (dots per inch), **100**
draft mode, **100**
drivers
defined, **100**
ODBC drivers, 173
drives, **100**. *See also* floppy disks; hard disks
Drop-Down Box tool, 204
drop-down boxes
adding to forms, 201, **203–205**
defined, **101**, **203**, *204*
drop-down menus
defined, **101**
in Windows, **306–307**, *307*
Dynamic Data Exchange (DDE), **97**, **110–112**
creating DDE links, **111–112**
defined, **97**, **110–111**
Enable DDE Refresh option, **225**
Ignore DDE Requests option, **225**
versus OLE, **110**
problems, **112**
timeout setting, **24–25**
dynasets. *See also* queries
changing data in, **244**
creating forms from, 15
defined, **12–14**, *13*, **101**, **243–244**
forms based on, **245**
Options dialog box settings, 228
printing as forms, **238**
read-only dynasets, **79**, 105
reports based on, **266**
select queries and, **245**
sorting on fields, 14, **253**
using as tables, **245**
viewing, **79**, **254**

E

Edit Filter/Sort button, 130
Edit menu. *See also* Undo feature
Copy command, 60–61, 112, 217
Cut command, 60–61
Delete command, 83
Find command, 84
Insert Object command, 207, 218, 220
Paste Append command, 61

Paste command, 60–61, 217
Paste Link command, 112
Relationships command, 186
Replace command, 87
Select Record command, 60, 83, 238
Edit/Sort property, 130
editing. *See also* changing
data with joins, 184
in Datasheet View, **11–12**, 76, **103**
defined, **103**
embedded objects, 221–222
with forms, 103–104
objects in Design View, 76
eliminating. *See also* deleting
empty fields, 8
redundancy and repetition, 25
embedding, **217–221**. *See also* Object Linking and Embedding
defined, **216**
editing embedded objects, 221–222
files, 218–220
with Object Packager, 220–221, *221*
objects, 217, *218*, *219*
empty fields
Allow Zero Length property, 200, 291
eliminating, 8
enabling. *See also* displaying; Options dialog box
action query confirmation, 225
Control Wizards, 227
document deletion confirmation, 225
Enable DDE Refresh option, 225
Objects Snap to Grid option, 227
record change confirmation, 225
toolbar customization, 225
ToolTips, 226
End key, 91
enforcing referential integrity, **185–186**, 190, **264**
engines, **104**, 248
Enter key, 226
entering. *See also* data entry
data
in Datasheet View, **11–12**, 76, **80–82**, **105–106**
with forms, **106**
dates, 77
default values, 77
field names, 43, 64

QUERY DATASHEET TOOLBAR

	Print Preview
	New Record
	Cut
	Copy
	Paste
	Find
	New Query
	New Form
	New Report
	Database Window
	AutoForm
	AutoReport
	Undo Current Field/Record
	Undo
	Cue Cards
	Help

FORM DESIGN TOOLBAR

	Design View
	Form View
	Datasheet View
	Save
	Print Preview
	Properties

	Field List
	Code Window
	Toolbox
	Palette
	Bold
	Italic
	Left-Align Text
	Center-Align Text
	Right-Align Text
	Database Window
	Undo
	Cue Cards
	Help

FORM VIEW TOOLBAR

	Design View
	Form View
	Datasheet View
	Print
	Print Preview
	New Record
	Cut
	Copy
	Paste
	Find

continued…